Anonymous

**Campaign text-book of the National Democratic party, 1896**

Anonymous

**Campaign text-book of the National Democratic party, 1896**

ISBN/EAN: 9783337810290

Printed in Europe, USA, Canada, Australia, Japan

Cover: Foto ©ninafisch / pixelio.de

More available books at **www.hansebooks.com**

# CAMPAIGN TEXT-BOOK

OF THE

# National Democratic Party

# 1896

NATIONAL DEMOCRATIC COMMITTEE
CHICAGO AND NEW YORK
1896

**SECOND EDITION, REVISED.**

## INTRODUCTION.

The preservation of Democratic principles and of the Democratic party demands the rejection of the platforms adopted by the Silver party at Chicago and St. Louis and of the candidates there put in nomination, whose victory would mean defeat to the Democratic party and disaster to the country which it was organized to serve.

This motive has caused the great uprising which the National Democratic organization represents.

The Populist Democratic representatives of the Chicago and St. Louis platforms can make successful appeal to their hearers only by disregard of facts, figures and human experiences.

This campaign text-book is issued by the National Democratic Committee to set forth the facts, the experiences and the arguments which refute their claims. It is intended for writers—especially for editors; and for speakers—particularly those engaged in debate; and it is put in handy form that it may be carried in the pocket and easily consulted. It is issued at a low price that it may also be used for general circulation, although it is not intended so much for a campaign document as for the use of those preparing campaign documents and speeches. It is intended, should the development of the campaign make it desirable, to issue early in October a supplement which will present additional facts and arguments. A newspaper supplement is also in preparation, giving documents, speeches, etc., in connection with the movement, to be issued at a low price ($12 per 1,000) for general use.

Part first includes the address and platform of the National Democratic movement; sketches of the two tried Democrats who are the candidates of the Indianapolis Convention for President and Vice-President; their speeches of acceptance; and evidence as to which is the true Democratic party as witnessed by true Democrats.

Part second sets forth, in successive chapters, the arguments, with the historical facts and statistical figures which justify them, refuting the position of the Silver party and, to some extent, the economic and financial heresies and errors which should prevent Democrats from supporting the sound money candidate of their historical opponents. The first chapter shows that the free-silver plunge is an experiment as new as it is dangerous. The second shows from the history of the Latin Monetary Union and the record of the

International Conferences how impossible it has been to base permanent coinage on the ratio of 15, 15½ or 16 to 1. The third chapter shows how contradictory are the claims of the Silver party that silver can be raised to $1.29 per ounce and the so-called benefits of free silver obtained. The fourth chapter deals with the question of public faith. The fifth chapter treats of the relations of the farmer to free silver, and gives the facts and figures showing how disastrous free coinage would be to him. The sixth deals with silver and prices. The seventh shows the relation of the wage-earner to free silver; proves that wages have not decreased during the gold period, but the contrary; and gives special attention to the case of railway employees. The eighth handles the Republican heresies of. "protection." The ninth shows the absolute necessity of maintaining law and order, and deals with the attack upon the Supreme Court. The tenth deals with the record of the Democratic Administration, in relation to sound money, the tariff and civil service reform. The eleventh treats specifically of the National finances, showing that our revenue has not been increased by the McKinley act or impaired by the Wilson bill.

Part third comprises a Free Coinage Catechism, reprinted by permission of the "Evening Post;" chapters on the principles of Money and Banking from Bowker's "Economics for the People," reprinted by permission of Messrs. Harper & Bros.; a statement of the history and the principles of the Democratic Party, from an address by Edw. M. Shepard; and extracts from "the fathers," from the Presidents of the United States, both Democratic and Republican, and from later Democratic statesmen, showing how thoroughly sound money has been an American and a Democratic doctrine, and how entirely the platforms of the Silver party have rejected Democratic principles.

Part fourth includes many statistical tables, giving the figures as to money, coin, wages, prices, etc., etc.

The National Democratic Committee presents this compilation in the belief that facts will tell and that it pays to tell the facts.

The National Democratic party, which has put forth as its candidates men linked with the past, in emphasis of the fact that it represents the historical Democracy, faces the future, in its platform, in belief that its work is necessary to preserve the Democratic party for 1900; that with the dawn of the twentieth century, if not at the close of the nineteenth, the Democratic party will again be charged by the American people with the upholding of American principles in the administration of the people's government.

## CONTENTS.

### Part I—Platform, Candidates, etc.

| | |
|---|---|
| Address of Executive Committee | 1 |
| The National Democratic Platform | 3 |
| True and False Democracy on the Money Question—The Platforms Compared | 10 |
| The Candidates: | |
| For President—John M. Palmer | 12 |
| For Vice-President—Simon B. Buckner | 14 |
| Speeches of Acceptance: | |
| General Palmer's Speech | 18 |
| General Buckner's Speech | 22 |
| The True Democratic Party—the Witness of True Democrats | 25 |

### Part II—Issues of the Campaign.

| | |
|---|---|
| The "Free Silver" Plunge a New Experiment | 1.01 |
| The Latin Monetary Union and the International Conferences | 1.09 |
| The Claim that Silver Can be Raised to Gold Value | 1.23 |
| A Question of Public Faith | 1.31 |
| The Farmer and Free Silver | 1.42 |
| Silver and Prices | 1.56 |
| Labor and Free Coinage | 1.67 |
| Protection the Parent of National Disaster | 1.82 |
| The Question of Law and Order | 1.91 |
| Record of the Democratic Administration | 2.00 |

### Part III—Principles Underlying the Campaign.

| | |
|---|---|
| A Free Coinage Catechism | 3.01 |
| Principles of Money and Banking | 3.16 |
| The Democratic Party; its History and Principles | 3.32 |
| Public Men on Sound Money | 3.40 |

### Part IV—Statistical Tables, etc.

(*Note.*—Most of the tables in the body of the book are repeated in this part for convenience of reference.)

| | |
|---|---|
| Production of Gold and Silver in the World, 1492–1895 | 4.01 |

## CONTENTS.

| | |
|---|---|
| Monetary Systems and Approximate Stocks of Money in Principal Countries............................................................ | 4.02 |
| Products of Gold and Silver from Mines in the U. S., 1873-95......... | 4.04 |
| Average Yearly Wages in the U. S. in Manufacturing Industries, 1860-1890............................................................ | 4.04 |
| Statement of Coin and Paper Circulation of the U. S., 1860-96....... | 4.05 |
| Prices of Silver Bullion and Bullion Value of U. S. Silver Dollars since 1873............................................................ | 4.06 |
| Commercial Ratio of Silver and Gold since 1687..................... | 4.07 |
| Comparative Statement of Clearing House Exchanges in U.S., 1892-95.. | 4.08 |
| Transactions of the N. Y. Clearing House, 1860-95................... | 4.08 |
| Coinage of U. S. Mints, 1792-1896 ................................. | 4.09 |
| Railroad Freight Earnings and Rates per Ton, 1873-95 ............... | 4.09 |
| Crop and Yearly Prices of Cotton, 1872-95.......................... | 4.10 |
| Gold Values of Wheat per Bushel, 1862-94........................... | 4.10 |
| Average Farm Prices in Illinois, 1863-94............................ | 4.11 |
| Farm Prices in Indiana, 1862-95.................................... | 4.11 |
| Prices of Farm Implements in Bushels of Grain, 1873 and 1889........ | 4.11 |
| Freight Rates on Wheat, by Lake, Canal and Rail, Chicago to N. Y., 1860-95............................................................ | 4.12 |
| Freight Rates on Grain and Flour from St. Louis, 1876-95............ | 4.12 |
| Time Table of Procedure—The Act of 1873........................... | 4.13 |
| Prices, Wages, Purchasing Power, 1845-90 .......................... | 4.13 |
| Wages in U. S. and Other Countries................................. | 4.14 |
| Diagram showing Prices of Silver, Wheat, Pork, Freight, Telegrams, etc., 1873-1895.................................................. | 4.15 |
| Diagram showing Prices, Wages and Purchasing Power, 1860-90...... | 4.16 |

# THE NATIONAL DEMOCRATIC PARTY.

ADDRESS OF THE EXECUTIVE COMMITTEE.

CHICAGO August 17, 1896.

*To the Democrats of the United States:*

The Democratic party is the only existing political organization with a history extending back to the birth of the Republic. Party after party has attempted its overthrow. Some have achieved temporary triumphs. With each triumph was heard the prophecy that the Democratic party would surely die. It has survived all defeats. By virtue of its indestructible principles it has witnessed the birth and death of every rival save one, and this, its present great antagonist, with a history of more than forty years, had no part in laying the foundations of constitutional government..

For more than a century men of high principles, noble ambitions, unselfish and patriotic aims have adhered to the Democratic party with a constancy of devotion unparalleled in the history of politics.

For more than a century, through good and evil report, in times of prosperity and in days of adversity, it has kept its faith. "Without variableness or shadow of turning," it has kept fast to the fundamental principles of free government formulated by its founders and subsequently enforced by its great leaders, from Jefferson to Cleveland.

For more than a century no man was ever in doubt as to what constituted Democracy. He who proclaimed himself a Democrat defined his principles. He believed, and this was the cardinal article of his political faith, in the ability of every individual, unassisted, if unfettered by law, to achieve his own happiness, and, therefore, that to every citizen there should be secured the right and opportunity peaceably to pursue whatever course of conduct he would, provided such conduct deprived no other individual of the equal enjoyment of the same right and opportunity. He stood for freedom of speech, freedom of conscience, freedom of trade, and freedom of contract, all of which are implied by the century-old battle-cry of the Democratic party, "Individual Liberty." As a consequence, every Democrat believed in the rule of law, and the rule of an impartial law, in the unhesitating protection not only of the lives of citizens but of private rights and property, and in the enforcement of obedience to duly constituted authority.

Every true Democrat insisted upon a strict observance of the mandates of the Federal Constitution and of the limitations therein prescribed, as well as upon a loyal support of all the institutions thereby created to be guaranties of the liberty it sought to perpetuate. He profoundly disbelieved in the ability of government, through paternal legislation or supervision, to increase the happiness of the nation. He was opposed to all attempts to conjure comfort into the homes of its citizens, or wealth into their pockets. He believed that it is the function of government to provide the people with an honest and stable medium of exchange, thus enabling them to transact their business safely and conveniently in every market of the world. He reprobated every attempt to supply to money by means of legislation that value which it can possess only by return of those qualities that render it acceptable to the world when unsupported by legislative fiat. He believed in the greatest measure of freedom of trade and industry compatible with the necessity to obtain by constitutional means an adequate revenue for the support of the Government. He believed in a simple, economical, honest and efficient administration of the affairs of the nation, to the end that the prime object of government—the liberty of the people—should be preserved with the least possible resulting burden and the greatest possible certainty.

With such a record and such a creed, the President, moreover, being a Democrat, elected on a platform reaffirming the sound principles of Democracy, the Democratic Party was called upon to select delegates to a National Convention.

The delegates to the convention held at Chicago were authorized and had the power to proclaim a platform embodying their views of the true solution of the particular problems of government now agitating the nation, but upon the condition that such platform should be consistent with the cardinal principles held by the party throughout its existence. These principles constitute the essential element of the party's life. They distinguish it from all other political organizations. If they are abandoned, the party ceases to exist. It was, therefore, not within the power of any majority of the delegates assembled at Chicago to bind the Democrats of the United States to a platform inconsistent with the party's principles or to any action that should result in their surrender.

In violation of the trust committed to them, a majority of the delegates assembled in that convention, ignoring the rights of the minority, unseated regularly-elected delegates to make places for others in sympathy with themselves. They proclaimed a sectional combination of the South and West against the North and East. They impeached the honesty and patriotism of President Cleveland, who, under exceptional embarrassments, produced by past errors of legislation, has heroically maintained the honor and integrity of the Republic. Against the protest of one-third of the delegates, they promulgated a platform at variance with the essential principles of the Democratic party.

This platform is in its policies dangerous to the welfare and life of free government. It is mischievous in its tendencies. But even more threatening and mischievous was the spirit of the convention that adopted it—a spirit manifested not alone by its affirmative action, but as well by its reckless rejection of every proposition tending to temper the declarations of the convention with conservatism and justice.

The platform proposes to degrade the coin of the United States by means of the free, unlimited and independent coinage of silver by our Government, and by the exercise of the power of the nation to compel the acceptance of depreciated coins at their nominal value, thereby working an injustice to creditors, defrauding the laborer of a large part of his earnings and savings, robbing pensioned soldiers of a part of their pensions, contracting the currency by the expulsion of gold coin from circulation, injuring, if not destroying, domestic trade and foreign commerce.

While professing to advocate a policy of bimetallism, it censures the present Democratic administration for maintaining the parity of gold and silver. It proposes to reduce this country to a condition of silver monometallism, with its vacillating and unreliable standard of values, and tends to bring the farmer, the wage-earner and the salaried man to the wretched condition of the same classes in countries in which the silver standard prevails, and where the rewards of agriculture and labor are lower than anywhere else in the world.

With what seems to be a deliberate attempt to mislead the people, it asserts that by the Coinage Act of 1873 the United States abandoned the use of silver as money, and that gold has appreciated and commodities have fallen in price solely by reason of this legislation. It ignores the fact that the prices of commodities have fallen because of the enlarged use of labor-saving machinery, increased production and resulting competition. It suppresses the fact that a potent reason for the decline in the price of silver has been the discovery of new and cheaply-worked mines, resulting in an enormous increase in its production. Instead of recognizing these facts, it appeals to the prejudice of the people.

It demands the free coinage of silver at the arbitrary and fictitious ratio of 16 to 1, although the ratio established in the world's market is about 32 to 1, and although neither experience nor reason warrants the belief that the commercial ratio between the metals can be reduced by the action of this Government to any ratio even approximating that proposed.

It threatens, in certain contingencies, to increase to an unlimited extent the volume of legal tenders issued by the Federal Government, the ultimate effect of which would be to force the withdrawal of all coin from circulation and to compel public and private business to be transacted in depreciated paper currency, constantly fluctuating in value, and to invite the ruin and confusion that have always followed the adoption of such a policy.

Its declarations invite, and have almost produced, a financial panic, and many of its proponents announce that to accomplish their purposes they are prepared to involve their country in a disaster comparable to nothing in its history save the calamity of civil war.

It assails the independence of the judiciary by a covert threat to reorganize the courts whenever their decisions contravene the decree of the party caucus.

It seeks to allure office seekers and spoilsmen to its support by attacking the existing Civil Service laws, which good men of all parties have labored so long to establish and to extend to all departments of the public service.

The Chicago Convention, having thus departed from the recognized Democratic faith and promulgated doctrines new and strange to the Democracy, all Democrats are absolved from obligation to support its programme. More than this, as the doctrines announced are destructive of national honor and private obligation, and tend to create sectional and class distinctions and engender discord and strife among the people, all good citizens of the republic are bound to repudiate them and exert every lawful means to insure the defeat of the candidates that represent these false doctrines.

Democrats are told that they must accept the platform enunciated and the ticket nominated at Chicago because submission to the will of the majority is a fundamental principle of Democracy. It is true that when a majority of the people have expressed their will at a legal election, the will of such majority must be respected and obeyed. This is essential to the peace and existence of the Nation. But it is a monstrous perversion of this doctrine to apply it to a political party, which exists only by virtue of a common, voluntary assent to its principles. When a Democratic convention departs from the principles of the party no Democrat remains under any moral obligation to support its action, nor is there any tradition of the party that requires him so to do. On the contrary, it is evidence of moral weakness for any freeman to vote to enforce policies which, in his opinion, are inimical to the welfare of the people or to the integrity of the Nation.

The duty of the hour is to stand steadfast in the defense of our ancient faith. In this crisis there is at stake more than the possibility of temporary victory. The honor and perpetuity of the Democratic party are at stake. A political organization that is untrue to itself, its principles, its history and traditions, is disgraced and dishonored. The existence of our great historical party, that has withstood the assaults of every foe, is threatened by reason of the recreancy of many of its members. That this party, as we have known it, may not die, let the faithful of years rally round its historic banner, re-form its broken lines, and, with abiding faith in the final triumph of its principles, unite to restore the name "Democrat" to its former meaning and proud distinction.

To this end we request all Democrats who are opposed to the platform adopted and the candidates nominated at Chicago to organize in their respective States and to send representatives to the convention of the National Democratic party to be held at Indianapolis on Wednesday, September 2, 1896, in accordance with the call heretofore issued by the National Committee.

W. D. BYNUM, Chairman ;
JOHN R. WILSON, Secretary ;
CHARLES TRACEY,
J. M. FALKNER,
F. W. M. CUTCHEON,

ELLIS B. USHER,
S. H. HOLDING,
F. W. LEHMAN,
W. B. HALDEMAN,
JOHN P. HOPKINS,

Executive Committee of the National Democratic Party

# THE NATIONAL DEMOCRATIC PLATFORM.

ADOPTED AT THE CONVENTION OF THE NATIONAL DEMOCRATIC PARTY AT INDIANAPOLIS, IND., SEPTEMBER 3, 1896.

This convention has assembled to uphold the principles upon which depend the honor and welfare of the American people in order that Democrats throughout the Union may unite their patriotic efforts to avert disaster from their country and ruin from their party. The Democratic party is pledged to equal and exact justice to all men of every creed and condition; to the largest freedom of the individual consistent with good government; to the preservation of the Federal Government in its constitutional vigor and the support of the States in all their just rights; to economy in the public expenditures; to the maintenance of the public faith and sound money; and it is opposed to paternalism and all class legislation.

The declarations of the Chicago Convention attack individual freedom, the right of private contract, the independence of the judiciary, and the authority of the President to enforce Federal laws. They advocate a reckless attempt to increase the price of silver by legislation to the debasement of our monetary standard, and threaten unlimited issues of paper money by the Government. They abandon for Republican allies the Democratic cause of tariff reform to court the favor of protectionists to their fiscal heresy.

In view of these and other grave departures from Democratic principles, we cannot support the candidates of that convention, nor be bound by its acts. The Democratic party has survived many defeats, but could not survive a victory won in behalf of the doctrine and the policy proclaimed in its name at Chicago.

The conditions, however, which make possible such utterances from a national convention are a result of class legislation by the Republican party. It still proclaims, as it has for years, the power and duty of the Government to raise and maintain prices by law; and it proposes no remedy for existing evils except oppressive and unjust taxation.

## THE CONTINUITY OF DEMOCRATIC PRINCIPLES.

The National Democracy, here convened, therefore renews its declaration of faith in Democratic principles, especially as applicable to the conditions of the times.

Taxation, tariff, excise or direct, is rightfully imposed only for public purposes and not for private gain. Its amount is justly measured by public expenditures, which should be limited by scrupulous economy. The sum derived by the Treasury from tariff and excise levies is affected by the state of trade and volume of consumption. The amount required by the Treasury is determined by the appropriations made by Congress.

The demand of the Republican party for an increase in tariff taxation has its pretext in the deficiency of revenue, which has its causes in the stagnation of trade and reduced consumption, due entirely to the loss of confidence that has followed the Populist threat of free coinage and the depreciation of our money, and the Republican practice of extravagant appropriations beyond the needs of good government.

We arraign and condemn the Populistic conventions of Chicago and St. Louis for their co-operation with the Republican party in creating these conditions which are pleaded in justification of a heavy increase of the burdens of the people by a further resort to protection.

We therefore denounce protection and especially free coinage of silver, as schemes for the personal profit of a few at the expense of the masses, and oppose the two parties which stand for these schemes as hostile to the people of the Republic, whose food and shelter, comfort and prosperity, are attacked by higher taxes and depreciated money.

In fine, we reaffirm the historic Democratic doctrine of tariff for revenue only. We demand that henceforth modern and liberal policies toward American shipping shall take the place of our imitation of the restricted statutes of the eighteenth century, which were long ago abandoned by every maritime power but the United States, and which, to the nation's humiliation, have driven American capital and enterprise to the use of alien flags and alien crews, have made the stars and stripes an almost unknown emblem in foreign ports, and have virtually extinguished the race of American seamen. We oppose the pretense that discriminating duties will promote shipping; that scheme is an invitation to commercial warfare upon the United States, un-American in the light of our great commercial treaties, offering no gain whatever to American shipping, while greatly increasing ocean freights on our agricultural and manufactured products.

### GOLD AND SILVER IN THE CURRENCY.

The experience of mankind has shown that, by reason of its natural qualities, gold is the necessary money of the large affairs of commerce and business, while silver is conveniently adapted to minor transactions, and the most beneficial use of both together can be insured only by the adoption of the former as a standard of monetary measure, and the maintenance of silver at a parity with gold by its limited coinage under suitable safeguards of law. Thus the largest possible employment of both metals is gained, with a value universally accepted throughout the world, which involves the only practical bimetallic currency assuring the most stable standard, and especially the best and safest money for all who earn a livelihood by labor or the product of husbandry. They cannot suffer when paid in the best money known to man, but are the peculiar and most defenseless victims of a debased and fluctuating currency, which offers continual profits to the money changer at their cost.

Realizing these truths, demonstrated by long public inconvenience and loss, the Democratic party, in the interests of the masses and of equal justice to all, practically established by the legislation of 1834 and 1853 the gold standard of monetary measurement, and likewise entirely divorced the Government from banking and currency issues. To this long-established Democratic policy we adhere, and insist upon the maintenance of the gold standard and of the parity therewith of every dollar issued by the Government, and are firmly opposed to the free and unlimited coinage of silver and to the compulsory purchase of silver bullion. But we denounce also the further maintenance of the present costly patchwork system of national paper currency as a constant source of injury and peril.

We assert the necessity of such intelligent currency reform as will confine the Government to its legitimate functions, completely separated from the banking business, and afford to all sections of our country a uniform, safe, and elastic bank currency under governmental supervision, measured in volume by the needs of business.

### PRESIDENT CLEVELAND'S ADMINISTRATION.

The fidelity, patriotism and courage with which President Cleveland has fulfilled his great public trust, the high character of his administration, his wisdom and energy in the maintenance of civil order and the enforcement of the laws, its equal regard for the rights of every class and every section, its firm and dignified conduct of foreign affairs and its sturdy persistence in upholding the credit and honor of the nation, are fully recognized by the Democratic party and will secure to him a place in history beside the fathers of the republic.

We also commend the administration for the great progress made in the reform of the public service, and we indorse its effort to extend the merit system still further. We demand that no backward step be taken, but that the reform be supported and advanced until the undemocratic spoils system of appointments shall be eradicated.

### ECONOMY, PEACE, JUSTICE AND LAW.

We demand strict economy in the appropriations and in the administration of the government.

We favor arbitration for the settlement of international disputes.

We favor a liberal policy of pensions to the deserving soldiers and sailors of the United States.

The Supreme Court of the United States was wisely established by the framers of our Constitution as one of three co-ordinate branches of the government. Its independence and authority to interpret the law of the land without fear or favor must be maintained. We condemn all efforts to degrade that tribunal or impair the confidence and respect which it has deservedly held.

The Democratic party ever has maintained, and ever will maintain, the supremacy of law, the independence of its judicial administration, the inviolability of contract, and the obligations of all good citizens to resist every illegal trust, combination or attempt against the just rights of property and the good order of society, in which are bound up the peace and happiness of our people.

Believing these principles to be essential to the well-being of the public, we submit them to the consideration of the American people.

## THE TRUE DOCTRINE.

## TRUE AND FALSE DEMOCRACY

*From the National Democratic platform adopted at Chicago June 22, 1892.*

We denounce the Republican legislation known as the Sherman Act of 1890 as a cowardly makeshift, fraught with possibilities of danger in the future, which should make all of its supporters, as well as its author, anxious for its speedy repeal. We hold to the use of both gold and silver as the standard money of the country and to the coinage of both gold and silver without discriminating against either metal or charge for mintage, but the dollar unit of coinage of both metals must be of equal intrinsic and exchangeable value or be adjusted through international agreement or by such safeguards of legislation as shall insure the maintenance of the parity of the two metals and the equal power of every dollar at all times in the markets and in the payments of debt ; and we demand that all paper currency shall be kept at par with and redeemable in such coin. We insist upon this policy as especially necessary for the protection of the farmers and laboring classes, the first and most defenseless victims of unstable money and a fluctuating currency.

---

*From the platform of the National Democracy, adopted at Indianapolis September 3, 1896.*

The experience of mankind has shown that by reason of their natural qualities, gold is the necessary money of the large affairs of commerce and business, while silver is conveniently adapted to minor transactions, and the most beneficial use of both together can be ensured only by the adoption of the former as a standard of monetary measure, and the maintenance of silver at a parity with gold by its limited coinage under suitable safeguards at law.

Thus the largest possible enjoyment of both metals is gained with a value universally accepted throughout the world, which constitutes the only practical bimetallic currency, assuring the most stable standard, and especially the best and safest money for all who earn their livelihood by labor or the produce of husbandry. They cannot suffer when paid in the best money known to man, but are the peculiar and most defenseless victims of a debased and fluctuating currency which offers continual profits to the money changer at their cost.

Realizing the truths demonstrated by long and public inconvenience and loss, the Democratic party, in the interests of the masses and of equal justice to all, practically established by the legislation of 1834 and 1853 the gold standard of monetary measurement and likewise entirely divorced the Government from banking and currency issues. To this long established Democratic policy we adhere, and insist upon the maintenance of the gold standard, and of the parity therewith of every dollar issued by the Government ; and are firmly opposed to the free and unlimited coinage of silver, and to the compulsory purchase of silver bullion. But we denounce also the further maintenance of the present costly patchwork of national paper currency as a constant source of injury and peril.

We assert the necessity of such intelligent currency reform as will confine the Government to its legitimate functions, completely separated from the banking business, and afford to all sections of our country a uniform, safe and elastic bank currency under governmental supervision, measured in volume by the needs of business.

## ON THE MONEY QUESTION.

### THE FALSE DOCTRINE.

*From the so-called National Democratic platform adopted at Chicago, July 9, 1896.*

We declare that the Act of 1873, demonetizing silver without the knowledge or approval of the American people, has resulted in the appreciation of gold and a corresponding fall in the prices of commodities produced by the people, a heavy increase in the burden of taxation and of all debts public and private, the enrichment of the money-lending class at home and abroad, prostration of industry and impoverishment of the people.

We are unalterably opposed to the single gold standard, which has locked fast the prosperity of an industrial people in the paralysis of hard times. Gold monometallism is a British policy, and its adoption has brought other nations into financial servitude to London. It is not only un-American, but anti-American, and it can be fastened on the United States only by the stifling of that indomitable spirit and love of liberty which proclaimed our political independence in 1776 and won it in the War of the Revolution.

We demand the free and unlimited coinage of both gold and silver at the present legal ratio of 16 to 1 without waiting for the aid or consent of any other nation. We demand that the standard silver dollar shall be a full legal tender, equally with gold, for all debts, public and private, and we favor such legislation as will prevent the demonetization of any kind of legal tender money by private contract.

Congress alone has the power to coin and issue money, and President Jackson declared that this power could not be delegated to corporations or individuals. We therefore demand that the power to issue notes to circulate as money be taken from the national banks and that all paper money shall be issued directly by the Treasury Department.

---

*From the platform of the People's Party adopted at St. Louis July 24, 1896.*

We demand a national money, safe and sound, issued by the General Government only, without the intervention of banks of issue, to be a full legal tender for all debts, public and private, a just, equitable and efficient means of distribution direct to the people and through the lawful disbursements of the Government.

We demand the free and unrestricted coinage of silver and gold at the present legal ratio of 16 to 1, without waiting for the consent of foreign nations.

We demand that the volume of circulating medium be speedily increased to an amount sufficient to meet the demands of the business and population, and to restore the just level of prices of labor and production.

We demand such legislation as will prevent the demonetization of the lawful money of the United States by private contract.

## THE CANDIDATES.
### For President, John M. Palmer.

John McCauley Palmer was born in Eagle Creek, Scott County, Kentucky, September 13, 1817. When he was fifteen years old, his father removed to the State of Illinois, settling at Carlingville, in Macoupin County. The family did not prosper, and two years later the father gave John "his time," which meant in the vernacular of those days liberty to shift for himself. John Palmer was then seventeen years old. His first ambition was for a higher education than he had been able to obtain in the country schools, and he sought it in a school at Alton where pupils were permitted to pay their way with manual labor. The young student's greatest difficulty was to keep himself decently clothed. It was an unequal struggle, and ended in his leaving the school in debt. This debt he shortly after paid with money earned in the making of flour barrels, he having quickly learned the cooper's trade.

The young man's next venture was in peddling clocks. He was intrusted with the driving of one of several peddlers' wagons maintained by a Yankee peddler from Connecticut. The turning point in his life came while thus engaged. One night he vainly sought lodging at a crowded hotel in Carthage until Stephen A. Douglas, then on a stumping tour in a congressional campaign, offered to share his room with him. Douglas engaged him in conversation, and finding him fairly well educated and of a well-balanced intellect, advised him to abandon trade and to study law. The advice was taken, and after surmounting many difficulties Mr. Palmer was admitted to the bar in 1839. His entry into politics followed quickly, the campaign of 1840 finding him fighting with Douglas against the whigs. His first office was the probate judgeship of Macoupin County, to which he was elected in 1843. He held the office through successive terms until 1847, when he was defeated because of his anti-slavery convictions, to which he had given vigorous expression in the Illinois Constitutional Convention of 1846, where he opposed the adoption of an article to prohibit free negroes from entering Illinois. His personal popularity conquered prejudice, however, and in 1348 he was re-elected to the office, and in the following year he was chosen County Judge.

In 1851 Mr. Palmer was sent to the State Senate, where he again distinguished himself as an opponent of slavery by fighting against the bill to prohibit negro immigration. He continued, however, in full fellowship with the Democratic party, and in 1853 was selected to renominate Stephen A. Douglas for United States Senator. Soon thereafter, however, came his break with Douglas. The latter endeavored to make support of the Kansas-

Nebraska act a test of Democratic fealty. Palmer spurned the test and ran as an independent cadidate in his legislative district, defeating the Douglas candidate. He and the other anti-Nebraska Democrats held the balance of power in the Legislature, which had the choice of a United States Senator to succeed Shields. It appearing that defections from the independents might give Shields the election, Palmer sprung the name of Lyman Trumbull, an independent Democrat, who was elected with the aid of the forty-eight votes thrown to him by Abraham Lincoln.

When Mr. Palmer severed relations with Mr. Douglas, he also severed connection with the Democratic party. He was one of the founders of the Republican party, and was chairman of the first state convention of that party in Illinois. Then came the national convention of the party in Philadelphia, to which Palmer was a delegate. Returning home, he refused a nomination as Representative in Congress, and took the stump for Fremont. He had to face the most violent partisan abuse. In a debate with Major Harris at Plainview he was constrained to meet some of Harris's scurrilous remarks with the word "liar," and then to face Harris's irate friends with a pistol in his hand. When it came his time to speak, the crowd tried to howl him down. In a voice which rose above the howls, Palmer told the "cowardly scoundrels" that they had listened while he was being maligned and that now they must listen to him. The demand was effective and the crowd heard him to the end. After Fremont's defeat Mr. Palmer ran as a candidate for Representative from his Congress district, but was defeated.

In the campaign in which Lincoln was elected, Palmer was an elector-at-large in Illinois. He returned from the peace conference in Washington in 1861 to raise the Fourteenth Illinois Regiment, of which he was made Colonel. A few months later he was made a Brigadier-General, and eventually he became a Major-General of volunteers. He was with Gen. Pope in the capture of New Madrid and Island No. 10, commanding the First Brigade, First Division of the Army of the Mississippi, and later a division of Gen. Grant's army, leading a division at the battle of Stony River. He also participated in the battle of Chickamauga and the Atlanta campaign. One year after the war he was a candidate for United States Senator from Illinois, but was defeated by John A. Logan. The next year he was elected Governor of the state, which office he filled for four years, declining a renomination, in 1872, on the ground that the convention would be controlled by men whose leading object would be the renomination of President Grant. He opposed Grant's re-election, and has since that time acted with the Democrats. One of the leading causes of Mr. Palmer's opposition to Grant was because the President had permitted General Sheridan to use four companies of United States soldiers as police after the great fire in Chicago, thus reflecting upon the ability of the state to maintain order. And so Mr. Palmer supported Greeley.

Governor Palmer was at the Liberal Republican convention in Cincinnati and objected even to a mention of his name as a presidential candidate. He was importuned so persistently for a declaration of his principles that he finally said: "I will make no pledges, promises or declarations of principles or purposes to secure a presidential nomination." He gave a hearty support to Horace Greeley and took the stump in his behalf. In 1872, when the Liberal and Democratic parties in Illinois were fused, Governor Palmer became a recognized Democratic leader, and was at once the champion of hard money, urging the adoption of a hard-money platform in the coming state convention. On August 26 the convention met and Governor Palmer was made chairman, and in a powerful speech he advocated his views. A model hard-money and State's rights platform was the result, and the party went before the people. But the independent and prohibition vote of 75,000 stepped in between and gave the Republicans a plurality of 84,805.

Since then General Palmer has been a Democrat, and was elected to the State Senate by that party in 1877. In 1890 he was elected United States Senator from Illinois, which position he still holds.

## For Vice-President, Simon B. Buckner.

Simon Bolivar Buckner was bred a soldier and is now a farmer. No better representative of that sturdy yeomanry for which Kentucky, like England, is celebrated, has ever been offered to the world. Unostentatious in his manner of living and holding himself in no respect above his neighbors, Gen. Buckner is one of the most finished gentlemen in America; he is "a scholar and a ripe and good one." He has distinguished himself as a statesman, but he was never an office-seeker.

Gen. Buckner was born in Hart County in 1823, on the farm and in the house in which he now lives. His father was one of the first iron manufacturers of the State, and built and operated the Clay Furnace, on Green river, only a short distance from the family residence. He was a member of a Virginia family of English descent, and was a man of means and standing. During his son's early life he moved to Munfordville, where Simon received the rudiments of his education. The schools of that day were much better than many now believe, as the teachers were usually graduates of Virginia or Eastern colleges.

The elder Buckner moved to Muhlenberg County later, and from there his son was given a cadetship to West Point. Simon Bolivar's record was a good one, and when he was graduated in 1844 he was assigned to the Second Infantry regiment. In August, 1845, he was made Assistant Professor of Ethics at West Point, at which post he remained until the following May. Upon the breaking out of the war with Mexico he applied for transfer to the scene of operations. This was delayed, but he reached Mexico in time to take a very active part in that brief but brilliant conflict. He was attached to the Sixth

Regiment, and was breveted first lieutenant for gallantry at Contreras and Cherubusco. At Molino del Rey he won the captain's brevet.

After the war he was an instructor at West Point for some time, then served on the frontier among the Indians. He resigned March 25, 1855, and during that year superintended the building of the Chicago Custom-house. Returning to Louisville he took an interest in militia matters, and Gov. Magoffin appointed him Adjutant and Inspector General of the State Guard. He organized the Guard and brought it to a high state of efficiency, showing his great executive ability in the work.

When the war broke out every effort was made by the Federal authorities to secure Gen. Buckner for the Union. He was then in the prime of a handsome young manhood, confessedly an able soldier and of the greatest personal influence in his State. The most tempting offers were made him—a general's commission and promises of high command—but all were refused. He felt that he should go with the South, and, though all his property lay in the North, he went as conscience dictated. A large part of the State Guard followed their commander.

Gen. Buckner invaded Kentucky from Camp Boone and threatened Louisville, but advanced no further than Bowling Green. From there he went to Fort Donelson, where the incapacity of his superior officers, Gens. Pillow and Floyd, forced him to choose between abandoning his men or surrendering them. He first commanded a brigade, and distinguished himself in the battles of February 13, 14 and 15. On the last day a gallant sortie was made, the Federals were driven back and the way was opened for the army's escape, but Gen. Pillow ordered them back. Gen. Buckner protested, but was overruled. That afternoon Gen. Grant so arranged his forces that retreat was cut off. A conference was held in the evening and Gens. Floyd and Pillow announced that as they would probably be hanged if captured they would make their escape by river that night. Gen. Buckner would not hear to leaving their troops, so the command was turned over to him. Floyd and Pillow made good their flight; Buckner remained to undergo the mortification of the inevitable surrender.

A pleasant incident was the conduct of the Union General, who privately placed his purse at his old friend's disposal. They were cadets together at West Point. They had scarcely met since then, except on a visit by Gen. Grant to New York, when Grant had left the army and Buckner was on staff duty in that city and was able to do a kindly favor for his West Point friend. They did not meet again till Gen. Grant was dying at Mount Macgregor, when Gen. Buckner called to give thanks to the great Union leader for the stout and successful resistance he had made to Andrew Johnson's intention to try the Confederate Generals for treason, after their parole had been accepted and had been honorably maintained. The association of Gen. Buckner and Gen. Johnston as pall-bearers at Gen. Grant's funeral was one of the first proofs of the reconciliation that is now complete between North and South.

After his surrender the young Confederate was sent to Fort Warren, Boston, where he remained until exchanged in August of that year. He was then given the command of the First Division of Gen. Hardee's corps in Bragg's army. He was made a Major General, and distinguished himself in the battles of Murfreesboro and Chickamauga. As Lieutenant General he succeeded to the command of Kirby Smith's army which he surrendered at Baton Rouge May 26, 1865.

Like all other Southern soldiers, Gen. Buckner found himself practically reduced to poverty by the war. He owned valuable property in Chicago, which he had deeded to his brother-in-law, Lieut. Kingsbury, of the Federal Army, to save it from confiscation at the breaking out of hostilities. Lieut. Kingsbury was mortally wounded in battle, though he made a nuncupative will bequeathing the property back to Gen. Buckner. It took many years of litigation to establish the claim. After the property had been improved the great fire came, and there was another struggle. Only first-class business capacity could have saved the real estate, though it had constantly increased in value, but it was done.

Before he had succeeded in straightening up his affairs Gen. Buckner engaged in journalism. For a year or so he edited one of the New Orleans newspapers and then came to Louisville and occupied the same post on the "Courier." When that was united with the "Journal" he engaged in business in Louisville and in Chicago. It was to him the State is indebted for the excellent Insurance Law framed about that time.

Since 1870, the General has spent nearly all his time upon his farm in Hart County. He took great delight in improving it with new roads, and gave his neighbors and the whole country the benefit of his engineering skill. The house he occupies is a roomy log-structure, and, though he has made many additions to it, he has never had the heart to pull it down and build anew.

In 1883, about a month or six weeks before the State Convention was held, Gen. Buckner's friends and neighbors held a meeting at Munfordville and asked him to make the race for Governor. He complied and made a brief but satisfactory canvass. He carried every county that he visited, and ranked a close third in the number of instructed votes he had received. The Hon. Proctor Knott got the nomination, but four years later it went to Gen. Buckner almost without a contest. He was elected over Col. W. O. Bradley by a plurality of 17,000 votes, and after a canvass that was as hot as Col. Bradley could make it.

As Governor, Gen. Buckner demonstrated that a new career lay before him. His knowledge and grasp of public business were remarkable, and what was even more surprising than his executive ability was the profound knowledge of constitutional law that he displayed. He used the veto power rather freely, but though this often provoked bitter hostility, he was almost invariably sustained. His veto of the bill reducing the tax levy was one of the exceptions, and because his act was disapproved the State has ever since been seriously cramped and has now for over a year been compelled to dishonor its bills. It was in accordance with his recommendation for an investigation that Treasurer Tate's defalcation was discovered. During his term at one time there was required a large amount of money to answer pressing needs, and he advanced $50,000 out of his own pocket to the Commonwealth without a cent of charge for interest. In many ways he improved the public service, and when he retired from office it was in the midst of universal approbation.

While he was Governor, at the request of his neighbors, Gen. Buckner made the race for delegate to the Constitutional Convention. He was elected and took an important part in framing that instrument.

Gen. Buckner has been twice married. His first wife was a Miss Kingsbury, of Old Lyme, Conn. She died when young. A daughter, who became Mrs. Morris Belknap, of Louisville, and who was her father's confidant and idol, died a few years ago. Gov. Buckner's second wife was Miss Delia Claiborne, a Richmond (Va.) belle. Mrs. Buckner is a relative of Washington, and has made the Executive Mansion at Frankfort and Glen Lily, their home, famous for hospitality.

The Governor's popularity does not stop with the confines of Kentucky or the South. His friendship with Gen. Grant, and the fact that he was one of that great soldier's pall-bearers, have made him widely known all over the North and East wherever there is a comrade of the Grand Army. When the encampment was held here last year he took a conspicuous part in the welcoming, and was one of the most sought after veterans that gathered here. He has been a frequent and welcome guest at military reunions both North and South.

# SPEECHES OF ACCEPTANCE.

## Gen. Palmer's Speech.

You give me official information that delegates representing the National Democracy of forty-one States lately assembled in convention in the City of Indianapolis honored me by designating me the National Democratic candidate for the Presidency, and that the convention associated with me in the formal temporary leadership of that great historic party of the United States, an eminent citizen of Kentucky—a citizen distinguished in arms and as a patriotic Chief Magistrate of his and my own native Commonwealth.

Mr. Chairman and Gentlemen—Gen. Buckner and I were once, in a modest sense, representatives of opposing opinions upon fundamental questions relating to the powers of the United States and of the respective States under the Constitution. We met on the battlefield, where great public controversies that admit of no other method of solution are determined. I know he did his duty, and I trust the country believes that I did mine.

### A REUNITED PEOPLE.

The nominations made by the National Democratic Convention at Indianapolis prove more conclusively than anything which has occurred within the last thirty years that the American people are again united; that our hopes, our rights, our duties, and our interests are the same; that the lofty and patriotic mission of the National Democracy is to maintain peace and order, defend Constitutional liberty, regulated by just and equal laws, and if possible avert from the country repudiation, bankruptcy, and National dishonor.

I accept the unsought honor and responsibilities imposed upon me by the National Democratic Convention. I accept them as proof that my Democratic fellow-citizens confide in my devotion to Democratic principles so clearly and accurately defined in the proceedings of the convention. It was known to the delegates to the convention before this honor was conferred upon me, and is well understood by the country, that my public services commenced more than fifty years ago, and that since that time I have taken an active, earnest part in the discussion and settlement of every public question which had at the time sufficient importance to attract popular attention.

### THE EXPERIENCES OF FIFTY YEARS.

My opinions and my public acts have been an open book, to be read by my contemporaries. I have been at all times controlled by my own convictions of duty, and I have now no one whom I can properly invite to share my responsibilities. Taught by Jefferson, I opposed slavery when it existed. Inspired by Jackson, I defended the Union of the States to the extent of my ability, and, influenced by his example, when my conduct as a military officer was challenged as violative of law, I voluntarily submitted myself to the jurisdiction of the civil courts.

When Governor of my adopted State, while I opposed and by peaceful means successfully resisted the interference of the United States by its military forces in the purely local concerns of the State, I distinctly conceded the right and asserted the duty of that Government to enforce within the States or elsewhere its own laws by its own agencies.

Mr. Chairman and gentlemen, the matters to which I have adverted are but reminiscences—they relate and belong to the past. Our duties as lovers of our country are present and we must meet and deal with existing conditions, and to these the late National Democratic Convention addressed itself.

## TRUTHFUL AND DEMOCRATIC.

Its platform asserts truths which can be demonstrated, and it correctly defines Democratic principles. It asserts 'that the Democratic party is pledged to equal and exact justice to all men of every creed and condition; to the largest freedom of the individual consistent with good government; to the preservation of the Federal Government in its constitutional vigor, and to the support of the States in all their just rights; to economy in the public expenditures; to the maintenance of the public faith and sound money, and it is opposed to paternalism and all class legislation.'

It also asserts that 'the declarations of the Chicago Convention attack individual freedom, the right of private contract, the independence of the judiciary, and the authority of the President to enforce Federal laws. They advocate a reckless attempt to increase the price of silver by legislation to the debasement of our monetary standard, and threaten unlimited issues of paper money by the Government. They abandon for Republican allies the Democratic cause of tariff reform to court the favor of protectionists to their fiscal heresy.'

It then asserts, with earnestness and in terms which will not satisfy those who assert it to be 'the duty of a Democrat to first vote the ticket and then read the platform,' that, in view of these and other grave departures from Democratic principles, 'we cannot support the candidates of that convention nor be bound by its acts.'

The convention held in Indianapolis then declares, with force and exactness, the Democratic doctrines with respect to taxation, whether by tariffs, excises or by direct imposition, and asserts that none of these can be rightfully imposed except for public purposes, and not for private gain, and reaffirms the historic Democratic doctrine of a 'tariff for revenue only.'

### GOLD MUST BE THE STANDARD.

It is then asserted by the convention in its declaration of principles that 'the experience of mankind has shown that, by reason of their natural qualities, gold is the necessary money of the large affairs in commerce and business, while silver is conveniently adapted to minor transactions, and the most beneficial use of both together can be insured only by the adoption of the former as a standard of monetary measure, and the maintenance of silver at a parity with gold by its limited coinage under suitable safeguards of law. Thus the largest possible enjoyment of both metals is gained with a value universally accepted throughout the world, which constitutes the only practical bimetallic currency, assuring the most stable standard, and especially the best and safest money for all who earn their livelihood by labor or the produce of husbandry. They cannot suffer when paid in the best money known to man, but are the peculiar and most defenseless victims of a debased and fluctuating currency which offer continual profits to the money changer at their cost.

'Realizing these truths, demonstrated by long public inconvenience and loss, the Democratic party, in the interests of the masses and of equal justice to all, practically established by the legislation of 1834 and 1853 the gold standard of monetary measurement and likewise entirely divorced the Government from banking and currency issues. To this long-established Democratic policy we adhere, and insist upon the maintenance of the gold standard and of the parity therewith of every dollar issued by the Government, and are firmly opposed to the free and unlimited coinage of silver and to the compulsory purchase of silver bullion.'

### THE SAME DEMAND IN 1892.

This language is but a reiteration of the terse demand of the Democratic platform of 1892, that 'every dollar coined or issued by the Government shall have equal power in the market and in the payments of debts.'

The convention which assembled in Chicago in July of the present year, in demanding the unlimited coinage of silver dollars on the ratio of $412\frac{1}{2}$ grains of standard silver to 25.8 grains of standard gold, with full legal-tender quality for all debts and dues, public and private offers to the country a scheme from which every voter may expect whatever advantage to the country or himself his reason or even his imagination can suggest.

The advocates of the unlimited coinage of full legal-tender silver do not agree as to what will be the consequence of the adoption by the United States of their favorite measure. The more intelligent know that it is impossible by law to give to silver bullion or silver coin a local value in the United States; and, therefore, Mr. Bryan who must be regarded as the official interpreter of the free silver dogma, asserts his belief that the unlimited coinage of legal-tender silver by the United States alone would increase the value of silver bullion, which is to-day 67 cents per ounce, to $1.29, and he asserts his belief that under unlimited coinage the silver dollar, containing 412½ grains of standard silver, coined by the authority of the United States, would be of equal acceptability and value with the dollar containing 25.8 grains of standard gold in all the markets of the world.

### AGAINST THE EXPERIENCE OF MANKIND.

It is something that this opinion has no support in the experience of mankind. It is enough for present purposes to say it has no foundation other than the confident assertions of those who share in that belief. No party in the country ever undertook so much as do the advocates of the unlimited coinage of silver. They not only undertake to maintain commercial parity in value of about 434,502,041 silver dollars already coined by the United States under the authority of the acts of the 28th of February, 1878, and of July 14, 1890, and of all the silver dollars that hereafter may be coined, but they assume the task of advancing the value of silver coinage of all the nations of the world to an equal acceptability and value with coins of gold.

If the expectations of such of the advocates of free coinage of silver are realized it would be difficult upon their own promises to perceive what could be gained by those who expect cheap money.

Accepting their claim that under free coinage the dollar of silver would become of equal power in the markets and in the payment of debts throughout the civilized world, the silver dollar would then be as difficult to procure as the dollar of gold is now. They complain now that the dollar of gold has too much purchasing power and is too difficult to obtain.

### A CHEAP DOLLAR MOVEMENT.

But the real expectation of the great body of supporters of the free coinage of silver, and one much more in harmony with the experience of mankind, is that the unlimited coinage of silver would give to the country a depreciated and cheaper dollar, which would enhance nominal values and be used in the payment of debts, but would be attended and followed by the ruin of all industries, the destruction of public and private credit, and irreparable mischief.

Mr. Chairman and Gentlemen: Our platform commits us to the maintenance of the Democratic faith. Many of our associates, deluded by deceptive sophistries, are supporting a coalition which disavows the traditional faith of the Democratic party. The best we can hope for them is that they may be defeated, and when defeated, they may return to the safe paths that they have heretofore trodden.

## Gen. Buckner's Speech.

I cannot fittingly express my acknowledgment for the very graceful and eloquent terms in which you have announced to me the action of the National Democracy. I know, sir, that a spirit actuated that convention at Indianapolis which looked more to that general principle of Democracy, that spirit of nationalism, than to any merit in me in selecting its candidates. It was known that I had been prominent on the border in advocating the true principles of Democracy, but not, Mr. Chairman, for any merit in me, but because of that spirit of nationalism which always pervaded the Democratic party, that feeling crystalized around me as an object to be associated with this gallant chieftain in blotting out all past differences and sectionalism. I accept that position, Mr. Chairman, and discharge that duty with as much willingness as I ever discharged any on earth (applause); to be associated with the movement which blots out all sectional lines forever and makes us one people and one nationality.

### THE ANCIENT SPIRIT.

It is time that this ancient spirit of Democracy should be revived. We have had amongst us parties builded up heretofore upon sectional hate; parties which had advocated special interests at the expense of all other interests. We have had the great Republican party, ruling and controlling the destinies of this country, built upon hate and antagonism to one-half of the country. But now, at the very moment that that party has announced that it will cease the contention of one section against another, that hereafter it will be a national party, there springs up again among us another party, professedly built upon sectionalism, urgently insisting that one special interest in this country, that of the greedy silver miner, shall be built up at the expense of every other citizen in the land. And what is that party?

### THE SILVER MINERS' PARTY.

It is not proper that I should discuss the particular platforms of the different parties here, but it is well for us as patriots to ask the origin of this party, calling itself falsely the Democratic party, how it was constituted and what are the principles that it annunciates. They claim that they were regular. The delegates to that convention were appointed, it is true, under the regular authority of Democratic organization, but when the primary conventions met to choose delegates to the State conventions nearly every primary meeting began their proceeding by reaffirming the uniform principles of the Democratic party. The delegates sent to their State convention were therefore bound by the instructions they received to adherence to the principles of Democracy. When the State conventions themselves met, almost without exception, they, too, reaffirmed the fundamental principles of the Democratic party and sent their delegates to Chicago, bound in honor and by every political duty, to adhere to the principles of the Democratic party.

### THE ABANDONMENT OF DEMOCRACY'S PRINCIPLES.

Did they do it? You have been told by the gentlemen who have preceded me how they violated their instructions; how they abandoned the principles of Democracy; how they betrayed their own party to the enemy and went over to false doctrines. But they said that that was regular; and, therefore, that we, and every one who has been associated with the Democratic party are bound to follow their lead, because they regularly proclaimed that the principles of Democracy were dead and those of Populism should be hereafter those of Democracy. You, sir, I heard a few days ago, make an admirable illustration of this on another point. These gentlemen at Chicago claim that they were regular. Benedict Arnold was regular in his proceeding. He was regularly commissioned by his government; he wore its uniform; he was regularly assigned by Washington to the command at West Point and the island; he issued regularly his orders through the chosen staff officers to his troops, disbursing them broadcast, in order that the enemy might come in and massacre all of them. All that proceeding was regular, but when he was detected, when his rank treason was discovered, Washington and his associates refused to follow such regular proceedings.

And yet, according to the theory of our friends at Chicago, Washington and the patriots of the Revolution were bolters of the regular proceedings; and in the same sense are we bolters, refusing to follow the leaders of this treachery, adhering as of old to the true principles and standard of Democracy The convention which met at Chicago was not Democratic. When they abandoned Democratic principles, it ceased to be a Democratic convention, and became that of the principles which it adopted.

The Democratic faith has always claimed that the United States Government is supreme within the limits of the authority they have received from the States and from the people; that it has a right to go wherever that flag goes and it is its duty to enforce the laws of the land in accordance with the powers conferred on it; yet the Chicago convention would wipe virtually out of existence that Supreme Court which interprets the law, forgetting that our ancestors in England fought for hundreds of years to obtain a tribunal of justice which was free from executive control. They would wipe that out of existence and subject it to the control of party leaders to carry out the dictates of the party—they would paralyze the arm of the General Government and forbid the powers to protect the lives and property of its citizens. That convention in terms almost placed a lighted torch in the hands of the incendiary and urged the mob to proceed without restraint to pillage and murder at their discretion.

Mr. Chairman, the Democratic party can never endorse such heresy. We proclaim now as we proclaimed at Indianapolis the ancient principles of Democracy, obedience to law, a court untrammeled either by legislative or by executive control, a tribunal which is the last resort of the weak against the powerful. Though our friends at Chicago would destroy, we insist on upholding and supporting its decrees by the whole power of the State and national authority.

## THE THREE PLATFORMS.

We have before us three platforms, representing three parties in this country, and it is for you, fellow-citizens, to choose which you will sustain. The Republican party, still adhering to its principles of protection, where all classes are taxed for the benefit of one, and not regarding its fiatism, which two things together have brought all the commercial disasters on the country at this stage. It adheres to those doctrines. Then you have the true Democratic platform, which announces still the old Democratic doctrine which may be summarized in a single sentence, the Jeffersonion doctrine of equal and exact justice to all and exclusive privileges to none.

We insist that for every one hundred cents' worth of work done by the laborer he shall receive one hundred cents. We advocate the freest possible trade and we insist that the commerce of the world shall be brought to our ports in free ships, untaxed for the benefit of any special interest in this country. These were the fundamental doctrines of Democracy we proclaimed and over that the flag of Democracy waves as proudly as ever in the hour of victory.

But there is another party, that represented by the conclave at Chicago, and what flag is over it? Not the flag representing their principles, but like some pirate on the ocean, they hoist false colors, in order to allure the unsuspecting within their reach, and over that deck, which is a platform in reality, the illegitimate offspring of Republican protection and fiatism and Populistic communism, repudiation and anarchism, that true flag does not reveal the death's-head of the pirate until you are lured within their reach, and then, for the first time, you find yourself engulfed in the chasm which they dig for the prosperity of the country.

I accept the task imposed upon me by the National Democracy. It was unsought and undesired further than as one who believes he is a patriot is willing to devote the few remaining years of his life to the interests of his country. Not only do I accept the charge imposed upon me, but acknowledging the authority of that great Democracy to place its members wherever it chooses, I obey their mandate and bear the flag, which, through you, they have placed in my hands, under our distinguished leader in that vast concourse of true Democrats who follow his steps, knowing that in the future, as in the past, they lead only in the pathway of duty, of honor, of principle and of patriotism.

# THE TRUE DEMOCRATIC PARTY—THE WITNESS OF TRUE DEMOCRATS.

PRESIDENT CLEVELAND.

BUZZARD'S BAY, MASS., September 10, 1896.

Hon. W. D. BYNUM, Indianapolis, Ind. :

I regret that I cannot accept your invitation to attend the notification meeting at Louisville Saturday evening.

As a Democrat devoted to the principles and integrity of my party, I should be delighted to be present on an occasion so significant, and to mingle with those who are determined that the voice of true Democracy shall not be smothered, and who insist that the glorious standard shall be borne aloft as of old in faithful hands.

GROVER CLEVELAND.

SECRETARY CARLISLE.

BAR HARBOR, ME., September 12, 1896.

Hon. W. D. BYNUM, Louisville, Ky. :

Your telegram inviting me to attend the meeting at Louisville to-day has been forwarded to me at this place, and I greatly regret my inability to accept.

The conservative and patriotic declaration of the Indianapolis Convention on the public questions involved in the pending contest, and the high character of its nominees, cannot fail to arouse the real Democratic sentiment of the country and command the hearty support of all who sincerely believe in the preservation of the public honor, the public peace, and the stability and value of the currency used by our people.

I am proud to take my stand with the old-fashioned Democrats who have refused to abandon their honest convictions in order to form unnatural alliances with political and social organizations, whose purposes are dangerous to the country and wholly inconsistent with the fundamental principles of our party, and I pledge to you and your associates such support and assistance as I can properly give during the campaign.

J. G. CARLISLE.

SECRETARY LAMONT.

WASHINGTON, D. C., Sept. 9, 1896.

Hon. WILLIAM D. BYNUM, Chairman, etc. :

I regret that I am unable to accept the invitation of your committee to be present at the notification to Senator John M. Palmer and ex-Gov.

Simon B. Buckner of their nomination by the National Democratic party for President and Vice-President of the United States. The outcome of the Indianapolis convention in candidates and platform is inspiring to every Democrat who refuses to abandon the principles established by the fathers and steadfastly maintained with pride and honor, and who declines to adopt the new and strange creed proclaimed in a moment of delirium at Chicago and promptly recognized and ratified as its own by the Populist party at St. Louis. I prefer to keep the old faith and remain a Democrat, and shall accordingly cast my vote for Palmer and Buckner.

DANIEL S. LAMONT.

SECRETARY FRANCIS.

WASHINGTON, D. C., Sept. 10, 1896.

Hon. W. D. BYNUM, Chairman, Indianapolis, Ind.:

I regret can not accept your invitation to attend the notification of Gens. Palmer and Buckner at Louisville, Saturday evening. Those old heroes have fought valiantly for their convictions on many battle fields, but no patriot ever enlisted in a nobler cause than that which they have consented to lead. It is the maintenance of the country's honor and the preservation of the integrity of Democratic principles, on whose perpetuity depends the survival of our institutions. May the nominees receive that earnest and zealous support which their high character and the National Democratic party's pure aims so richly merit.

DAVID R. FRANCIS.

# THE "FREE SILVER" PLUNGE A NEW EXPERIMENT.

The proposal of the Free Silver party differs absolutely from anything yet attempted in the history of the country. It is made in disregard of all experience and common sense and could have but one result—to land every interest in the country in a common abyss of ruin.

The demands of both wings of the Free Silver party in regard to the coinage of silver are substantially identical.

The Chicago platform says: "We demand the free and unlimited coinage of both gold and silver at the present legal ratio of 16 to 1 without waiting for the aid or consent of any other nation. We demand that the standard silver dollar shall be a full legal tender equally with gold, for all debts, public and private."

The St. Louis platform says: "We demand the free and unrestricted coinage of silver and gold at the present legal ratio of 16 to 1, without waiting for the consent of foreign nations."

The candidate of both conventions has declared in his speech accepting the nomination of the Chicago Convention: "As against the maintenance of a gold standard, either permanently or until other nations can be united for its overthrow, the Chicago platform presents a clear and emphatic demand for the immediate restoration of the free and unlimited coinage of silver and gold at the present legal ratio of 16 to 1, without waiting for the aid or consent of any other nation. We are not asking that a new experiment be tried; we are insisting upon a return to a financial policy approved by the experience of history and supported by all the prominent statesmen of our nation from the days of the first President down to 1873."

"When we ask that our mints be opened to the free and unlimited coinage of silver into full legal-tender money, we are simply asking that the same mint privileges be accorded to silver that are now accorded to gold. When we ask that this coinage be at the ratio of 16 to 1, we simply ask that our gold coins and the standard silver dollar—which, be it remembered, contains the same amount of pure silver as the first silver dollar coined at our mints—retain their present weight and fineness."

### CIRCUMSTANCES ALTER CASES.

In stating that the proposed free coinage of silver is not a new experiment, Mr. Bryan is manifestly mistaken. When all the conditions under which an experiment is made have changed, the experiment itself changes in character also. That the conditions surrounding free coinage have changed may be easily demonstrated by a reference to the facts of history. In declaring that no State shall make anything but gold and silver a legal tender in payment of debts, the Constitution merely confirms the power of the general government to have the sole regulation of the coinage. What the relations of the two metals in that coinage should be was left to Congress to determine.

The monetary unit of the first coinage act, as of all subsequent coinage acts, was the dollar. The Law of 1792 was drafted in strict conformity with the recommendations of Alexander Hamilton in his celebrated mint report, and what Hamilton aimed at was a monetary unit of two terms between which there should be strict equivalence. The two terms were 24.75 grains of pure gold to 371.25 grains of pure silver, either, in coins bearing the mint stamp of the United States and combined with a certain proportion of alloy, being equivalent to the value of one dollar. But by this ratio of one to fifteen it was found that gold was undervalued, an ounce of gold being held in the other markets of the world to be worth 15.5 ounces of silver. The mints of France were open to its free coinage at that ratio, so it was impossible to keep gold in the country.

Up to the time when the Act of 1834 came in to redress the lack of equivalence between the two terms of the monetary unit, the most important element of the coinage was the silver half-dollar. This had full legal tender power and quality, the grains of standard silver it contained being just half of the weight of the dollar. The Act of 1834 reduced the amount of pure gold in the dollar to 23.20 grains, and later the Act of 1837 made it 23.22 grains. As the amount of pure silver in the dollar remained unchanged, its weight only being reduced to 412.5 grains by a reduction of the amount of copper alloy, the ratio of 1834 was a fraction more than 16 to 1, and the ratio of 1837 a fraction less. This ratio was adopted in opposition to the advice of Albert Gallatin, who advised the fixing of the intermediate ratio of 15.5 to 1, which continued to be that of the nations of Continental Europe. The ratio of 1834–37 erred on the one side as much as the ratio of 1792 had erred on the other, and silver was driven out of circulation under the new system as thoroughly as gold had been under the old one.

Down to 1873, when the place of the non-existent silver dollar was taken by a trade dollar designed to facilitate commerce with the East, and the statutory bimetallism which had become a dead letter more than a generation before, was formally abandoned, all the attempts made to secure equivalence between gold and silver had failed.

### GOOD-BYE TO COMMON SENSE!

And yet these experiments had been made under conditions much more favorable to their success than any that exist now. For over a hundred and fifty years, the market ratio between gold and silver had varied comparatively little. In 1717 it was 15.13 to 1, and in 1873 it was 15.92 to 1. Even during the period, 1848–68, of the immense production of gold, amounting to $2,757,-

000,000 against only $813,000,000 of silver, the change in the ratio did not exceed 1.6 per cent. There was that much difference between the commercial ratio of 1873 and 1874, and ten times that difference between the commercial ratio of 1874 and 1884.

If the error, amounting to less than three per cent., in the ratio of 1792, prevented gold from entering into circulation for forty-five years, and a similar error on the other side in 1837 brought gold into circulation but banished silver, how much more certain would the proposal of the Silver Party Conventions be to cause the wholesale exportation of gold and make silver the sole standard of value? If the experience of the founders of the Republic is to be brought into this controversy, it ought to be as a lesson and a warning. Now that one ounce of gold will buy over thirty ounces of silver, the proposed restoration of the equivalence of the two elements of the monetary unit, on the theory that one ounce of gold will buy only sixteen ounces of silver, is an affront to ordinary intelligence.

The recent legislation of the United States, which was passed with a view to arrest the fall in the price of silver, and so to bring the commercial and legal ratio into closer accord, reserved the privilege of coinage to the Government, placed a limit on its volume, looked to the co-operation of foreign nations, and declared it to be the policy of the country to maintain the silver coinage at equal and interchangeable value with gold. The act of February 28, 1878, declares in its second section: "That immediately after the passage of this act the President shall invite the governments of the countries composing the Latin Union, so called, and of such other European nations as he may deem advisable, to join the United States in a conference to adopt a common ratio between gold and silver, for the purpose of establishing internationally the use of bimetallic money and securing fixity of relative value between those metals."

The act of July 14, 1890, provided: "That upon demand of the holder of any of the Treasury notes herein provided for the Secretary of the Treasury shall, under such regulations as he may prescribe, redeem such notes in gold or silver coin, at his discretion, it being the established policy of the United States to maintain the two metals on a parity with each other upon the present legal ratio, or such ratio as may be provided by law."

The act of November 1, 1893, repealing this latter statute, has for its concluding sentences the following: "And it is hereby declared to be the policy of the United States to continue the use of both gold and silver as standard money of equal intrinsic and exchangeable value, such equality to be secured through international agreement, or by such safeguards of legislation as will insure the maintenance of the parity in value of the coins of the two metals, and the equal power of every dollar at all times in the markets and in payment of debts. And it is hereby further declared that the efforts of the Government should be steadily directed to the establishment of such a safe system of bimetallism as will maintain at all times the equal power of every dollar coined or issued by the United States, in the markets and in the payment of debts."

The legislation proposed in the Chicago and St. Louis platforms proceeds on a repudiation of the principles of all the legislation that has preceded it. The idea that was uppermost in the minds of the authors of our earliest coinage legislation, that the closest possible correspondence in the legal and the commercial ratio between gold and silver should be maintained, is thrown to the winds, and the idea of the later legislation that a dollar in any and every one of the constituent elements of the currency of the United States, gold, silver and paper, should be maintained as of equal value is alike discarded. The proposal is that the monetary unit should be a dollar containing 371.25 grains of pure silver, worth to-day in the markets of the world about 53 cents, and that this should be the measure of all values and the standard for the payment of all debts.

This, obviously, is silver monometallism, pure and simple, and one of its first effects would be to drive all the gold in the country either abroad or into hiding. For, manifestly, no possessor of gold coin or bullion would exchange 23.22 grains of pure gold, now called a dollar, for 371.25 grains of pure silver, which the Government of the United States had stamped as a dollar and returned to its owner, when he could buy for every 23.22 grains of his gold 700 grains of pure silver and have them stamped on his own account. The fact that 23.22 grains of pure gold are now freely exchanged for coins containing only 371.25 grains of pure silver, or for their paper equivalents, is simply due to the other fact that the credit of the Government is pledged to maintain such silver coins, notes or certificates as good as the gold dollar. No such pledge could be given or maintained under free silver coinage, because, among other reasons, it would bankrupt any government that gave it. The repeal of the Bullion Purchase Act of 1890 became a pressing necessity in 1893, because even under its limitations of coinage and with the Government taking all the profits of the transaction, it was demonstrated to be impossible to keep the growing volume of silver and of paper based on silver in the currency or a parity with gold.

### AN OBJECT LESSON IN SILVER.

The preliminaries of the crisis which preceded the repeal of the law of 1890 (usually known as the Sherman Act) are thus outlined by Congressman John DeWitt Warner:

"As is pretty generally agreed, the growing dullness of business had left our currency superabundant as far back as 1890; while in that year the rate at which depreciated silver was poured into it was increased from $24,000,000 a year to more than double that rate. The effect was as though water were poured into a measure already filled with oil. The Sherman notes, whose circulation was bounded by national lines, went to the bottom of the measure—that is, stayed in this country; the gold, free to move—that is, current everywhere—overflowed to foreign countries.

"Another effect now began to be prominent. To a small extent our holders of mortgages (which in this country are usually for short terms, even though intended as permanent investments) promptly secured themselves by requiring renewals under contracts payable in gold; but many lenders—to some extent from individual hesitancy in exacting unusual terms of borrowers, and to some extent from apprehension lest the legislation threatened in many States against such discrimination might prove valid—refused to make or renew time loans, thus forcing a stagnation of enterprise in many directions and in many others a realization of assets under unfavorable circumstances.

"Concurrent with this was developed a disposition to hoard gold and to discriminate in its favor by withholding it from payments. That this was markedly true in 1893 is universally understood. It seems to have been forgotten in many quarters how much earlier than that year this practice became general; though an inspection of the treasury accounts shows that in September, 1890, the first month after the passage of the Sherman Act, the Treasury lost \$58,000,000 of its gold reserve.

"June 30, 1890, the net treasury assets were \$255,893,000, of which \$190,232,000 was in gold and gold bullion. A year later similar assets were \$176,459,000, of which \$117,667,000 was in gold and gold bullion—the "free gold," that is the amount above the \$100,000,000 reserve for greenback redemption, having been reduced during the year from \$90,232,000 to \$17,667,000.

"Recalling that the customs receipts are the principal streams which feed the Treasury, we can investigate one step further. In June, 1890, above 90 per cent. of our customs receipts were in gold. The proportion of gold steadily declined thereafter until in June, 1891, but twelve per cent. of the customs receipts were in gold.

"The circle of investigation is complete for the period. The Treasury was diluting the currency by silver inflation at the rate of \$4,500,000 each month; and at the same time it was rapidly losing power to maintain its parity in gold; while the selection by which gold was retained and silver used for payments to Government indicated that gold was being hoarded outside.

"The National Administration, though doing nothing to avert the crisis, was sensible of its approach. In the spring of 1891 the Treasury, by refusing to furnish gold bars, of which it had plenty, practically charged gold exporters one-tenth per cent. premium, at which price during that year they took above \$60,000,000; and during the summer of 1891, the Government attempted to gain gold by selling legal-tender Western exchange at a price sixty cents per

$1,000 less than the normal rates, on condition of being paid in gold, some $12,000,000 of which was promptly thus secured.

"Finally, to accelerate the rate at which we were moving toward disaster, the joint effect of the tariff revision of 1890 and the liberal appropriations of the Fifty-second Congress had been to turn the late annual surplus, averaging $110,000,000 per annum for the year 1888–1890, into a deficit which for the year beginning July 1, 1893, amounted to more than $69,000,000; so that a constantly weaker Treasury faced a steadily increasing responsibility. The time thus rapidly approached when the sole resource to maintain our currency upon a natural basis would be the steadily diminishing gold receipts of the Treasury ; which, so far as concerned customs revenues, had shrunken to less than four per cent. in September, 1892, and never again rose above ten per cent. until in the currency famine of 1893, the hoarded gold coin was forced from the bank vaults.

"Such was the course along which the Treasury steadily drifted for years, until in February, 1893, the outgoing Administration, by private appeal to its friends, secured some $6,500,000 of gold from New York bankers, just in time to enable it, going out on the 4th of March, to escape the breaking of the dam behind which for years it had seen the waters steadily piling.

"As the Cleveland Administration settled into its place the flood was still rising, though not faster than had been the case for months previous. But soon the actual impairment of the $100,000,000 Treasury gold reserve showed the water trickling over the levee, and on every side each weak spot about to give way."

### A COMPREHENSIVE PROPOSAL.

Disastrous as were the results of the experiments in "rehabilitating" silver which culminated in the Sherman Act, the result of any such experiment as is demanded by the Chicago platform and echoed in the Populist platform adopted at St. Louis must be more disastrous still. That experiment consists of three main conditions : (1) that the coinage of silver—instead of being under the control of the Government, as at present, and therefore restricted in amount—shall be so far free that any citizen may, on demand, have any amount of silver bullion converted into silver dollars without charge or seigniorage; (2) that the fine silver so coined shall be only 16 times the weight of fine gold contained in the gold dollar, though it would require over 30 times the silver to equal the value of the gold ; and (3) that the silver dollars so coined shall be legal tender for the payment of debts, without limit as to amount. It is not even proposed to limit this privilege of coinage to bullion of domestic production, but to throw open the mint to supplies coming from any part of the world.

Though there is in every country in Europe a party, more or less considerable in numbers and influence, that is in hearty sympathy with this financial programme, there is nowhere, outside of the United States, a party that believes in the possibility of any one nation being able to restore the parity of silver with gold. This profound and all but universal European distrust of the ability of this nation to accomplish alone a task likely to prove hard enough for a combination of the great civilized powers of the world, has a vital bearing on the feasibility of the American silver programme. It so happens that our external indebtedness is the largest of any nation in the world, being estimated at between $1,500,000,000 and $2,000,000,000. If our foreign creditors had confidence in our ability to restore the value of silver in the way proposed by the silver industry, they might be expected to at least assent to a fair trial of free coinage before recalling their loans. But having only one opinion as to the certain failure of such an experiment, the course they would take, in the contingency of free coinage being authorized, admits of no doubt. With a fixed conviction that unlimited coinage would force us upon the silver basis and precipitate a fall in the current value of the silver dollar to the market value of silver bullion, they would immediately proceed to realize upon our obligations in our own markets. That would be an inevitable result of investors' prudence. The force of this factor would be felt, indeed, before the revolution could be put in operation; and there can be no uncertainty about the effects which it would develop.

So soon as the prospect of the enactment of free coinage became reasonably sure, the return of these foreign-held securities would set in. The reflux would intensify the distrust of our creditors; and the remittances of gold against their realizations would compel a suspension of gold payments before the new law could be put in operation. There would follow an inevitable demoralization and disorganization of banking and credit operations, a prostration of all commerce and a paralysis of all industry. The catastrophe would in magnitude and violence transcend any in all our history; the crisis attending the outbreak of the Civil War would be a small matter compared with it. Of course we could not liquidate our whole foreign indebtedness, for we should have no available means for making such enormous settlements. Our entire stock of gold would not suffice to pay more than one-third of our obligations. There would be a point at which the return of securities must cease, but only to be renewed the moment there was any recovery in our ability to pay for them; and those obligations would interminably press like a millstone upon our finance and prevent the recovery of our prostrated credit.

Concurrently with the apparent triumph of the course of free silver coinage would necessarily come the abandonment of the efforts of the Government to maintain, in the language of the National Democratic platform of 1892 and of the act of November 1, 1893, "the equal power of every dollar at all times in the markets and in the payment of debts." There would be a wild rush by every one holding the paper obligations of the Government to convert them into gold and a compulsory recourse by the Treasury to payments in silver. Gold would at once go to a premium, and the paper money in the pockets of the people would shrink in purchasing power with each advance in the gold premium that marked the decline in value of the silver coinage and the notes payable in it to the market price of 371.25 grains of silver bullion. All trade would be thrown out of joint, factories would close and the wholesale transactions in every class of merchandise would cease, till the people had learned to adapt themselves to the new conditions. Recovery would necessarily be slow, unless indeed a revelation of the gulf of ruin opened up before the country should produce a change in public sentiment so sudden and complete as to compel a return to the safe ground which had been so heedlessly abandoned. But the lesson, even were it so quickly perceived and promptly acted on, would be a frightfully costly one, and would have to be paid for by years of patient toil by the producers of the country's wealth.

# THE LATIN MONETARY UNION AND THE INTERNATIONAL CONFERENCES.

This union of the five nations, France, Belgium, Switzerland, Italy and Greece, containing about eighty million people, is usually credited with having demonstrated the success of a system of bimetallism. In point of fact its experience below demonstrates the impossibility of maintaining such a system under trifling variations between the legal and commercial ratio of the two metals, and its absolute and costly failure when these variations become large.

In what goes before, certain statements have been made which may seem to require proof. First among these is that in regard to European opinion as to the possibility of the United States restoring, unaided, the parity between gold and silver under a system of free coinage.

Europe has seen in the last thirty years a succession of efforts to work out the problem of keeping gold and silver circulating side by side at a fixed ratio, and the conclusion which it has drawn from these is that no nation or combination of nations can accomplish this under a system of free and unlimited coinage. It can be done with restricted coinage under the Government control, but not otherwise. That conclusion is a necessary induction from the experience of the nations comprising the Latin Monetary Union, whose history has been written by Pierre des Essars, the Chief of the Department of Economics of the Bank of France, as a chapter in that monumental work "A History of Banking in All Nations," published by the New York "Journal of Commerce and Commercial Bulletin." From this chapter is extracted the following summary of facts:

The law of the 7th Germinal, Year XI., which established the French monetary system, provided that "Five grammes of silver of a standard fineness of .9 shall constitute the monetary unit, designated by the name franc." Articles 6, 7 and 8 added: "Gold pieces of 20 and 40 francs shall be struck. Their standard is fixed at .9 fine and .1 alloy. The pieces of 20 francs shall be 155 to the kilogramme, and those of 40 francs 77.5 to the kilogramme." According to these provisions, gold of equal weight and standard is considered to be worth 15.5 times as much as silver. This was the ratio fixed by royal decree of October 30, 1785.

The simplicity and admirable convenience of the French monetary system, with its great advantage of a decimal basis, procured for it adoption by Belgium on June 5, 1832, Switzerland May 7, 1850, and Italy August 24, 1862. In consequence of this identity of system, the moneys of each of the four countries circulated freely in the others, and thus a kind of monetary union was improvised without formal understanding. But in 1850, as a result of the discovery of gold deposits in California and Australia, the monetary circulation of Europe was profoundly disturbed. Here was a case, apparently, of the depreciation of gold and a reflection on the stability of value claimed for that metal. But it will be observed that the extreme range of gold fluctuation was less than one per cent., while the depreciation of silver has been over 50 per cent. Whereas gold was abundant and commonly used even for payments of slight importance, silver, whose production had remained stationary, rose in value. The ratio between gold and silver, which, during the ten years 1841–50, had averaged 1 to 15.835, declined in the fifteen succeeding years, falling below 15.5 from 1852 to 1861, the lowest point, 15.21, being reached in 1859. The average ratio of gold and silver during that period was 15.37. The relative increase in the value of silver, amounting to 0.846 or less than ⅞ of one per cent., was sufficient to attract speculators, who, by continuous manipulations with large quantities of metal, gained tempting profits. At the very start the money-changers drained the market of five-franc pieces, which disappeared from circulation. The fractional coins were melted, and France suffered from a genuine silver money famine, affecting the supply both of five-franc pieces and subsidiary coins. Among the varied devices suggested for putting an end to the dearth of fractional money, one was seized upon that had eminently the characteristics of an expedient. The intrinsic value was reduced to do away with the profits obtained from melting. Switzerland, by a Federal Act of 1860, lowered the standard of the silver franc and its multiples up to five francs, and of its fractions, to .8 fine, so that the franc coin was worth only 0.889 franc. Italy, adopting the French system in 1862, struck coins in denominations below five francs at a standard of 0.835, which gave the franc an intrinsic worth of 0.928 franc. In France a law was enacted May 24, 1864, on the model of the Italian measure, adopting the standard of 0.835 for the twenty and fifty centime pieces, but maintaining the 0.9 standard for the higher denominations. Belgium made no change in her coinage. These measures, taken without previous agreement, altered the conditions of the monetary exchange of four nations and opened a new field for speculation. Swiss pieces were exchanged for Belgian, and the latter were brought to Switzerland for recoinage at a reduced standard.

### THE FORMATION OF THE UNION.

Belgium, taking alarm at these abuses, made overtures to the French Government with a view to a conference in Paris, at which Switzerland and Italy should be represented, and which should have for its object to establish a uniform system for the coinage and circulation of fractional moneys in the four coutries. It was further proposed that the conference should have full liberty of action, and might either confine its work to a consideration of monetary regulations for the four states concerned, or extend its scope by laying the foundation of a uniform circulation for the whole of Europe.

The conference proposition was approved by Switzerland and Italy, and the International Commission began its deliberations in Paris, November 20, 1865. After a protracted debate, in which Belgium declared for the standard already established in France and Italy, Switzerland consented to the 0.835 standard. However, the period fixed by the conference for the withdrawal of the coins that had been issued by the various countries under conditions other than those provided for, which was to expire January 1, 1868, was extended in the case of Switzerland until January 1, 1879. After this obstacle had been got over, all parties being in hearty sympathy with the project for a monetary union, the other matters at issue were not such as to cause any decided conflict of opinion. At the meeting of December 21, 1865, the conference adopted the fifteen articles of the famous agreement consolidating Belgium, France, Italy and Switzerland in a monetary union. The following is a summary of that agreement:

The four contracting States were to issue coins of the same weight, standard, and diameter. The percentage of allowable loss of weight by use was to be uniform in all the States. The standard for the five-franc silver piece was to be .900 fine, and for the pieces below five francs .835 fine. The coins struck by each of the contracting States were to be accepted in the public offices of all, under these conditions: The five-franc piece without restriction, and the fractional coins up to 100 francs, provided that coins which had been reduced in weight by use one per cent. below the legal limit, or whose effigies have been effaced, might be excluded. In the latter case, if their weight has been reduced by use five per cent. below the legal limit, they were to be restruck by the Government that issued them.

Each of the contracting governments engaged to accept from individuals or from the public offices of the other States the fractional silver coin that it had issued, and to exchange it for an equal value of current money (gold pieces or five-franc pieces), provided the sum presented for exchange should not be less than 100 francs. The quantity of fractional money to be issued was fixed at six francs per head of the population. The year of coinage was to be stamped upon the gold and silver pieces of each State. The same agreement conceded the privilege of joining in the compact to other countries adopting the Union's monetary system, and named January 1, 1880, as the date of expiration of the compact, with a tacit extension fifteen years longer, unless notice of withdrawal should be given at least a year before the specified date of expiration.

### BEGINNING OF TROUBLE.

These were the broad provisions of the Convention of December 23, 1865. A brief experience made its imperfections and deficiencies felt. It was not foreseen that the money market, which in 1865 was favorable to silver, might change and favor gold; and that, in such not impossible contingency, a grave problem would arise respecting the final settlement of the five-franc pieces—a problem, which, indeed, would be much more serious than that of subsidiary coins. Several countries that were expected to join the Union entertained misgivings and were slow to decide. Austria, in 1867, seriously contemplated giving in her adhesion, but finally only Greece and the Papal States came over. By a law enacted August 10, 1867, Greece adopted the French monetary system, and, profiting by the privilege vouchsafed by Article 12 of the convention, on November 18, 1868, signified her desire for membership of the Latin Union, which was accorded to her by the associated governments without any dissent.

The whole policy of the Second Empire displayed a tendency toward groupings of nationalities and the formation of a sort of European confederation. The Latin Union seemed to be a first step in that direction, and the next question opened up was whether the system adopted by the four countries might not be extended to embrace all Europe. The Exposition of 1867 appeared to offer a favorable opportunity. At the instance of the French Government, an international conference was held, at which eighteen nations were represented. It had its sessions in Paris from June 17 to July 6, 1867. As had been done in 1865, a list of questions was made up, which were brought forward successively for discussion. Nothing practical came of this conference so far as the Latin countries were concerned, but useful hints of the inclinations of the different powers were obtained. Mr. Meinecke, the Prussian delegate, signified his preference for the single gold standard, and the conference, with one dissenting vote—that of the delegate of the Netherlands—expressed itself affirmatively upon the following question: "Is there a possibility to attain this end (uniformity in coinages) upon the basis and with the condition of the adoption of the exclusive gold standard, leaving to each country liberty to retain temporarily the silver standard?" Indeed, from the opening of the conference, it was evident that there was little prospect for gaining adherents for the system of the Latin Union, whose essential feature was the simultaneous use of gold and silver. This indication was not permitted to go unheeded; for the conclusions arrived at by the Conference of 1867 led Prince Bismarck, promptly after the war of 1870, to substitute in Germany the single gold standard for the old silver standard. Germany was soon followed by the Scandinavian countries—Denmark, Sweden and Norway—which also profited by the decisions of the Conference of 1867. Since 1873, Holland had seriously taken up the coinage question, manifesting a preference for the gold standard, which she accordingly adopted on June 6, 1875.

### DOWNWARD COURSE OF SILVER.

Meanwhile China and the other far Eastern countries did not take quantities to at all compensate for the excessive production. Thus three agencies worked together for depressing the price of silver; the increase in the output of the mines, the change in the monetary systems of Germany, the Netherlands and the Scandinavian nations, and the decrease in the Asiatic demand. Moreover, the price of silver on the London market, which should have stood at 60⅛d. per ounce if the 15.5 ratio is correct, took this downward course:

| | Maximum Per Ounce. | Minimum Per Ounce. |
|---|---|---|
| 1865 | 61⅞d. | 60⅛d. |
| 1869 | 61d. | 60d. |
| 1870 | 62d. | 60¼d. |
| 1871 | 61⅛d. | 59¼d. |
| 1874 | 59½d. | 57¼d. |
| 1875 | 57⅝d. | 55½d. |

With the right of unlimited coinage allowed to the contracting States, the Latin Union served to drain off the larger part of the surplus silver. As the average intrinsic ratio of gold and silver rose from 15.64 in 1872 to 15.93 in 1873, this left, notwithstanding the loss of interest on mint vouchers, a sufficient margin for speculation, since the piece that circulated for five francs was worth barely 4.85 francs at the rate of the day. The coinage of five-franc pieces took great strides. In 1873 there were coined:

| | Five-Franc Pieces. |
|---|---|
| In Belgium | 111,704,795 |
| In Italy | 42,273,935 |
| In France | 154,649,045 |
| Grand total | 308,627,775 |

This aggregate of 308,627,775 francs represents the coinage of only three governments, Switzerland having for a long time abstained from minting. The over-supply of the depreciated money alarmed the public. The Bank of France rejected Belgian and Italian five-franc coins, as it had the right to do. The Chambers of Commerce, particularly those of Antwerp and Lyons, gave decided expressions to their solicitude, and demanded that the gold standard be adopted. To soothe these apprehensions, the French and Belgian Ministers caused a slackening in the coinage of five-franc pieces, but more energetic measures were needful. Mr. Malou, Belgian Minister of Finance, took the initiative. On November 11, 1873, he presented the draft of a law authorizing the Government to limit or suspend the minting of five-franc pieces until July 1, 1875.

A conference between the representatives of the countries belonging to the Union was held in 1874 and another in 1875. The result of both was the same—to place further limits on the coinage of silver. A third conference met in

Paris on January 20, 1876. The considerations that had rendered limitation of the silver coinage imperative in former years had acquired added strength during 1875. The standard ounce of silver had fallen to 55.5 pence on the London market on June 11, making the ratio of gold and silver intrinsically 16.989. Throughout the year, the ratio ranged above 16.3. The Bank of France saw its stock of silver coin augmented enormously, having increased as follows from 1871 to 1875:

|  | Francs |
|---|---|
| 1871 | 131,700,000 |
| 1872 | 145,500,000 |
| 1873 | 150,300,000 |
| 1874 | 329,500,000 |
| 1875 | 508,700,000 |

### SUSPENSION OF FREE COINAGE.

Thus, in a period of five years, despite all endeavors to maintain silver in circulation, the stock had nearly quadrupled. It was consequently needful to preserve the restrictions on coinage. In France, M. Leon Say, Minister of Finance, deeming it inexpedient to have the coinage conducted at the sole pleasure of individuals, submitted to the Senate, on March 21, 1876, the draft of a measure authorizing the restriction or entire discontinuance of minting by decree. He said in his explanatory statement: "Since 1865, there has occurred a certain depreciation in the value of silver. The Powers subscribing to the Convention have considered it prudent, since 1874, to put a check upon the coinage of five-franc silver pieces. A maximum coinage has been designated for the countries of the Union, amounting in 1874 to 120,000,000 francs, in 1875 to 150,000,000 francs, and in 1876 again to 120,000,000 francs. The share allotted to France was 60,000,000 francs in 1874, and 75,000,000 francs in 1875. This year (1876) it is 54,000,000 francs, with the privilege to coin at least 27,000,000 francs in 1877; which implies that our mints are limited to 81,000,000 francs until a new arrangement shall obtain. But as the home legislation of France has not meantime been altered, the amount which is maximum from the point of view of the State is minimum as regarded by interested individuals. Indeed, from the very day that France was empowered to strike 54,000,000 francs of five-franc pieces, the owners of silver have had a perfect right to insist that the Government neither can nor should deny them the privilege to convert their bullion into coin, so long as the international convention is not violated—in other words, so long as the prescribed bounds are not overstepped. They are therefore entitled to demand that five-franc pieces be minted for them until the quota apportioned to France shall have been exhausted." After calling attention to Belgium's suspension of silver coinage in 1873, M. Say concluded by declaring that, in view of the depression of silver, respecting which it was difficult to form a definite judgment, he believed it to be convenient, without wishing to solve the question whether the single or double standard was preferable, to assume a waiting attitude and not increase the quantity of silver pieces.

On August 6, 1876, a decree was issued announcing that bullion and other material for the coinage of five-franc pieces for private account would no longer be accepted. Meanwhile, in the Belgian Parliament, M. Frere-Orban had interpellated M. Malou, Minister of Finance, on the coinage question. It is well to remember that the allowances successively granted to the several countries bore no relation to their legitimate needs, excepting, probably, in the case of Greece, and that in various instances they served only as a means to levy a convenient tax upon the circulation of neighboring States, the effect of which was not immediately felt. To levy such a tax the only thing needful was to buy silver at the rate of the day—ten to twenty-five per cent. less than the nominal legal value—and throw it upon the market after transformation into five-franc pieces at face value. M. Frere Orban's interpellation bore upon such transactions. M. Malou confessed that he had bought bar silver for 10,800,000 francs with three per cent. consols for the purpose of making a profit for the State. In his defense he said : "Is the five-franc piece false money ? It is worth five francs, and, therefore, I could not make scandalous profits." This provided his interrogator with an inviting opportunity, which was availed of in the following severe words: "Why has the Government bought and coined for the account of the State ? By its own admission, to make a profit. The five-franc piece is always worth five francs, but whence comes the profit ? It comes from the circumstances that you legislate in recognition of fundamental wrong, proclaiming against truth, against plain evidence, and against the nature of things—proclaiming, I say, in perpetuity that fifteen and a half kilos of silver shall always exchange for one kilo of gold. The Government, to gain a miserable profit, has swelled the burdens of the State in the event that demonetization shall occur, and has increased the amount of the coinage, as you admit." The incident had no practical issue, but it afforded a demonstration of the spirit of speculation that actuated the demands for unnecessary coinage. M. Frere-Orban enjoyed a sort of satisfaction afterward when the Belgian Chambers were convoked by the Ministry to vote upon an extension of the law of December 18, 1873, until January 1, 1879.

### A SERIES OF CONFERENCES.

On the 18th of February, 1878, the United States Congress had passed the Bland Bill, authorizing the coinage of silver dollars and making them legal tender. It had, moreover, decided that an international conference should be called to establish an international understanding as to the ratio between the two metals. General Noyes, Minister of the United States to France, made overtures to that effect to the French Government, which led to the resultless international conference held in Paris in August, 1878. As soon as the French Government received the invitation of the United States it sought the advice of the other governments comprised in the Latin Union regarding the reply to be given. All were of opinion that the international conference should be preceded by an exchange of views on the part of the delegates from the Latin Union countries; and for this purpose a conference was called for August 30, 1878, to examine the conditions for a renewal of the compact that was to expire in 1880. At a preliminary meeting, the Italian representatives once more brought forward the old demand for legal tender for gold and five-franc silver coins of each of the contracting States in all the nations of the Union. This Italian demand, rejected in the former conferences, was the logical outcome of the Convention of 1865, which required the public officers of each nation to take unrestrictedly and without possibility of exchange and settlement a foreign money which, nevertheless, might be refused by the people to whom the State makes payments, since among them it is not legal tender. If, on the other hand, to forestall this danger, the coins should be invested with the legal-tender quality, individuals would then compulsorily have to receive foreign money— not note money, but actual—struck without the concurrence or surveillance of the Government to which they owe allegiance, and which would hold itself responsible without power of control. All this applies equally to gold money ; but the ready preference of the public for the yellow metal always assures foreign gold of easy circulation, and so it is the less necessary to pronounce it legal tender in order to keep it current. To finally secure assent to her claim, Italy agreed to a modifying provision, whereby each country, in the case of a breach of the Convention, was to take back its own five-franc pieces that might be in the possession of the other States and pay gold for them. Upon this modifying clause turned subsequently the transactions of the Conference of 1885.

### THE DIFFICULTIES OF A SETTLEMENT CLAUSE.

The management of the Bank of France did not feel at all satisfied with the outlook, observing that the practical effect would be to deprive the bank of all right to refuse, if necessary, foreign coins, and thus further swell the stock in its vaults, which amounted nearly to 270,000,000 francs, whereon the loss in exchange was thirteen to fourteen per cent. Moreover, the question of State responsibility for the redemption of foreign coins held by the bank had never been settled, and on that score the management had grave anxieties, which found expression in the reply sent, December 5th, to the Minister. In this the bank, after explaining that the consequences of the 1865 Convention were very burdensome, and that the receipts of foreign silver grew daily because of the public's aversion for the heavy and inconvenient five-franc pieces, rejected with all its energy the proposition to establish legal tender for foreign coins, whether silver or gold. It added that, while it had consented temporarily, upon the State's demand and in the general interest, to take foreign pieces, it would none the less be entitled to protection under the principles of the common law. In plainer words, it intimated that it would be able to throw upon the State the loss that it might have to suffer from the depreciation of silver. Finally, it was stated that although the Convention of 1865 had not provided a method for the liquidation of the five-franc silver pieces, the decline of ten to fifteen per cent. which silver had undergone required imperatively that the Conference should not leave the question without solution. This letter furnished the Minister of Finance a reason for rejecting the legal-tender proposal, which accordingly was ultimately set aside.

The Convention of 1878, so laboriously constructed, was to terminate on the 1st of January, 1886, unless extended by general agreement. Early in 1884 Italy showed anxiety for a new convention. The Minister of Finance, Signor Magliani, seemed desirous of creating a situation in which gold should be the predominating element, awaiting circumstances for placing the country on a basis of absolute bimetallism. Switzerland, having suffered some losses from the Convention of 1878, demanded, on January 11, 1884, the calling of a new conference, to consider details for a new understanding. The conference, after being several times delayed, began its deliberations on July 20, 1885. The wishes of France were: 1, The continuance of the Latin Union ; 2, insertion of a settlement clause ; 3, provision for taking measures to insure equal treatment of gold and silver ; 4, prohibition of all the States of the Latin Union issuing and maintaining in circulation small scrip as injurious to the circulation of silver ; 5, revision of the per capita basis of fractional coins. Items 3 and 4 had reference mainly to Italy. Her decree concerning the composition of the metallic reserves of the banks had been an interference with the equality of treatment due the two metals, which was indicated by the spirit, if not the letter, of the Union's conventions. By preserving 350,000,000 francs of small scrip in circulation, she arbitrarily narrowed the field open to five-franc pieces and fractional coins. But the principal matter of difficulty was the proposed settlement clause—a clause which should bind the different countries, at the expiration of the Union, to take back the silver pieces struck by them and, after making mutual exchanges, to settle balances in gold or equivalent values. It is easily understood how strong an interest France had in urging such a clause (which, by the way, Italy and Switzerland approved) when it is stated that on November 5, 1878, the Bank of France had on hand 1,031,700,000 francs in silver, and on July 20, 1835, 1,150,900,000 francs—an increase of 119,200,000 francs. Of the 1885 sum, according to an estimate made at the time, 23.76 per cent. was in foreign pieces. The depreciation of silver, which in 1878 was ten to twelve per cent., had reached seventeen to eighteen per cent. in 1885. But the reasons that caused France to be so solicitous for a settlement clause were precisely the reasons inducing Belgium (which, more than any other country, had contributed to the plethora of silver by coinages far beyond her needs) to oppose the plan.

### THE BASIS OF SETTLEMENT.

The settlement clause was the occasion for protracted debate, at one stage of which the Belgium delegates withdrew from the conference. Finally, toward the close of 1885, the Belgian Government suggested the following arrangement: "If a settlement shall occur, France will amass the Belgian coins circulating in the States of the Union, and will herself proceed to exchange them with Belgium. If, after balancing, Belgium shall still be debtor to France, the difference shall be divided into two parts. The Belgian Government will, within five years, pay for the one-half in gold and drafts on France, and the other half shall be sent back through commercial and exchange channels. Belgium shall make no change in her monetary system of a character to interfere with this taking back of coins, and she guarantees that the balance to be settled shall not be in excess of 200,000,000 francs." This was regarded as an acceptable offer, and it was approved by the French Government in principle.

But another stumbling block had to be got over. In the protocol of November 6, 1885, it was said in substance: "In the event that one of the governments of the Union, either directly or through the instrumentality of bank issue, shall effect an arrangement with the Belgian Government for again redeeming its own five-franc pieces, such arrangement shall be submitted to the other States of the Union for approval. In case of non-approval, each of the other States will have, with regard to the State effecting such arrangement, the choice between agreeing to the arrangement or acting in pursuance of the settlement clause already adopted." The Italian Government, informed of the understanding arrived at between France and Belgium, claimed the right to reserve to itself the privileges granted by the protocol. This gave rise to a possibility that circumstances might come to pass which would make it preferable for France to hold Italy to the settlement clause, and to send back the Belgian pieces at the risk and peril of France. Nevertheless, as it was all-important that Belgium should stay in the Union, it was determined, after long negotiation, that France and Italy should mutually claim the benefit of the conditions given to the Belgian Government as to the regulation of their accounts, so that the maximum balance of the repatriated coin should be 200,000,000 francs so far as Belgium was concerned. Greece reserved the right of choice at the time when she should abandon the régime of forced currency.

To provide for the special case of Switzerland—which, having struck no five-franc pieces, might have suffered from dearth of coin under the proposed mode of settlement—it was decided that France, Italy and Belgium should settle "at sight" in Swiss five-franc silver pieces and ten-franc gold pieces and higher denominations for the moneys presented to them by the Swiss Confederation.

The Union of 1865 was prolonged to December 31, 1890, by the terms of the additional act of December 12, 1885, which restored Belgium to membership in it. Silver coinage was further suspended, not to be resumed without the unanimous assent of the contracting States. Any State desiring to have free coinage again, was required as a preliminary to redeem in gold and at sight the silver coins of its mintage that circulated in other nations. The Convention was for five years, and therefore was to expire December 31, 1890. But none of the contracting States had any interest in its dissolution, and it was extended from year to year by tacit agreement. Since December 31, 1890, the Bank of France has yearly engaged to receive over its counters the coins of the Latin Union for the account of the Treasury. The Convention survives mainly because the circumstances of the associated nations render it impossible for them to dissolve it. Switzerland, having coined but a practically insignificant amount of five-franc pieces, might step out without harm; but Italy and Belgium would be exposed to very grave embarassment if they should be obliged to take back the five-franc pieces that France holds. As for France, she fears that by giving notice of her retirement from the Union the exchanges of her neighbors would be deranged, and she would suffer from the counter-shock. Notwithstanding, therefore, the precarious footing on which it stands, the Latin Union is renewed from year to year tacitly, and the probability is that it may continue for a long time to come.

After passing through an experience like this, it would be strange, indeed, if in any of the countries of the Latin Union there should be any faith in the ability of the United States to maintain, single-handed, the double monetary standard with the privilege of the free and unrestricted coinage of silver at the ratio of 16 to 1. In the other countries which have been more or less interested spectators of the experiment there never has been any serious doubt about the certain failure of such an experiment.

### A SERIES OF CONFERENCES.

The United States have made numerous efforts to secure by international agreement an enlarged use for silver, as the following brief summary of the work of successive monetary conferences will show. As already stated, the first international monetary conference was that of 1867. It met on the invitation of the French Government "to consider the question of uniformity of coinage, and to seek for the basis of ulterior negotiations." It came together in the City of Paris on June 17. Eighteen of the principal countries of Europe and the United States were represented at it, the latter by Hon. Samuel B. Ruggles, of New York. The conference voted unanimously against the adoption by the countries represented by the silver standard exclusively, and unanimously, with the exception of the Netherlands, in favor of the single gold standard. At the final session of the conference it was voted to refer these and other decisions reached to the several States for diplomatic action, and that information of the action of the States should be transmitted to the French Government, which should have power to reassemble the conference. The conference adjourned July 6, and was not reassembled.

The second international monetary conference was that of 1878. It was called by the United States. The Act of February 28, 1878, directed the President to invite the governments of Europe to join in a conference to adopt a common ratio between gold and silver for the purpose of establishing internationally the use of bimetallic money and securing fixity of relative value between these metals. The conference met at Paris on the 16th of August. Twelve countries were represented, the United States by Reuben E. Fenton, of New York; W. S. Groesbeck, of Ohio, and Francis A. Walker, of Conn. S. Dana Horton, the secretary of the American delegation, was admitted as a member. It is worthy of note that Germany declined to send delegates to this conference.

At the second session Mr. Groesbeck, on behalf of the United States, laid two propositions before the conference: (1) That it was not to be desired that silver be excluded from free coinage in Europe and the United States. (2) That the use of both gold and silver as unlimited legal tender may be safely adopted by equalizing them at a ratio fixed by international agreement.

These propositions were discussed in every phase by the delegates of the various States during the seven sessions of the conference. The collective answers to them of all the European delegates, save those of Italy, were presented by the president, Mr. Leon Say, and were:

(1) That it was necessary to preserve in the world the monetary function of silver as well as of gold, but that the choice of one or the other, or both simultaneously, should be governed by the special situation of each State or group of States. (2) That the question of the restriction of the coinage of silver also should be left to the discretion of each State or group of States. (3) That the difference of opinion that had appeared excluded the adoption of a common ratio between the two metals. The conference adjourned on the 29th of August.

The third international monetary conference, that of 1881, was called in January of that year by the Governments of France and the United States "to examine and adopt, for the purpose of submitting the same to the governments represented, a plan and a system for the establishment of the use of gold and silver as bimetallic money, according to a settled relative value between these metals." Nineteen countries were represented. The representatives of the United States were Hon. William M. Evarts, of New York; Allen G. Thurman, of Ohio; Timothy O. Howe, of Wisconsin, and S. Dana Horton

Like the delegates of the previous conferences, those of the present one were marked with the highest ability and by a thorough mastery on the part of the several delegates of monetary science. They covered twelve sessions. At the thirteenth Mr. Evarts, on behalf of the delegates of France and the United States, and in the name of their respective governments, read a declaration in which they stated.

(1) That the depression and great fluctuations of the value of silver relatively to gold are injurious to commerce and to the general prosperity, and the establishment of a fixed ratio of value between them would produce the most important benefits to the commerce of the world.

(2) That a bimetallic convention entered into between an important group of States for free coinage of both silver and gold at a fixed ratio and with full legal-tender faculty would cause and maintain a stability in the relative value of the two metals suitable to the interests and requirements of commerce.

(3) That any ratio now or lately in use by any commercial nation, if so adopted, could be maintained, but that the adoption of the ratio of $15\frac{1}{2}$ to 1 would accomplish the object with less disturbance to existing monetary systems than any other ratio.

(4) That a convention which should include England, France, Germany and the United States, with the concurrence of other States, which this combination would assure, would be adequate to produce and maintain throughout the commercial world the relation between the two metals that such convention should adopt.

After this declaration had been read, certain members, through the president, expressed a desire for adjournment, but this met with opposition from Mr. Forsell, delegate from Sweden, who thought that an adjournment would give a character of permanence to the conference, whereas it was better to acknowledge at once that bimetallism had collapsed and that the resolutions of the European delegates at the conference of 1878 should be reaffirmed. After a short recess the president read a resolution reciting that, in view of the speeches and observations of the delegates and the declarations of the several governments, there was ground for believing that an understanding might be established between the States that had taken part in the conference, but that it was expedient to suspend its meetings; that the monetary situation might in some States call for governmental action, and that there was reason for giving opportunity for diplomatic negotiations. The conference was adjourned to April 12, 1882. It was never reconvened.

The fourth international monetary conference was called by the Government of the United States "for the purpose of conferring as to what measures, if any, can be taken to increase the use of silver as money in the currency system of nations." The conference met at Brussels on the 22d of November, 1892. Twenty countries were represented. The delegates of the United

States were Hon. William B. Allison, Hon. John P. Jones, Hon. James B. McCreary Mr. Henry W. Cannon, Mr. E. Benjamin Andrews, and Hon. Edwin H. Terrell.

In accordance with the wish expressed by the conference, the delegates of the United States, after full consultation, prepared a declaration and programme which embodied the following resolution:

"That in the opinion of this conference it is desirable that some measure should be found for increasing the use of silver in the currency systems of the nations."

This resolution was presented to the conference at the second session. On that occasion, Sir Rivers Wilson, speaking in the name of the entire delegation of Great Britain said:

"We accept the resolution of the delegates of the United States as it stands, adding only this reservation and this explanation, that we consider it as being in fact a recapitulation of the substance of the invitation which has been addressed to the different governments, and which has been accepted by them."

Similar declarations were made by France, Spain, the Netherlands and other nations.

The programme of the United States was discussed in all its phases by the conference substantially in the order presented. Conformably to the suggestions of the programme, several projects, having in view the enlarged use of silver without contemplating its complete rehabilitation, were presented to the conference. These plans, together with the subordinate projects mentioned in the programme, were referred at the third session of the conference to a committee of twelve. This committee made two reports. The committee reported affirmatively upon one proposition, namely: That it was wise to withdraw from monetary circulation all the gold coins, and all paper money redeemable in gold of a less denomination than 1 pound, 20 francs, or 20 marks, and substitute silver money for them. As to the other plans, though some of them were favored in principle, they were not reported upon affirmatively, because they were not broad enough nor presented in sufficient detail to justify a favorable report upon them.

In the discussion of these various proposals and plans in the full meetings of the conference, the attitudes of all, or nearly all, the governments were disclosed. The utterances of the delegates indicated, however, what measures the governments were unwilling to adopt rather than how far they were willing to go to secure the enlarged use of silver as proposed by the President in his invitation.

The conference adjourned on December 17, 1892, after deciding, should the governments approve, to meet again on May 30, 1893. The governments whose adhesion was indispensable to any international agreement did not approve, and the conference, as an accredited representative body, did not reassemble.

## THE CLAIM THAT SILVER CAN BE RAISED TO GOLD VALUE.

In addition to the claim made by the candidate of the two divisions of the Silver party that the policy which he represents is not a new one, there is the additional claim that under that policy the bullion value of silver would so advance that the commercial and legal ratio between the two metals would be identical. All experience shows the absurdity of this latter claim, which is also at variance with the promise that free silver would mean higher prices for all products. The idea that the quantity of money in circulation governs the rise or fall of prices has been proved to be baseless.

In face, however, of the demonstrated impossibility of maintaining parity between gold and silver under a system of free silver coinage, the candidate of the two wings of the Silver party is rash enough to contend that the free and unlimited coinage by the United States alone will raise the bullion value of silver to its coinage value and thus make silver bullion worth $1.29 per ounce in gold throughout the world. He has the temerity to add that this proposition is in keeping with natural laws, not in defiance of them. It is a fundamental fact of finance that gold and silver have a relative international value which no nation alone can do more than temporarily disturb ; and the conclusion that the inferior will drive out the superior currency is at least as old as the 14th century, when Nicholas Oresme, Bishop of Lisieux, told Charles V. of France that if the fixed legal ratio of coins differs from the natural or market value of the metals, the coin which is underrated entirely disappears from circulation, and the base coin alone remains current, to the ruin of commerce. The same conclusion was stamped with the authority of Copernicus, 160 years later, and was explained to Queen Elizabeth by Sir Thomas Gresham half a century later still. The fundamental law of coinage which has come to be known as Gresham's law has been found to be universally true. As MacLeod remarks : "It is not confined to single and separate states ; it is not limited in time or space ; it is absolutely universal ; and it is equally impossible for the whole world to maintain coins of two or more metals in circulation together in unlimited quantities at a fixed legal ratio which differs from the natural or market value of the metals as it is for single and separate states to do so."

"It is exactly the same in all cases in which persons are allowed to pay their debts in things which have nominally the same value, but in reality are of different values. When persons are allowed to pay their rents in kind, they naturally select the worst portions of the produce to pay their landlords, and keep the best portions for themselves."

"If merchants received an order for so many yards of cloth, and the law allowed two different yard measures to be used—one of three feet and one of two feet—merchants would naturally fulfill their orders in yards of two feet rather than in yards of three feet. It is only natural that persons should pay their debts in the cheapest form to themselves.

"So if the law allows debtors to pay their debts in coin of different metals which are rated equally in law, but whose values differ in the market of the world, they will naturally pay their debts in the coin which is overrated, and keep the coin which is underrated at home. Then inevitably the coin which is underrated disappears from circulation, and the coin which is rated above its natural or market value alone remains current; and this is true whether single and separate states do so, or whether the whole world does it. If, then, the whole world were to agree to rate a coin below its market value, it would inevitably disappear from circulation; for the whole world can no more by universal agreement make nine equal to twelve than any separate states can."

But the Silver party and its candidate argue that they merely apply the law of supply and demand to silver when they say that a new demand for silver, created by law, will raise the price of silver bullion. It is unquestionably true that the suspension of the coinage of silver in the most important civilized states has tended to depress its price. But in all the world's history there never was a time in which so much silver was coined as during the period that has witnessed its greatest decline. Leaving Mexico and the South American states entirely out of consideration, there were coined in Europe, the United States and India in the years 1851 to 1860 an annual average (at the old ratio) of $38,794,000. During the decade 1861–1870, when the production of silver in the United States began to be developed, and when the cotton famine enormously increased the payments due to India on account of international trade, this annual average coinage amounted to $80,020,000. But even this figure, which up to that period had never been reached, is exceeded by the average amount of coinage (Mexico and South America not included) in the years 1887 to 1891, when the price of silver had fallen as low as 43½d. in London. The average coinage of those years amounted to no less than $113,000,000 (at the old ratio of value), and this sum does not include the storage of silver bullion by the United States.

The known aggregate coinage of silver during the sixteen years 1876–1891 —that is, during the period of the greatest depreciation of the metal— amounted to $2,110,560,000. From this we must deduct $71,000,000, which were recoined from old coins into German and Scandinavian divisional coins; but this amount is offset by the monetary silver bullion brough into the United States Treasury under the law of July 14, 1890. Moreover, this sum embraces about $950,000,000 of Mexican piasters, one-half of which may have served as coinage material. The remainder went to China, or may be considered the equivalent of the bar silver exported to China, which serves monetary purposes. The net silver coinages, therefore, of this metal would have to be put at at least $1,560,000,000. On the other hand, the production of silver during the same period, according to Soetbeer, amounted to $2,109,894,000. Thus, the net coinage was fully 74 per cent. of the production, while the gross amount of coinage shows that a quantity of silver as large as or even larger than that of the silver newly produced passed through the mints. The coinage of silver, it is true, had been suspended in France. It could no longer be turned, for the convenience of holders, into five-franc pieces, but in lieu thereof it found a place in the currency of the United States, to the amount annually of $70,000,000—a sum six times as great as the average annual coinage of France during the time of silver's supremacy.

### FOR WHOSE BENEFIT?

But if it were to be conceded that the United States should be able to achieve the impossible, and so raise the price of silver that its mercantile ratio with gold should correspond to the legal ratio, who would be benefited? Would prices rise, the burden of debts diminish and everybody feel sensibly richer? It is $1.29 per ounce *in gold* that silver is to be worth in the markets of the world, according to the candidate of the silver party, and the prices of other products of human labor will, of course, be measured in gold too. The standard of price will be the same as it is now, only silver will have advanced, by a miracle, to the price at which the coinage ratio of 16 to 1 expresses its market value. Precisely how it is to be kept there is a detail to which the candidate does not give any attention. If the operation of the law of supply and demand can raise the value of silver, it must also be able to depress it.

There must come a time, even assuming, what is palpably untrue, that there is a universal desire for an increase of the silver coinage by the people of this country, when there will be silver enough coined and stored to satisfy all demands for it. Then the price will go down again, for, Mr. Bryan to the contrary notwithstanding, there will be no interruption, but rather a tremendous impetus in the supply. When St. Clair-Duport published his book on Mexico, some fifty years ago, he said that the time would come, sooner or later, when the production of silver would have no other limits than those imposed on it by the constantly increasing decline of its value. The old Frenchman knew more about his subject than Mr. Bryan does, and even that eminent advocate of the use of silver, the late Professor Suess, writing in 1893, adds to the statement above quoted the following: "This limit, however, is as yet far from being attained, despite the considerable fall in price. Even at the present day, on the Andes of South America, dry ores are worked with profit, under the most unfavorable external circumstances. Even at the present day in Peru small smelting furnaces are in profitable operation, for which at these great altitudes there is no other fuel than the droppings of the llamas. In those regions there is yet ample room for lightening the labor. It must be said openly that all hope of improvement in monetary relations through decline of silver production presupposes as yet a very material fall in the price of silver."

### THE "QUANTITY THEORY."

The Bryan idea appears to be that the Government could accomplish more easily under a system of free silver coinage what it does now under coinage for its own account only—the maintenance of parity between all the elements of the currency. But according to the axiom that things which are equal to the same thing are equal to one another, the prices of the Bryan regime, measured by the same gold standard as now prevails, or by a silver standard absolutely convertible with it, would still be the prices of to-day. The only theory on which a different result could be predicated would be what is known as the "quantity theory" of money value, and which is, indeed, one of the most obstinate of the fallacies held by the free silver party. The theory is that the prices of commodities are determined by the ratio which the quantity of metallic money bears to the quantity of commodities, or that changes in the volume of money, or in the transactions to be carried out by money, have as complete an effect on the prices of commodities as changes in the supply and demand for commodities. Hence the assumption that there is not gold enough in existence to affect the commercial exchanges of the world, and hence the claim of the Populistic-Democratic platform that there has been from the suspension of silver coinage an appreciation of gold and a corresponding fall in the price of commodities.

It may be useless to argue against the silver delusion by pointing out how relatively insignificant are the proportion of the world's stock of either or both of the metals called precious to the volume of the transactions of the world's trade. For if the significance of that point were understood there would be no delusion. But it may be worth while to insist on the truth of the somewhat trite statement that trade, in its most advanced form, has not ceased to be barter—the exchange of the results of one man's labor against those of another. As a matter of relative value, it is just as accurate to say that a bushel of wheat is worth two pounds of a certain grade of tea in New York as it is to say that either can be exchanged for the equivalent of 70 cents in gold. A cargo of wheat can be exchanged for a certain number of boxes of tea without any gold being used in the transaction. It is only when the difference in value between a great mass of commercial exchanges, involving perhaps a great many countries, comes to be adjusted, that the country which has nothing to offer in settlement which the rest of the world is ready to take is called on to pay in gold. The United States can buy coffee in Brazil by means of cotton delivered in Liverpool, just as readily as it can buy the product of English potteries by the same kind of exchange. The exchangeable value of a bushel of wheat or a bale of cotton may depend on the world's stock in these commodities, because they are things actually exchanged, and their price is naturally governed by the law of supply and demand; but millions of transactions in all forms of merchandise may be conducted without the use of any "standard money" whatever, and in point of fact the proportion that the amount of coin used bears to the sum of the world's exchanges is not only an insignificant but a constantly diminishing fraction of the whole. The combined value of the foreign commerce of England, Germany and the United States, which was $2,449,000,000 in 1850, had increased to $8,904,000,000 in 1890, and there was probably more gold employed in the settlement of the balance between these countries in the former year than in the latter, though the value of the transactions had nearly quadrupled, and their volume very much more than quadrupled.

#### ECONOMIES IN THE USE OF MONEY.

To illustrate the rôle played by money in commerce, take the simplest form of a commercial transaction: A and B are indebted to each other. A owes B $50, and B owes A $65. If each sends a clerk to the other to demand payment in money; it would require $115 in money to discharge the two debts. If A sends $50 to B to discharge his debt, and B sends back the same $50 with $15 added in settlement of his debt, the amount of money needed to discharge the two debts is reduced to $65. But if A and B meet and set off their mutual amounts of debt against each other and pay only the difference in money, the two debts are discharged by the use of only $15. The amount of money required to carry on any given amount of business must vary, therefore, according to the method adopted of settling debts. But the most economical of the three methods above described represents only a slight approach to the refinement of the actual practice of the commercial world. If debtors and creditors deal at the same bank, they settle their obligations to each other by what amounts simply to the transfer of a credit from one account to another, and there is complete payment without the use of any money whatever. Under the Clearing-house system, a number of associated banks become for all practical purposes one great bank, and there is a daily aggregate of transactions reaching enormous figures, balanced with an infinitesimal amount of exchange of "standard money." The theory that the prices of commodities are determined by the ratio which the quantity of metallic money bears to the quantity of commodities is the exploded fallacy of the last generation, which had indeed been rejected by generations preceding. The French merchants of two or three hundred years ago discovered that the nearer debts could be made to balance each other the less need there was for the employment of money. Instead, therefore, of making their debts payable at their own houses, where they would have to keep large amounts of specie to meet them, they made them payable at the great continental fairs, which were held every three months. On a fixed day at the fair the merchants met together and exchanged their acceptances against each other. It is related that once at the fair of Lyons eighty millions in bills were paid and discharged against each other without the use of a single coin.

### THE INCREASED GOLD PRODUCT.

The spokesmen of the Silver party are disposed to ignore the recent enormous increase in the world's product of gold, and the further fact that in the ten years—1885-1894—the coinage of gold by the civilized nations of the world exceeded the production of gold by $305,886,000. It is impossible to say how much of this was the recoinage of abraded pieces or the conversion of existing stocks of bullion. The annual average of gold production between 1885 and 1894, inclusive, was $128,836,400, while the annual average of gold coinage was $159,425,000. Of the amount of gold employed in the arts, there are only estimates, as, for example, that for 1894 the amount was $51,250,000, of which England used $12,000,000; the United States, $10,750,000; France, $8,375.000; Switzerland, $4,175,000, and other countries in diminishing proportions The amount of gold held in bank vaults is unprecedentedly large, and the proportion of notes outstanding against it unprecedentedly small. It was for many years regarded as a safe rule that the great European banks of issue should maintain a note circulation three times as great as their metallic reserve. The Bank of England has to day a note issue of $313,000,000, of which $176,-000,000 is retained by the banking department in its reserve, but instead of holding against this issue gold to the amount of $105,000,000, it has the enormous gold reserve of $229,000,000. In France and Germany a similar state of things exists, and yet there are people who still insist that gold is scarce.

There began with the second half of the century a period of gold production such as the world had never seen. The average annual product of the five years 1851-55, was 264.5 per cent. above the average of the preceding ten years, and during the following five years this average was somewhat exceeded. There was $400,000,000 of gold mined between 1841 and 1850 and $1,400,000,000 mined between 1851 and 1860, of which the larger part found its way to the mints. Between 1493 and 1840 the whole gold product of the world was. $3,800,000,000, so that in the twenty years 1841-60 nearly as much gold was mined as in the 347 years preceding. If the comparison be carried to 1870, it will be found that the annual product of the thirty years—1841-70—was nearly ten times as great as the annual average of the 347 years which began with the discovery of America. If there be any merit in what is known as the quantity theory, prices ought to have gone up by leaps and bounds between 1850 and 1870. But nothing of the kind happened. The price of labor advanced 15 or 20 per cent., as a part of the general process that has gone on without any regard whatever to the world's stock of precious metals. The articles that showed a well-marked rise in price were those whose production did not increase in proportion to the demand, and chiefly the growth of tropical countries, just as coffee and India rubber have gone up in price of late years while most other products were going down.

The world's production of gold, which fell off after 1860, resumed its upward course in 1888, and has increased to such an extent that in the last two years the value of gold extracted was greater than that of both the gold and silver during the palmy days of early Californian and Australian mining. Considering that the amount of gold and gold notes reported in actual circulation in the United States at the end of last year was $528,600,000 against $487,700,000 in silver dollars, silver certificates and treasury notes of 1890, it would seem that among the other incidents of the triumph of the cause of free silver would be a sudden and violent contraction of the currency. As the purchasing power of every dollar would suffer an immediate and severe diminution, the dilemma presents itself to the silver men—would prices contract with the contraction of the currency, or would they expand with the debasement of the dollar? If since the virtual stoppage of silver coinage the stock of metallic money in the country is not large enough for the needs of its commerce, a frightful deficit in the circulating medium would surely be effected by the expulsion of gold. The assumption that it would not be driven out is too preposterous for argument. If the contention of the silver men be true that it is the gold in the dollar that has depreciated and not the silver that has gone down, the fact remains that the gold dollar could by no possible exercise of ingenuity be made to circulate side by side with the silver dollar.

But the most serious charge against the silver men is that it is credit they are tampering with in their attempt to change the standard of value. As ex-Secretary of the Treasury Hon. Charles S. Fairchild has well said:

"All the time we hear, and I believe it is uncontradicted, that about five per cent. of all the transactions of the people of this country are made in money. All the rest of the transactions are made with the other media—checks, notes, and all kinds of things. If this is true, suppose we could double the amount of money in an instant, what would we have done? We would have doubled five per cent. of the whole. What would we have added? We would have added five per cent. to the whole. In a thousand dollars what would we have added? We would have added $50. But suppose in adding that $50 you have disturbed the minds of men so that the other 95 per cent. was diminished, as has been done from time to time during the last few years; suppose you apply your percentage to $950, and cut that in two, owing to the uncertainty you have created in the minds of men as to the quality of their money; suppose you have only affected it by 10 per cent.—what is the result? Why, you have diminished that by $95, and when you come to add the $50 that you have credited by doubling your money and deduct your $95, you will find that you are $45 worse off than when you started. You are 4½ per cent. worse off so far as the circulating medium that really transacts your affairs is concerned. That is one of the great reasons why we find these great disturbances in business when men tamper with currency."

## A QUESTION OF PUBLIC FAITH.

Up to this time the Government of the United States has accepted the responsibility for the mint stamp on its coins by keeping the legal and the commercial ratio of the bullion they contained as nearly identical as possible, or by pledging itself to the maintenance of parity between them in presence of a wide disparity between the legal and commercial ratio. The free-silver proposal does away with any such responsibility, and places in private hands the regulation of the currency. But in making the depreciated coinage a legal tender for all debts, public and private, it compels the Government to adopt a policy of repudiation. This would be a step attended by the most disastrous and far-reaching consequences. It would wreck the whole edifice of domestic credit as well as affix a lasting stain to the good name of the United States. The disgrace of such a line of public policy would be fairly matched by the monumental proportions of the losses it would entail.

By opening the mints to the free coinage of silver at a ratio of 16 to 1, the Government would at once surrender all its power to maintain parity in gold among the various elements of the national currency. The real arbiter of the value of the dollar would be the owner of silver bullion at home and abroad. On the rapidity with which the tons of silver offered for coinage could be passed through the mint, or certificates having the quality of legal tender could be issued in exchange for the deposits of bullion, would mainly depend alike the volume and the value of the currency under the new conditions. The bullion value in the markets of the world of 371.25 grains of pure silver would be its ultimate standard, disturbed at first only by considerations due to the demand for currency, the amount of silver bullion offering, and the facilities provided by law for the prompt conversion of new or old silver into some form of money. The Treasury would be compelled to accept this currency in payment of public dues, and would be compelled to use it in the payment of its own debts. The first tender of this depreciated currency to the holders of the bonds of the United States, would be accepted by the world as an act of repudiation. The faith of the United States has been held to be pledged to the payment of its debt, principal and interest in gold, the country has profited to the extent of many millions a year by this interpretation of the Law of 1869, and to set it aside now would be a conspicuous act of public dishonor, differing in degree, not in kind, from a formal act of repudiation.

### "PAYABLE IN COIN."

The advantages of redeeming the bonds in silver were first mooted twenty years ago when the fall in the price of the white metal had become considerable enough to make the substitution appear a profitable operation. The subject was then taken up and discussed by Hon. Lot M. Morrill, Secretary of the Treasury in the second administration of President Grant. In his report of

December 4, 1876, Mr. Morrill makes the following dispassionate review of the considerations affecting this subject:

"Since the fall of silver, propositions for the revival of the silver dollar have been made, and the position which it would occupy with reference to unexpired coin obligations, should its coinage with unlimited tender be again authorized, has been the subject of considerable discussion. The question whether the pledged faith of the United States to pay its obligations in coin would justify their payment in the silver dollar is of no small importance as affecting the public securities of the United States. In any discussion of the question it must be conceded at the outset that the silver dollar was the unit of value, having the quality of legal tender for all sums and in all cases, and that the terms of the United States obligations do not exclude payment therein, and that the Act of 1869, in which is the pledge of payment in coin, does not in terms, discriminate against silver. These provisions are broad enough in terms, to include payment in either gold or silver, and compel an inquiry into the history, production, issue, and subsequent treatment of these obligations, and the relative condition of gold and silver coin as money of payment in order to a correct interpretation of the meaning of the language, 'payment to be made in coin.'

"Not long after the close of the civil war, which gave rise to these obligations, doubts arose as to the kind of money in which these securities were payable and which led to the passage of the Act of 1869, entitled 'An act to strengthen the public credit,' and it was intended to dispel all hesitation or doubt as to the purpose of the Government upon the question, and by which the faith of the United States was pledged to the payment in coin of all obligations except those expressly otherwise provided for. This legislative action was in harmony with that of the executive administration."

"What, then, was intended and understood to be intended by this pledge of the Government? Was it that the public securities were to be paid in gold coin or in silver, or might be in either?"

"It will not be questioned by anyone conversant with the question at that time that the popular impression, not to say general conviction, was that the pledge was for payment in gold. This belief may have been obtained from the fact that the interest on this class of obligations, payable in coin, had uniformly been paid in gold, that the customs receipts had been set apart to this end, and that those were paid in gold, and that the silver dollar had, as money of payment, therefore gone into general disuse, especially in all large transactions, and should scarcely be considered as contemplated in any measure having for its object to provide for payment of sums so ample as the interest on the public debt, at that time amounting to the sum of $130,000,000. This view of the subject receives no inconsiderable support, also, in the legislation of Congress of 1873, by which the legal-tender quality of the silver coin was limited to $5.

By force of the laws of trade, quite independent of those of Congress, the legal-tender silver dollar had actually disappeared from circulation as money, and, although not abolished by act of Congress, it did not, as matter of fact, exist for commercial purposes, and did not enter into money payments. The object and intent of the Act of 1873 was confessedly to give to gold the precedence in the statutes of the country it held in the commercial world practically, and to declare the gold dollar in law to be what it was in fact—the representative of the money unit. Gold had for many years been treated as the principal money of coin payments in legislation and in the transactions of the Treasury Department:"

### THE PROFIT OF HONEST REDEMPTION.

"By the Act of 1863 the Treasury was authorized to receive deposits of gold coin and bullion and to issue certificates therefor redeemable in gold coin, thus indicating that its obligations called for payment in gold and not in silver. This provision, it will be seen, is in consonance with the fact that our foreign exchanges for many years have been made upon the gold basis, and thus it is apparent that the general understanding has been of late years, for the consideration stated, that the money of coin payments was gold, and an obligation to pay in coin required payment in gold coin."

"As was contemplated by Congress in the policy declared in 1869, the public securities, then depressed, immediately arose to par in gold, and have since maintained an enviable position at the money centres of the world. The 5-20 6 per cent. bonds, then selling at 88 cents on the dollar, soon arose to par in gold, and have since borne the average premium of 5 per cent. at home and abroad. At the present time the borrowing power of the Government is somewhat less than 4½ per cent. bonds, on short time, are really taken at par in gold, and sold at a premium in this country and in Europe. If no disturbing element enters into our present monetary system, affecting the present policy of the Government, it is believed that it will be found practicable at no remote period to fund the national debt into a 4 per cent. bond having from thirty to fifty years to run, and this at an annual saving in the interest of the public debt of $25,800,000, a sum which, if invested in a sinking fund at 4 per cent. annually would pay off the present national funded debt in a fraction over thirty years."

"It is a matter of deep public concern that a policy so beneficent in results and advantageous to the future should receive no detriment from conflicting interests, policies or theories. Whatever may be thought of the right to pay these public securities in cheaper money, it will remain true that it is lawful to pay them in gold coin; that the belief that they were to be so paid has a practicable value in the probable reduction of the public debt equal to one-fourth of the amount of the interest thereon."

"It is respectfully submitted that the coin payment to which the faith of the nation was pledged in 1869 was gold and not silver, and that any other view of it, whatever technical construction the language may be susceptible of, would be regarded as of doubtful good faith and its probable effect prejudicial to the public credit."

### "THE CRIME OF '73."

But it is part of the free-silver contention that the Coinage Act of 1873, which made the gold dollar by law what for a generation it had been in fact, the unit of monetary value in the United States, was part of a conspiracy to rob the American people by compelling them to pay their debts in a dollar of greater value than that in which these debts were contracted. Accordingly, the Coinage Act of 1873 is referred to in free-silver literature as "the crime of '73"; it is declared in the Chicago platform to have "demonetized" silver without the knowledge or approval of the American people, and to have resulted in the appreciation of gold and a corresponding fall in the prices of commodities produced by the people. So the question is asked by those who seek to apologize for the act of repudiation proposed by giving a legal-tender quality to depreciated dollars: "Is not a dollar that has appreciated in value as fraudulent to the debtor as a dollar that has depreciated in value is fraudulent to the creditor?"

It is unquestionably true that the purchasing power of a dollar has considerably increased since 1873. That is part of the progress of humanity, of which we have had our full share, and by which the laboring man has been the greatest gainer. But the prices of some things have increased, notably the wages of labor, and this would hardly be the case if the appreciation of the dollar were the primary fact of the situation. And, as Secretary Carlisle has pointed out, "it is not true that our people owe any debts contracted as far back as 1873, though it may be that some of our great corporations which issued bonds before that date still owe them, but they have all been refunded at a low rate of interest, so that our free-coinage friends need not be disturbed on their account." That the demonetization of silver reduced prices is founded upon an assumption absolutely baseless, for silver constituted no part of the money in use or in existence in this country before or at the time of that legislation. As the Act of 1873 did not reduce by a dollar the amount of money in the country, it could not, even accepting the theory of the silver party, have reduced prices. As Secretary Manning put the case in his report for 1885: "Free coinage of a full-tender silver dollar was all that was withdrawn by the Act of 1873 or changed. The right withdrawn was a right long unused because it was a right unprofitable to any owner of silver in the United States. The unlimited legal-tender quality of any silver dollar still existing, unmelted, unexported, in the cabinets of collectors or the strong boxes of hoarders, whether the dollar of 1792 or the dollar of 1834, was not withdrawn." In his Covington speech of May, 1895, Secretary Carlisle put the question in a nutshell when he said : " The only metallic or redemption money in use here at that time was gold, which amounted to only $135,000,000, including what the Government was using, whereas we now have about $625,000,000 in gold and $397,652,878 in full legal-tender silver, beside about $77,000,000 in subsidiary silver coin. If, therefore, prices have fallen since 1873, the decline has taken place in spite of the fact that our full legal-tender metallic money has been increased, until now it amounts to more than seven times as much as it did at that date, and consequently the alleged decline in prices must be attributed to some other cause than the demonetization of silver. These facts prove not only that the demonetization of silver did not reduce the amount of redemption money in this country, but they prove also that the fundamental proposition of the advocates of free coinage is erroneous, and that prices are not fixed or regulated by the amount of redemption money alone, for if so, prices should have increased since 1873."

### THE DISPLACEMENT OF SILVER.

The assertion that there was anything furtive, secret or sinister in the Coinage Act of 1873, or in the methods of its passage, is one that frequent repetition does not render less ridiculous. No codification of the mint laws had been made since 1837, and, as part of the preparation for the resumption of specie payments, a complete revision of all technical matters of assayage and coinage was undertaken in 1870. An act had been passed in 1853 making the half dollar and coins of lower denomination subsidiary pieces with a limited legal-tender quality, and placing their coinage entirely in the hands of the Government. Silver dollars had disappeared from circulation because they were worth 104 cents of a gold dollar. But as the smaller silver coins contained their full proportion of silver bullion, and were, like the dollar, worth more than their stamped value, the difficulty of keeping small change in circulation became very great. So the ratio was changed for the smaller coins, that there might be no temptation to hoard or melt them, and the Government reserved to itself the profit on making them, that there might be no excess in the supply.

This was the beginning of the end of the free coinage of silver. As Mr. Dunham, who had the Act of 1853 in charge in the House, said : " Another objection urged against this proposed change is that it gives us a standard of gold only. What advantage is to be obtained by a standard of the two metals, which is as well, if not much better, attained by a single standard, I am unable to perceive ; while there are very great disadvantages resulting from it, as the experience of every nation which has attempted to maintain it has proved. Indeed, it is utterly impossible that you should, long at a time, maintain a double standard. Gentlemen talk about a double standard of gold and silver as a thing that exists and we propose to change. We have had but a single standard for the last three or four years. That has been, and now is, gold. We propose to let it remain so, and to adapt silver to it—to regulate it by it." The use of silver as unlimited legal tender equally with gold was practically abandoned in 1853, and a subsidiary currency of 345.6 grains to the dollar's worth was enacted. It was the deliberate purpose to complete in 1870 the work begun in 1853, but so far from there being any secrecy or haste about it, three years of discussion was required to accomplish the task. The amendment to the coinage laws over which there has been so interminable a mass of misrepresentation was described at the time by Robert Patterson, of Philadelphia, as follows: "The silver dollar, half-dime and three-cent piece are dispensed with by this amendment. Gold becomes the standard money, of which the gold dollar is the unit. Silver is subsidiary." How little of a novelty this was deemed may be inferred from the following remarks in the House in April, 1872, by Mr. W. L. Stoughton : "Aside from the three-dollar gold piece, which is a deviation from our metrical ratio, and, therefore, objectionable, the only change in the present law is in more clearly specifying the gold dollar as the unit of value. This was probably the intention, and perhaps the effect, of the Act of March 3, 1849, but it ought not to be left to inference or implication. The value of silver depends, in a great measure, upon the fluctuations of the market and the supply and demand. Gold is practically the standard of value among all civilized nations, and the time has come in this country when the gold dollar should be distinctly declared to be the coin representative of the money unit." How clearly some of the men who afterward espoused the cause of free silver understood the significance of the proposed legislation is plain from the following remarks made by Mr. W. D. Kelley of Pennsylvania : "I wish to ask the gentleman who has just spoken (Mr. Potter) if he knows of any government in the world which makes its subsidiary coinage of full value? The silver coin of England is ten per cent. below the value of gold coin. And, acting under the advice of the experts of this country and of England and France, Japan has made her silver coinage, within the last year, twelve per cent. below the value of gold, and for this reason : It is impossible to retain the double standard. The values of gold and silver continually fluctuate. You cannot determine this year what will be the relative values of gold and silver next year. They were fifteen to one a short time ago ; they are sixteen to one now."

### VERY DELIBERATE LEGISLATION.

If other proof were needed that there was nothing surreptitious about the passage of the Coinage Act of 1873, the legislative history of the bill ought to furnish it. The date of its introduction in the Senate was April 25, 1870; it reached the House two months later. It reappeared in both House and Senate in the winter session, but it failed to pass as part of the business of that, the Forty-first Congress. It was reintroduced in the extra session of the Senate of the Forty-second Congress on March 9, 1871, and after much reporting, recommitting and amending, extending pretty well over the whole term, it finally became law on February 12, 1873. The following brief summary of the history of the act is by Professor Laughlin as are the few lines of comment.

*Summary of Procedure—The Act of 1873.*

|  | SENATE. | HOUSE. |
|---|---|---|
| Submitted by Secretary of the Treasury................ | April 25, 1870 | ............. |
| Referred to Senate Finance Committee................. | April 28, 1870 | ............. |
| Five hundred copies ordered printed.................. | May 2, 1870 | ............. |
| Submitted to House, with supplementary report and correspondence .................................... | ............. | June 25, 1870 |
| Reported, amended and ordered printed............... | Dec. 19, 1870 | ............. |
| Debated ........................................... | Jan. 9, 1871 | ............. |
| Passed the Senate by a vote of 36 to 14.............. | Jan. 10, 1871 | ............. |
| Senate Bill ordered printed......................... | ............. | Jan. 18, 1871 |
| Bill reported with substitute, and recommitted........ | ............. | Feb. 25, 1871 |
| Original bill reintroduced and printed................ | ............. | Mar. 9, 1871 |
| Reported and debated ............................... | ............. | Jan. 9, 1872 |
| Recommitted ....................................... | ............. | Jan. 10, 1872 |
| Reported from Coinage Committee, printed and recommitted........................................ | ............. | Feb. 9, 1872 |
| Reported back, amended and printed.................. | ............. | Feb. 13, 1872 |
| Debated ........................................... | ............. | April 9, 1872 |
| Amended and passed by vote 110 to 13................ | ............. | May 27, 1872 |
| Printed in Senate................................... | May 29, 1872 | ............. |
| Reported with amendments and printed............... | Dec. 16, 1872 | ............. |
| Reported with additional amendments and printed.... | Jan. 7, 1873 | ............. |
| Passed Senate. .................................... | Jan. 17, 1873 | ............. |
| Printed with amendments........................... | ............. | Jan. 21, 1873 |
| Conference committee appointed..................... | Jan. 27, 1873 | Jan. 25, 1873 |
| Report of conference committee presented and concurred in.. | Feb. 6, 1873 | Feb. 7, 1873 |
| Became a law February 12, 1873..................... | ............. | ............. |

It is perfectly clear from this that there was no haste nor secrecy about the case; it was printed again and again; laid on the desks of members again and again; it was debated until 144 columns of the "Globe" were filled. How, then, can anyone of intelligence for a moment offer the charge that the bill was passed stealthily? Here are the facts of record, to be verified by any man in the land. They are as clear as day. In the debate no opposition was made whatever to the omission of the silver dollar from the list of coins permitted to be coined. The Senate occupied its time chiefly in debating affairs relating to seigniorage and abrasion, while the House was concerned with the salaries of officials. Why was this? Because everyone knew no silver dollar pieces had been in circulation for more than twenty-five years. That was all there was to do.

### THE "CRIME" OF 1806.

If a "crime" was perpretated against silver in 1873, the action of President Jefferson in 1806 under which the coinage of silver dollars was suspended for over thirty years must have been still more criminal. For here there was no appeal to Congress, no discussion, no reporting or consideration of the question involved, but simply the following brief communication to the Director of the Mint at Philadelphia from Jefferson's Secretary of State:

"DEPARTMENT OF STATE, May 1, 1806.

"SIR—In consequence of a representation from the Director of the Bank of the United States that considerable purchases have been made of silver dollars coined at the mint for the purposes of exporting them, and as it is probable further purchases and exportations will be made, the President directs that all the silver to be coined at the mint shall be of small denominations, so that the value of the largest piece shall not exceed half a dollar.

"I am, etc.,
"JAMES MADISON.
"ROBERT PATTERSON, Esq.,
 *Director of the Mint.*"

To urge so purely fanciful a public wrong as the so-called "Crime of '73" as justification for a comprehensive act of national repudiation is of a piece with the whole process of mental and moral distortion that underlies the free silver proposal. The national shame of it would be equaled only by the heritage of national disaster. As Pierre des Essars says of Portugal: "'There is a treacherous enemy who lays pitfalls for the prodigal and the defaulter among governments; this enemy is called exchange, which is the dial of national decline of credit. This exchange impoverishes day by day whoever receives a bank note; it makes money melt like snow, and like snow it trickles from his hands. The country is placed on every side, at the mercy of a discredit which keeps increasingly turning the exchanges against it." On certain classes of imports it has the effect of a prohibitory tariff, and only to those who believe in the Chinese-wall policy of commercial isolation, does it have anything to be commended. But it falls like a blight on all progress and tends to aggravate all the evils of industrial monopoly which the silver advocates take occasion to deplore.

### THE COST OF DISHONOR.

Consider more minutely, in the line indicated by Mr. W. L. Trenholm, the effect of discrediting the Government of the United States. Let the Government lose its credit with the bankers, can it be retained among the people? Surely not. The $100,000,000 of gold now held as a special redemption fund will be drawn out as fast as greenbacks can be handed in through every aperture of the redemption counters of the Treasury, and there will remain $246,000,000 of greenbacks in the hands of the people, and neither gold to redeem them with nor credit with which to get more gold. These will, of course, immediately depreciate, how much is immaterial to our immediate purpose; let us say, only 10 per cent. That will take 10 per cent. off the purchasing power of $380,000,000 of silver dollars, $246,000,000 of greenbacks, $150,000,000 of Treasury notes of 1890, about $200,000,000 of national bank notes (because they are redeemable in greenbacks), making $976,000,000 of currency, on which 10 per cent. is $97,600,000.

In the last report of the Comptroller of the Currency, deposits of all the State banks and trust companies are estimated at $1,129,000,000; savings bank deposits, $1,778,000,000; individual deposits in national banks, $1,728,000,000; private bankers' deposits, $66,000,000. The total debt of the banks, etc., to the people, payable in lawful money, is thus $4,701,000,000. These deposits would, of course, follow the value of lawful money in which they are payable. On the $4,701,000,000 of deposits above shown, the loss would be $470,100,000; and the loss on currency as above would be $97,600,000, aggregate loss on above items resulting from 10 per cent. depreciation of greenbacks, $567,700,000. Here, then, is the sword held over us. Here is the power that compels us to preserve the credit of our Government.

Our circulation now includes: Greenbacks, about $346,000,000; national bank notes, $212,000,000; silver dollars and silver coin certificates outstanding, say $490,000,000; making the total of paper and silver and coin held up to parity of value with gold by the credit of the Government, $1,048,000,000.

The entire value of the greenbacks and national bank notes depends upon credit, while the silver dollars and silver certificates derive more than a fourth of their value from credit. Impair that credit, and for every 1 per cent. of currency depreciation resulting from its impairment you will inflict upon the people who are holding the currency, a loss of $10,480,000; and upon depositors in banks, etc., $47,010,000; here is a loss, for every 1 per cent. depreciation of $57,440,000. If the currency drops to the intrinsic value of 412½ grains of silver to the dollar, now less than 53 cents, that will be a loss of over 47 per cent., or nearly $2,700,000,000, which is more than three times the entire volume of the national bonded debt still unpaid.

Let Congress say, now, that the standard is the silver dollar, and straightway a loss of $2,210,000,000 will fall upon those among the people of the United States who have no gold, no foreign exchange, no government bonds, no bank stock. The people, the masses, who have deposits in the various banks, and who hold the money provided by the Government, will have to bear the entire loss. What boots it that a large part of this fearful loss will be offset by gains to those (banks and bankers) who now owe this money, and who have been wise enough or fortunate enough to invest it abroad, or to hold it here in gold, or in securities convertible into gold? In the case supposed, the poor will all be made poorer, the great bulk of the people who are in moderate circumstances will bear the chief loss, while some few among the rich may possibly be made richer. If these things are clearly apprehended, either in Congress or among the people, will any voice be raised to disturb the public confidence now enjoyed by our money? No patriot, no statesman could wish to disturb it; no demagogue or fanatic would dare to do so.

### TO IMPAIR THE OBLIGATION OF CONTRACTS.

But the silver party does not propose to stop short at reducing the Government to the necessity of paying its debts in depreciated money; its platform declares for "such legislation as will prevent for the future the demonetization of any kind of legal-tender money by private contract." This is to say, it proposes to do its best to make unlawful all promises between individuals to pay in gold. If, however, there is to be a daily uncertainty, as there would inevitably be under the free coinage of silver, about the value of the monetary unit, it would obviously be very hard to adjust the terms of contracts to pay or receive money at a future time. The very existence of credit is dependent upon the certainty of the monetary unit, and if the Government failed to supply that certainty the people would have to make shift to do it for themselves, otherwise industry would be paralyzed and commerce reduced to a particularly risky form of gambling.

But, in this case, it is proposed not only that the Government shall commit itself to a shifting standard of value, but shall prevent any body of citizens or any State from adopting a stable one. This is an undertaking which would obviously transcend the power of Congress. The silver party apparently adopt the novel reading of the Constitution that there was reserved to Congress the power to pass any law impairing the obligation of contracts, because it was expressly forbidden to any State. If the enumeration in the Constitution of certain rights is not to be construed to deny or disparage others retained by the people, surely the fact that the sacredness of contracts is specially guaranteed against State violation is proof that Congress was expected to hold it in very strict regard. It would obviously require a special delegation of power to warrant any interference by Congress with one of the primary rights of the people, and it involves nothing short of a contradiction in terms to assume that in the fundamental law of this Republic any such delegation could have been expressed or implied.

It is not at all doubtful what view the Supreme Court would take of such a question, and here would probably come one of the very first shocks of the inevitable conflict between the Federal Judiciary and the Executive branches of a government founded on the Chicago platform. The former would remain, under such a government, the sole guardian of the public rights, the sole custodian of the national honor. But it would have no power to enforce its own decrees, no power even to preserve its own ranks against the intrusion of men deliberately selected to overthrow the whole fabric of its antecedent decisions. There can be no doubt as to the meaning of the allusion in the Chicago platform to the Court as it may "hereafter be constituted." Nor can there be any doubt that the keystone of the arch of Republican freedom will be removed when the tribunal that was created to protect the Constitution against legislative encroachment becomes so perverted in membership and in purpose as to be itself a menace to the integrity of the Constitution and a means of facilitating the betrayal of its guaranties.

## THE FARMER AND FREE SILVER.

The farmer is asked to believe that free silver means for him better prices and a lighter burden of debt. The prices would advance only in name and the present debt be scaled down only to have the loss made good in future loans. The farmer sells the great bulk of his crops in the home market, and anything that brings disaster to the country at large must be adverse to his interests. Like other men engaged in productive occupations, farmers have a constant necessity to borrow money, and they are as much interested as merchants and manufacturers are in averting a collapse of the whole fabric of credit. Farmers are also capitalists and creditors, they own the largest single aggregate of property in the country, they have accumulated savings, and they are lenders as well as borrowers. In any of these capacities, the farmer has nothing to gain, but everything to lose, by the demoralization attending the adoption of a debased currency system.

The idea that the farmer would be any better off by a resort to the free coinage of silver at a ratio of 16 to 1 rests upon two assumptions, both of which are demonstrably false. The first is that the prices of agricultural products have declined because of the fall in the price of silver, and the other is that with all values measured by silver, the farmer would not only get more money for his product, but that the new silver dollar would be quite as good for the purchase of things that he needs as the gold dollar.

In an inquiry relating to the greatest industry in the country, it is necessary to separate it into its component elements. The conditions that affect the sale of wheat and cotton, for example, are not the same as those which govern the prices of corn and hay. But if the prices of the whole range of the produce of American farms have been depressed by the fall in the price of silver, there must have been substantial uniformity in the process. In point of fact there has been no such thing. Some agricultural products are higher than they were before silver began to decline, and others are lower. The two which are notably lower are wheat and cotton. The cause of the fall in price of the former is simply the increase of the world's production beyond the demands of consumption. The competition with American wheat in Europe of Russia, India, Australia and Argentina—the exports from these countries increasing by 429,000,000 bushels in six years—is surely a sufficient explanation of the fall in the price of wheat, as the trebling in twenty years of the yield of cotton, readily accounts for its fall in price.

### CHEAP MONEY AND INCREASED EXPORTS.

But the silver men argue that we are at a disadvantage in competing with Russia and Argentina, because with a cheaper currency they can undersell us. In the same way, the French farmers were told by the bimetallist agitators that they were suffering from the low price of wheat made by the competition of India. It was declared that since the same quantity of gold will buy twice as many rupees as it did twenty years ago, it will also buy twice as much

Indian wheat, so that an enormous stimulus is given to the export trade, of which the people of India have the full benefit, because the purchasing power of the rupee remains unchanged. When it is revamped for use here, the proposition appears in some such form as this: The pound sterling is only worth $5 in America, whereas in purchasing power it is worth nearly $10 in India and the Argentine Republic, and the English merchant will not and can not pay $10 for merchandise in this country, when by reason of the difference of exchange, he could buy the same quantity for a little over $5 in South America and India.

The answer to statements like these is, simply, that they are not true. When they were doing duty in France, an economist of an inquiring turn of mind undertook to subject them to a practical test. He asked one of the great importing houses of London to find out for him what was the price of wheat in gold the second week of January at the chief shipping port of Argentina, Russia, the United States, and British India. Wheat is sold in France by the metric quintal, a measure of a little over 220 pounds, or say $3\frac{2}{3}$ bushels. This was, accordingly, the unit of comparison. He found that at Buenos Ayres the nominal price of the quintal was 30fr.75 in paper, which was then equal to 10fr.10 in gold. At Odessa "poods" enough of wheat to make a quintal could be bought for 19 fr.04 in paper roubles, worth 12 fr.73 in gold. In New York the price of the bushel was 69 cents, which made the quintal worth $2.53 or 13 fr. 10, from which was deducted 9 centimes, on account of a premium of exchange of $\frac{7}{8}$ths of one per cent on gold. At Bombay a "candy" of wheat cost 32 rupees, making the price per quintal 9 rupees or 21 fr. 42 at par of the rupee. But the rupee being worth on January 14th only $14\frac{1}{16}$ pence instead of 24 pence or 1fr. 50 instead of 2 fr. 38, the true price of the quintal, or the price paid for it in gold, resolved itself into 13fr. 50.

Here, then, in four of the world's markets for wheat separated by thousands of miles from each other, it required last January to buy $3\frac{2}{3}$ bushels the following sums in gold: $2.02, $2.55, $2.60 and $2.70 respectively. The lowest price was in a country where the paper currency is worth rather less than a third of its face value, and the highest in a country nominally on a silver basis, but really under a régime of suspended free coinage of silver as the preliminary to the establishment of a gold standard. Instead of the pound sterling being worth twice as much in Bombay as in New York, it is, obviously, worth a fraction less, and so far from the American farmer having to fear the competition of the Indian ryot, it would seem that the latter has, so far, rather the worst of the game. That is, if the presentation of his product at a price calculated to tempt purchasers be deemed an advantage, the American has it over the farmer in India, while the farmers in Russia and the Argentine have it over him. Apparently, the Populist argument requires that the country should get back with all possible dispatch to a currency of irredeemable paper.

## FARM PRICES AND FOREIGN PRICES.

Tested by its price at the centre of production the fall in the price of wheat has a much narrower range than when tested by the foreign quotations. But even tested by the standard value for the world, set for wheat by the price of an imperial quarter of grain at Mark Lane, London, it will be found that the decline of wheat began in 1855, nearly twenty years before silver was "demonetized." In 1855 the average price for the year was 74s. 9d. The average price for the year 1894 for an imperial quarter of wheat was 22s. 10d. ; that is, hardly more than 30 per cent. what it had been in 1855. But in 1870, one year before Germany and three years before the United States had ruled silver out of their coinage as full legal tender, the price of wheat had tumbled to 46s. 11d. per quarter ; that is, it had dropped nearly half of the value it had in 1855, before the question of silver came up as a factor of any practical or theoretical importance. There were fluctuations in price from 1855 to 1870, just as there have been fluctuations in price between 1870 and 1895, ups and downs, controlled by good and bad harvests ; but on the whole the tendency of values had been downhill at an even more rapid rate in the fifteen years between 1855 and 1870 than in the twenty-five years between 1870 and 1895. Coming to the centre of production in the Mississippi valley, it would appear that gold has depreciated there since 1860, because the prices of wheat in Minnesota from 1862 to 1866 averaged 56.5 cents a bushel, if the currency price of a part of that period be reduced to a gold basis. In 1891 to 1894 the average was 62 cents. The following extract from a report made by Mr. L. G. Powers, Chief of the Bureau of Statistics of Minnesota, brings out this point very clearly, as also the still more important point, that by far the largest part of the decline in the London quotations for wheat has been brought about by economies in transportation and in intermediate charges.

"A comparative statement of the average gold values for wheat per bushel upon the farms of Minnesota and New York, and the market value in cents of American wheat in London, England, from 1862 to 1894 :

| YEAR. | MINN. | NEW YORK. | LONDON. | DIFFERENCES. ||
|---|---|---|---|---|---|
| | | | | Minn. and New York. | Minn. and London. |
| 1862–66 | 56.5 | 115.0 | .... | 58.5 | .... |
| 1867–70 | 65.3 | 138.6 | 175.6 | 73.3 | 110.3 |
| 1871–74 | 73.1 | 134.1 | 176.3 | 61.1 | 103.2 |
| 1875–78 | 72.7 | 110.5 | 149.2 | 37.8 | 76.5 |
| 1879–82 | 92.2 | 132.4 | 149.6 | 40.2 | 57.4 |
| 1883–86 | 64.2 | 92.4 | 113.5 | 38.2 | 44.3 |
| 1887–90 | 73.4 | 95.3 | 106.1 | 21.9 | 38.7 |
| 1891–94 | 62.1 | 83.5 | .... | 21.4 | .... |

"An examination of the foregoing table shows that from 1867 to 1870 the Minnesota farmer, on an average, realized in gold only a trifle over one-third of what his wheat was quoted at in London. He received 65.3 cents a bushel, while 110.3 cents were absorbed by the middlemen, the dealers and transportation companies, between him and the London miller, who paid for the wheat 175.6 cents. This great difference between the Minnesota figures for wheat and those of London has steadily declined, and this decline measures the fall of grain prices in Europe."

"The Minnesota wheat farmer realizes a general advance in the prices obtained by him from 1867 to 1882, and thereafter a decline. Some of the advance between 1867 and 1882 arose from the introduction of the roller process in milling in Minneapolis, which raised the price of hard spring wheat from a level of 10 cents a bushel below to 10 cents a bushel above the best white winter wheat of New York. The fact that other, and more recent, milling inventions have raised the price of winter wheat to nearly the same as that of hard spring, accounts for some of the subsequent decline shown in the table for Minnesota."

"The average price of wheat advanced in Minnesota after the legislation of 1873 as well as declined. The silver legislation could not produce both. The great decline in the average prices in the Eastern States took place between 1862 and 1873, and not after. The silver legislation of 1873 cannot be said to have caused the decline in grain prices."

### THE INFLUENCE AFFECTING COTTON.

The special reasons affecting the price of cotton are equally unmistakable. As Professor Laughlin remarks : Silver had no more to do with the fall of the price of cotton than it had to do with the fall of Icarus when the wax on his wings gave out. From 1876 to 1878 cotton sold at about 11 cents per pound ; and in 1890 it sold at the same price. It is only in the last five years, 1891–1895, that exceptionally low prices prevailed. The explanation of these low prices is to be found in the fact that the consumption has not kept pace with the steadily increasing production of cotton in the United States. The crop of to-day is about triple that of 1872. Still, up to 1890 increasing consumption kept up fairly well with the increasing production. The depression of trade in 1890, following the Baring failure, reduced the consumption of cotton, but just at this time came two or the largest crops of cotton ever produced. At the very time when the demand fell off the supply of cotton enormously increased. In 1891 the cotton crop rose to 8,652,597 bales, followed in 1892 by a still larger crop of 9,035,379 bales. Cotton fell in price from $12\frac{3}{4}$ cents in May, 1890, to $6\frac{7}{8}$ cents in March, 1892. The low prices led to a reduction of the acreage planted in cotton, and in 1893 the crop fell to 6,700,365 bales. Thereupon prices improved slightly. But the prospect of a crop of 9,875,000 bales in 1895, beyond the demand for consumption, again depressed prices. Just so soon as the coming recovery from the crisis of 1893 allows a readjustment of consumption to supply, the price of cotton will rise to a point at which the production of cotton will again be profitable. And then, if not before, it will be seen how absurd it has been to connect the price of cotton with the "demonetization" of silver, or any such thing. It is arrant demagoguism to try to make cotton growers believe that free coinage of silver can in any way restore the price of cotton, when its fall is due to excessive crops. This may be seen in the following table.

| Year. | Annual Crop of Cotton in Bales. | Year's Price, N. Y., in Cents. |
|---|---|---|
| 1872 | 2,974,851 | 22.19 |
| 1873 | 3,930,508 | 20.14 |
| 1874 | 4,170,388 | 17.95 |
| 1875 | 3,827,845 | 15.46 |
| 1876 | 4,632,313 | 12.98 |
| 1877 | 4,474,069 | 11.82 |
| 1878 | 4,773,865 | 11.22 |
| 1879 | 5,074,155 | 10.84 |
| 1880 | 5,761,252 | 11.51 |
| 1881 | 6,605,750 | 12.03 |
| 1882 | 5,456,048 | 11.56 |
| 1883 | 6,949,756 | 11.88 |
| 1884 | 5,513,200 | 10.88 |
| 1885 | 5,706,165 | 10.45 |
| 1886 | 6,575,691 | 9.28 |
| 1887 | 6,505,087 | 10.21 |
| 1888 | 7,046,833 | 10.03 |
| 1889 | 6,938,290 | 10.65 |
| 1890 | 7,311,322 | 11.07 |
| 1891 | 8,652,597 | 8.60 |
| 1892 | 9,035,379 | 7.71 |
| 1893 | 6,700,365 | 8.56 |
| 1894 | 7,549,817 | 6.9 |
| 1895 | 9,901,251 | 7.44 |

### PURCHASING POWER OF A BUSHEL OF WHEAT.

Professor Laughlin has made an interesting study of the purchasing power of a bushel of wheat and he finds that even though wheat has fallen in price, it will buy as much and even more than ever. A less number of bushels of wheat would buy the agricultural implements of the farmer in 1889 than in 1873, because there had been such a marked reduction in the cost of manufacturing these implements. Foreign competition may have reduced the Liverpool price of wheat, but the implements to be bought by the farmer have fallen still more. This is so important a point that it should be reiterated and repeated; for it has been taken for granted that the fall in the price of wheat means an absolute loss to the farmer, when, in fact, other things have fallen as well, and in greater proportion. Examine, then, the number of bushels of wheat, corn or oats required to buy the following implements of general use on a farm in 1873 and 1889 :

| IMPLEMENTS. | BUSH. WHEAT. | | BUSH. CORN. | | BUSH. OATS. | |
|---|---|---|---|---|---|---|
| | 1873. | 1889. | 1873. | 1889. | 1873. | 1889. |
| One-horse steel plow (wood beam)........ | 6.4 | 3.8 | 19.1 | 8.5 | 27.0 | 11.5 |
| One-horse iron plow (wood beam) .... ... | 4.9 | 2.7 | 14.7 | 6.2 | 20.8 | 8.3 |
| Two-horse side-hill, or reversible plow.... | 17.6 | 13.7 | 52.9 | 31.2 | 75.0 | 41.7 |
| One potato digger ........................ | 19.6 | 10.2 | 58.8 | 23.4 | 83.3 | 31.2 |
| Old-fashioned tooth harrow ............... | 14.7 | 8.9 | 44.1 | 20.3 | 62.5 | 27.0 |
| One-horse cultivator...................... | 6.8 | 4.7 | 20.5 | 10.9 | 29.1 | 14.5 |
| One-horse mower.......................... | 83.3 | 61.6 | 250.0 | 140.6 | 354.1 | 187.5 |
| Com. iron garden rake (10-tooth steel), doz. | 11.7 | 5.1 | 35.2 | 11.7 | 50.0 | 15.6 |
| One-horse horse-power.................... | 44.1 | 34.2 | 132.3 | 78.1 | 187.5 | 104.1 |
| Binder .................................... | 277.7 | 184.9 | 769.2 | 421.8 | 857.1 | 562.5 |
| Corn-sheller (1 hole)...................... | 11.2 | 8.2 | 33.8 | 18.7 | 47.9 | 25.0 |
| Common hoes (cast-steel socket), per doz.. | 6.3 | 4.7 | 19.1 | 10.9 | 27.0 | 14.5 |
| Common rakes (wood), per doz. .......... | 2.9 | 2.4 | 8.8 | 6.2 | 12.5 | 8.3 |
| Scythes (Ames' grass), per doz. .......... | 15.7 | 10.2 | 47.0 | 23.4 | 66.6 | 31.2 |
| Scythe snaths (patent), per doz. ........... | 10.8 | 6.1 | 32.3 | 14.0 | 45.8 | 18.7 |
| Shovel (Ames), per doz. .................. | 17.6 | 13 0 | 52.9 | 29.6 | 75.0 | 39.5 |
| Spades (Ames), per doz. ................. | 18.1 | 13.7 | 54.4 | 31.2 | 27.0 | 46.6 |
| Total.......................... | 569.4 | 388.1 | 1,645.1 | 886.7 | 2,048.2 | 1,187.7 |

The figures indicate the number of bushels it took in 1873 and 1889, respectively, to buy the implements opposite to which they are placed. For instance while it was necessary for a farmer to sell 83.3 bushels of wheat in 1873 to buy a one-horse mower, it required only 61.6 bushels in 1889 to purchase the same implement. That is, although wheat fell in price, mowers fell still more because of the cheapening in the cost of manufacture. Notice the final lesson as concerns wheat alone, even though it has fallen in price from 99.4 cents in 1873 to 69.8 cents in 1889. In 1873 all those seventeen kinds of implements would require 569.4 bushels of wheat to buy them, and after "the crime of 1873" it took only 388.1 bushels to buy the same articles. When the purchasing power of a bushel of the several crops is reckoned in other articles purchased by the farmer, the same story is told, as the tables of prices show. If there were any sense at all in this talk about "demonetization" in 1873, we might beg for more of it for the farmer.

FACTS ABOUT CORN AND OTHER CROPS.

If the comparison is made between implements and other cereal crops, the gain of the farmer since 1873 is still more marked. Whatever illusions foreigners may have on this subject, it need hardly be remarked here that wheat is not the most important crop in this country, and that it is in some sections rather an optional or alternative crop with the more important products of Indian corn, oats or hay. Mr. L. G. Powers, of Minnesota, has compiled a very interesting table which at once illustrates this point and shows the absolute absence of any relation between the price of silver and that of the great agricultural staples of the country. Dealing with the farm values of nine crops—corn, oats, wheat, rye, barley, buckwheat, potatoes, hay and tobacco—of the State of Illinois, he reaches the following somewhat astonishing results by giving the gold value of these farm products by four-year periods from 1862 to 1894, inclusive. Mr. Powers remarks that Illinois is a large State, and its agriculture is truly typical of the husbandry of all the vast territory extending from Ohio to Kansas, inclusive, and from Minnesota to the cotton belt of the South. In the years 1862 to 1894, inclusive, Illinois raised a total of 354,711,-827 tons of the nine crops, of a farm value of $5,038,150,906 in currency or $4,570,148,391 in gold.

*Average Farm Prices Per Ton in Gold in Illinois, 1862 to 1894.*

| CROPS. | 1862 to 1866 | 1867 to 1870 | 1871 to 1874 | 1875 to 1878 | 1879 to 1882 | 1883 to 1886 | 1887 to 1890 | 1891 to 1894 | 1862 to 1894 | Percentages. |
|---|---|---|---|---|---|---|---|---|---|---|
| Corn | $10.57 | $13.08 | $10.97 | $9.84 | $14.55 | $11.48 | $11.60 | $12.91 | $11.82 | 50.36 |
| Oats | 16.42 | 18.35 | 16.33 | 13.62 | 20.68 | 15.63 | 15.90 | 17.92 | 16.77 | 9.81 |
| Wheat | 29.17 | 30.44 | 32.49 | 28.34 | 33.10 | 24.59 | 26.18 | 20.96 | 29.55 | 8.49 |
| Barley | 24.22 | 29.60 | 28.16 | 24.74 | 29.41 | 22.39 | 24.77 | 18.25 | 25.72 | 0.27 |
| Buckwheat | 20.95 | 26.05 | 29.01 | 25.76 | 31.65 | 25.99 | 24.87 | 29.58 | 25.54 | 0.04 |
| Rye | 16.81 | 20.62 | 18.82 | 17.25 | 23.68 | 17.98 | 18.05 | 15.04 | 19.04 | 0.63 |
| Potatoes | 14.89 | 17.39 | 23.04 | 13.51 | 19.87 | 12.86 | 17.11 | 23.02 | 17.39 | 2.37 |
| Hay | 7.16 | 7.55 | 8.70 | 6.19 | 9.54 | 6.81 | 8.70 | 7.62 | 7.82 | 27.99 |
| Tobacco | 167.24 | 134.04 | 156.63 | 96.08 | 134.25 | 147.60 | 168.14 | 143.68 | 145.65 | 0.03 |
| Corn, Oats and Wheat (1) | 14.26 | 16.38 | 14.26 | 12.05 | 18.21 | 13.28 | 14.06 | 14.83 | 14.59 | ..... |
| Corn, Oats and Wheat (2) | 13.69 | 15.97 | 14.40 | 12.66 | 17.72 | 13.66 | 14.01 | 14.61 | 14.59 | ..... |
| All Crops (1) | 12.45 | 13.83 | 13.17 | 10.60 | 16.25 | 11.31 | 12.65 | 13.31 | 12.88 | ..... |
| All Crops (2) | 11.98 | 13.75 | 13.13 | 10.98 | 15.59 | 11.83 | 12.72 | 13.19 | 12.88 | ..... |

No. 1. General average of all.   No. 2. Averaged on relative importance.

Taking the average value per ton in gold of each of the nine crops above named, after combining the several products in fixed proportion by weight so as to give each its relative importance, and we reach as a final average the following gold value of all crops combined:

From 1862 to 1866, averaged in gold............ $11.98 per ton.
From 1871 to 1874, currency price being reduced
  to gold.................................... 13.13 "
From 1879 to 1882, the period of great scarcity in
  Europe, in gold............................ 15.59 "
From 1891 to 1894, in gold.................... 13.19 "

Dealing with the crops of maize or Indian corn, oats and wheat, as distinct from the other six crops included in the nine, we get the following results:

*Average Gold Value of Maize, Oats and Wheat.*

| | |
|---|---|
| 1862 to 1866, in gold.................... | $13.69 per ton. |
| 1871 to 1874, currency prices reduced to gold ... | 14.40 " |
| 1879 to 1882, in gold..................... | 17.72 " |
| 1891 to 1894, in gold..................... | 14.61 " |

These conclusions, verified by Mr. Edward Atkinson, are fully sustained by data furnished by Mr. Lucius B. Swift, of Indianapolis, in regard to the price of farm products in Indiana from 1873 to 1892. The prices are those nearest to the farm. They show approximately what the farmer realized. The prices during the suspension of specie payments are reduced to gold values, and the results are the following:

| | 1873–1877. | 1878–1882. | 1883–1887. | 1888–1892. |
|---|---|---|---|---|
| Corn, per bushel..................... | 35.6 | 41.8 | 37 | 39.8 |
| Oats, per bushel..................... | 29.6 | 31.6 | 28.8 | 35.2 |
| Wheat, per bushel................... | 95 | 102.6 | 79 | 87.2 |
| Rye, per bushel..................... | 52.8 | 70.4 | 57.6 | 68 |
| Potatoes, per bushel ................ | 58 | 60.6 | 50.8 | 59.4 |
| Hay, per ton........................ | $9.31 | $9.47 | $8.21 | $9.54 |

Of the six crops, it will be observed that wheat was the only one on which the Indiana farmers did not realize more in the last-named period than in the first. The increase of the purchasing power of corn is strikingly illustrated by Professor Loughlin. In 1873 a binder could be bought for no less than 769.2 bushels of corn and in 1889 for only 421.8.

### THE LAW OF PROGRESS.

While the American farmer has profited like other people from the scientific advance of recent years, he has also lost by it. The cheapening of ocean freights has served to place fields of competition farther removed from European markets on terms of equality with him. Improved machinery in the processes of production by minimizing the demands on human labor does not promote the multiplication of bread-eaters. The electric street railroad has displaced the horse, and the bicycle has aided the process to such an extent that while so recently as 1892 the 15,498,140 horses in the United States were valued at $1,007,593,636, the value in 1896 of 15,124,057 horses is set down at $500,140,186. This surely cannot be attributed to "the crime of '73," though a more sudden and startling contraction of value than any of the stock example of the free silverites.

The American grain farmer, in so far as he is a competitor in the markets of the world, is no more exempt from the penalty of having the supply of this product outrun the demand than the producer of calico or of steel rails. In so far as he is dependent on the consuming capacity of his home market he can be helped by increasing the number of wage-earners and bread-eaters, but certainly not by any movement calculated to paralyze industry, to throw hundreds of thousands of men out of employment and to reduce the purchasing ability of millions. The average annual value of the farm products of the United States is over $2,500,000,000. Of this the annual average exported of late years has been about $600,000,000, so that for the consumption of three-fourths of his products the American farmer is dependent on his home market. It is utterly impossible that prosperity should be brought to him by any process that brings ruin to the rest of the country. If the free coinage of silver offered him the means of paying his debts in dollars worth only 53 cents he would be no better off if he had not the dollars. In the dislocation of all business and the collapse of all credit that would attend the triumph of the free silver cause, it is absurd to assume that the farmer should enjoy the sunshine of prosperity. He would have his full share of the bitter consequences of a widespread and disastrous panic equally with the merchant, the manufacturer and the artisan; he might not be the first to feel the full force of the financial cataclysm, but he would certainly be the last to recover from it.

### THE FARMER AS A DEBTOR AND A CREDITOR.

The assumption that the farmers are universally or even generally in debt is manifestly false. Many of them are in debt on their current accounts, but a change in the currency system would have very little influence on these. According to the census returns, less than one farmer in five owes money on a mortgage, and the property mortgaged is valued at three times the total of the obligations. Dealing with ten great States in which the crops were grown on which his tabular comparisons are made, Mr. Powers says that: "An analysis of the mortgage debt of any one of these States will show that in 1890 the relative burden was not much, if any, over one-half as great as in 1880." The mortgage foreclosures of these States have been compiled over a long period for only one of these States—that of Minnesota. This compilation has been made by Mr. Powers himself. He says: "The statistics of this State disclose a relative frequency of foreclosures, less in 1893 than in any other year of Minnesota history. It shows that in that year it was less than one-fourth as great relatively as in 1873, or in the period before the noted silver legislation."

But, as Mr. Trenholm has pointed out: "The farmers are, in one sense, the great creditor class. The crop and the stock are debtors to the farmer not only for the capital invested, but also for the value of all labor bestowed on them by the farmer and his family. The farmers, therefore, are vitally interested in our money laws, for there is a long time between sowing and reaping, and the farmer needs to collect from the produce of his fields and flocks and herds as good money as he puts into these investments." When the farmer gets into debt it is usually for the purpose of increasing the yield of his crops, or securing improved machinery to sow, to cultivate and to reap. If he is a progressive man he will want to go on increasing the volume of his product in proportion to the cost of raising it, so that he may have a larger surplus. Like any other man engaged in productive industry, he is, in short, likely to be a borrower from time to time. Even if the free silver device could enable him to get more easily out of such debt as he may have for the moment, it would make it infinitely more difficult for him to borrow again. For it would drive capital out of the country and cause the United States to be avoided like a plague spot by all foreign investors. There would not only be far less money than before, but, what is fifty times more important than the actual stock of money, there would be very much less credit. The farmer is apt to regard himself now as the least favored of borrowers; under a colossal scheme of repudiation, which can be carried out only by his vote, his chances of getting credit would be very much worse. His probable gains at any point of the process, save perhaps in the scaling down of his debts, are purely visionary; his losses even before the force of the long and ruinous panic had spent itself, would easily exceed any gains that the most hopelessly indebted of his fellows could possibly secure.

### THE FOREIGN BALANCE OF TRADE.

The results in the foreign market would be not less disastrous and would be out of all proportion to any favor the farmer could do to the silver-mine owner by voting for the free coinage of silver. The product of silver from all the silver mines of the United States during the last five years, 1891-1895, has averaged, even in "coining value," but $74,000,000 a year, or at the actual commercial value of silver but $45,500,000 a year—less than 1-50, or 2 per cent. of the value of farm products and less than 1-12, or 8 per cent. of the actual export of farm products a year. Other countries would not buy more of our farm products unless the prices were lowered, while farmers would be driven to attempt to sell more abroad by lowered prices because of the lack of demand at home caused by hard times. The total returns of the increased export might not be greater than the present. It is with the product of our farms as well as our manufactures that we are to-day paying the interest on the moneys loaned us by the investment of capital from abroad. If it were at all true that the balance of trade is really settled in money, instead of by the process of exchange, Great Britain alone would have had to pay us in the past five years more gold than exists in Great Britain and the United States together. During those five years our trade with Great Britain alone averaged an export of $436,000,000 and an import of $160,000,000, leaving a "balance of trade" of $276,000,000 a year or $1,384,000,000 in five years. This balance is offset in a great measure by our interest payments abroad. If this country were to go upon a silver basis, the credit of the country would be weakened abroad and the rate of interest would rise and there would be still less net return for American products exported. Thus under "free silver" the farmer would be at disadvantage both in the home and in the foreign market.

## RAILROAD FREIGHT RATES.

Mr. Bryan has told farmers that railroad rates have not been reduced to keep pace with falling prices. On the contrary, transportation rates have fallen more than almost any other prices. In 1872 and 1873, all-rail rates per bushel of wheat, Chicago to New York were 33 cents; in 1895 but 12 cents. By lake-and-rail, the rate was 28 cents in 1872 and 7 cents in 1895; by lake-and-canal, 24 cents in 1872 and 4 cents in 1895. Canal freights between Buffalo and New York averaged 13 cents in 1872 and 2 1-5 cents in 1895. The average rate of freight per ton per mile on all railroads in the United States has fallen from 2 1-5 cents in 1872 to less than $\frac{3}{4}$ cent in 1895. These figures show that railroad rates have fallen more than crop prices. If free silver is to increase prices, the farmer will scarcely be benefited should this apply to railroad freight rates.

## INDEPENDENCE OF THE FARMER.

"The farmer," says Mr. Bryan, "is the most helpless victim of circumstances of all the producers of wealth." The contrary is true. Times may be hard, he may not make money, but he can live on what he raises. Corn and pork, chickens and eggs, vegetables and fruit will keep a man and his family alive and well, even if they do have to wear old clothes and stop buying groceries. But when the mill shuts down the workmen cannot eat the cloth or the shoes or the blankets he has made. If work stops and he has no savings, starvation stares him in the face. This is why Mr. Bryan's description of the farmer as driven between the bulls and bears of Wall street is so false. They cannot blight the corn or kill the pigs if they would. The farmer is really the only independent man. He can always live. But he wants to do more. He wants to make money. This he can only do when the country is prosperous—that is to say, when the mills are running and houses building, and everybody is earning a good living. And this is only possible in a country that has a fixed standard of value. Who will contract for the future to be paid in dollars when he knows not what a dollar will mean six months hence. It is just this uncertainty that has killed business for the last three years.

## CENSUS FACTS AS TO FARM VALUES AND MORTGAGES.

The final proof that the farming industry has not been ruined by the "crime of '73" is found in the statistics of the growth of that great interest given by the United States census. The number of farms in 1870 was 2,659,985; in 1890, 4,564,641—an increase of nearly 80 per cent. The acreage had increased from 407,735,041 in 1870 to 623,218,619 in 1890—over 50 per cent. The number of acres improved had increased from 188,921,099 in 1870 to 357,616,755 in 1890— or nearly double, and the percentage of unimproved land in farms had been reduced from 53 per cent. to 42 per cent. of the total. The average size of the farms had decreased from 153 acres in 1870 to 137 acres in 1890, but there had been an increase in the average size between 1880 and 1890. The decrease in size of farms had been chiefly in the New England States, New York, New Jersey and Pennsylvania, where the average holding has steadily gone down, and in the Southern States, where it has fallen very greatly, owing to the increased cultivation of small farms by the negroes, which has brought down the average. In the great central West, reaching from Ohio to the Dakotas, the average acreage of farms has greatly increased. The number of farms of the profitable size of from 100 to 500 acres has increased in larger proportion than any other kind; 1,695,983 farms in 1880 to 2,008,694 in 1890, the great part of this wholesome increase being in the central West. The valuation of farming property has increased for lands, fences and buildings, from $9,262,000,000 in 1870 to $13,279,000,000 in 1890; in implements and machinery from $336,000,000 in 1870 to $494,000,000 in 1890; in live stock from $1,525,000,000 in 1870 to $2,208,000,000 in 1890, these values having nearly doubled in the great central West, while they have actually decreased in the New England States, New York, New Jersey and Pennsylvania. This shows a steady increase in value in farming property except in the Eastern States, for the twenty years at the beginning of which silver was "demonetized."

In the census of 1890 a special investigation was made as to farm mortgages. This had not been made in previous census years, so that there are no statistics for comparison. These figures of 1890 show that out of $13,279,000,000 value of all farms $3,054,000,000 was the value of farms occupied by owners, on which there was a mortgaged indebtedness, and that the amount of the incumbrance was $1,085,000,000 or 35 per cent of the total value. This leaves $10,224,000,000, as the combined value of the farms owned free of any incumbrance and hired farms. The proportion of hired farms varies greatly in the different states, being highest in the New England and Southern States, and lowest in the great central West. This is undoubtedly because so many foreign immigrants have rented small holdings in the New England States and so many negroes have done the same of late years in the Southern States. At the same time careful investigations were made as to the average annual rate of interest paid on the farm mortgages in several States. The average for the whole country was just about 7 per cent, but the figures ranged from below 6 per cent. in the New England States to 7, 8 and 9 percent in the central West, and as high as 10 and even 12 per cent. in the far West. These figures furnish the key to the real difficulties of the American farmer, which are different in the East from what they are in the West.

## THE REAL DIFFICULTIES.

Farming in the Eastern States has been a declining industry because of the superior advantages of the West; farming in the West has been an increasing industry, which has nevertheless suffered a serious blow during the hard times of the past five years. The eastern farmer can no longer utilize the small and rocky farm of that section for the large crops which the West can produce in such profusion and at so much less cost; consequently, the Eastern States are being divided into smaller farms, utilized more and more by new comers—many of them of foreign nationalities—who are giving more attention to the small crops. The West has greatly increased the actual value of its farms and everything connected with them, but the value of farm products has not correspondingly increased. During the past few years not only has our product greatly increased—particularly in cotton—but new and vast countries have come into the world's competition, particularly in wheat. This enormous production—of great benefit to the world at large, in its provision against famine—as has already been shown, reduced the price of these particular crops with a very serious effect upon the southern planter and the western farmer. But it has had absolutely nothing to do with the demonetization of silver, and it is a cause beyond direct control. The remedy is that the arable acreage should be diverted more largely to other crops, as is more and more being done. But the figures suggest another great cause of the farmer's condition which is at this moment within his control. The western farmer who has incumbered his farm is paying something like 10 per cent. interest on the money borrowed. The reason for the high rate of interest in the Western States, increasing steadily from east to west, is the uncertainty which exists in the minds of the lenders as to the security of their money. During the past five years the interest has added up close to 50 per cent., or half of the money borrowed. The rate of interest has been enormously increased by the uncertainty, particularly of foreign loaners, as to the maintenance of the gold standard in this country. This was shown strikingly at the time of the bond issue, when the Secretary of the Treasury informed Congress that he could make a saving in the rate of interest amounting to $16,000,000, if Congress would declare the bonds "payable in gold" instead of merely "in coin." The election of Mr. Bryan would mean an increase in the rate of interest, and his defeat a decrease in the rate of interest, because of the action of those laws of credit which are beyond control of any men or set of men. The difference would mean millions of dollars to the American farmer. Least of all men can the American farmers, who are in debt, afford to vote for "free silver," which would not put any more dollars in their pockets with which to pay off their mortgages, and would surely and swiftly increase the rate of interest, which they must pay when they renew their mortgages. This is true of all farmers who have mortgaged their farms and to whom appeal is made by the orators of the silver party. To the great body of American farmers who are not in debt, no argument whatever can be made which should induce them to think for a moment of voting for "free silver."

## SILVER AND PRICES.

The alleged connection between the fall in the price of silver and that of various products of agriculture and manufacturing industry is disproved by the facts of experience no less than by the principles of political economy. If the theory of the silver party be a correct one all prices should have moved up and down in sympathy with the changing quotations of the white metal. That nothing of the sort has happened is but one of the many demonstrations of how destitute of foundation is the whole structure of the free silver argument.

Demonstration has already been offered of the fact that there is no possible relation between the use of silver in the coinage and the course of prices, and that, if there were, on the theory of free silver advocates, the general course of the prices of commodities would have been entirely different. Proof has also been presented that while the prices of certain products of the farm have gone down in the last twenty-five years, the prices of others have advanced, which would not have been possible had they been governed by the fluctuations in silver. There is, however, no point of the free silver creed so obstinately defended as this: "Stoppage of coinage without the stoppage of the production of commodities has limited the supply of money and increased the quantity of commodities. The cheapness of the commodities is but another expression for the dearness of money." One would like to know what is meant by the dearness of money at a time when there is in the great financial centres of the world a congestion of idle capital, when the amount of the paper circulation of the chief European banks is far within the volume which their gold reserve would justify, and when the returns paid by first-class securities have remained for a long time at a point unprecedentedly low. If this be a time of cheap commodities it is emphatically a time of cheap money, too, and one reason for the low rates which either is able to command is that there is more offering than the international market can absorb.

The history of the whole course of modern production is one of labor-saving devices, and hence of increasing cheapness. As has been remarked: In 1830, when we used to work fourteen hours a day in the manufacture of cotton goods, a single operator could produce only about four thousand yards in a year, in 1840 about nine thousand yards a year, and in 1890, with the working time reduced to ten hours a day, an operator produced over thirty thousand yards of the same goods.

The two great revolutionary changes affecting modern production and values have been in motive power and industrial mechanism. From the beginning of the change, it has been clear that the new motive powers of steam and electricity and the new labor-saving mechanisms must immensely reduce the cost of every form of manufactured product; and also that the reduction of the cost must bring about a proportionate increase in production; an increase not only of machine-made articles but also, in a lesser degree, of natural products.

### A QUACK REMEDY FOR HARD TIMES.

The claim that the free coinage of silver would restore prosperity by advancing prices proceeds upon three equally fallacious assumptions: 1. That high prices are, of themselves, a necessary accompaniment of prosperity; 2. That prices have fallen because of the fall in silver; and, 3. That prices would advance with the appreciation of the price of silver. As to the first illusion, the criticism of Professor Laughlin is apt and exhaustive:

"Goods, after all, are the basis of all exchange. Money should not be mixed up in idea with all goods. Money is only one article. There are thousands of other articles, which we are daily using. These articles vastly outnumber money itself. There may be $1,600,000,000 of all kinds of money in the United States, but the other articles of wealth are enormously greater in value. People sometimes assume that money and goods are the same thing, and that demand comes only from money, when, in truth, the demand depends upon the goods primarily, and the money is only a go-between, or like a gate through which the goods go to get to other goods. No man's wealth is merely money in his pocket. His wealth and his demand are synonymous with the salable goods and property he owns.

"So when we see a restoration of prosperity, accompanied by rising prices in some industries, note that this has not been due to a change in the quantity of the circulation, but to an increasing offer of purchasing power, merely expressed in terms of money, for the products of these particular industries. And, after a depression, this will spread until the value and prices of all goods formerly produced at a loss will sell at such prices relative to other goods that their production will be remunerative to both employer and employed. But what is back of it is the generally increasing purchasing power of the community, due to owning or producing more goods, and not to any increasing 'volume of the currency.' This explains why it is that a good wheat or corn crop means a general quickening of trade and prosperity. When more goods are produced men have more purchasing power. And this further explains why it is that, when prosperity returns and men generally have more goods, and so more purchasing power, they cease to talk about the need of 'more circulating medium.' There is no need of quack medicines when health returns. And when healthy industrial conditions return there will be no more place for the quack silver medicines at 16 to 1."

### THE ILLUSION OF HIGH PRICES.

"There is absolutely no gain derived from a general change in all prices brought about by altering the value of money. Industry is not boomed by raising all prices alike. No manufacturer makes more profit by higher prices of hi product when all the materials he uses have risen in the same proportion. To suppose that one is made richer by merely expressing the same old property and goods in terms of a money that has become less valuable is a stupid delusion. To believe in it is to follow a momentary will-o'-the-wisp. The object is forever receding.

"The only way in which a rise of his prices can be of advantage to a producer is by a partial, not a general, rise. That is, since a general rise in all prices leaves every commodity in just the same unaltered relations to every other commodity, the only gain to a single producer arises from the fact that his goods have risen when others have not. Such a partial change of prices indicates a change in the value of some goods to other goods. One man thus gains at the expense of other men. Some goods buy more than before solely because other goods have not risen in price. If, for example, the leather industry had been depressed, prices low and employment irregular because demand had fallen off, then, when people begin to find that their stocks of leather are used up, and more leather is needed, a perceptible increase in demand for leather is noticed in the trade. The additional leather will not be furnished until the price (owing to a better demand) rises so that a fair profit can be made. This rise of price is merely the result of a changed and improving demand. It restores leather to a better relation to other goods than before. It has altered its value relatively to other articles solely because the change affected leather in particular.

"Such a rise in prices, affecting only a few industries, shows an altered value of their products and is a distinct gain to persons in the industries affected. Observers of such a process, seeing this unmistakable gain, jump to the conclusion that, if a raise of prices is gainful to one industry, it must be for all industries. Just here lies the fallacy. The delusion that a rise in prices in general is a gain has been punctured. Just as soon as the rise is general, and not peculiar to only a few industries, it ceases to be of advantage to anyone. For, in that event, no one has any advantage relatively to anyone else. It is perfectly true that a rise of prices in particular cases gives a gain to employer or employed ; but it is decidedly not true if this rise of prices is general and affects all industries. The delusion consists of mixing the particular with the general ; in supposing that what is true of particular industries is true of industries in general. It is an error of dwelling upon a gain due to relative advantages which must disappear the moment the relative advantage ceases to exist."

### PRICES THAT ADVANCED AS SILVER DECLINED.

The claim that the fall in the price of silver is alike the measure and the cause of the fall in the price of commodities has already been disposed of in dealing with the prices of products of American agriculture. Outside of our chief cereal crops, however, there is a considerable range of products of the soil whose course of price absolutely disproves the theory of the free silver advocates. Consulting the record of wholesale prices of commodities which has been kept for fifty years by the London "Economist" and it will be found, for example, that the price of coffee which between 1845 and 1850 ranged from 44 to 54 shillings per hundred weight in London, was quoted from 59 to 82 shillings on January 1, 1883, from 78 to 85 shillings on January 1, 1888 and from 80 to 92 shillings on January 1, 1895. There is here obviously no connection whatever with any changes in the price of silver, and there is a price movement extending over ten or twelve years absolutely contrary to that of silver. On a lesser scale, the prices of flax in London have fluctuated out of all correspondence with the price of silver. It was as high as 35 pounds per ton on January 1, 1879, and as low as 27 pounds on January 1, 1884, it rose to 32 pounds by January 1, 1887 and fell again to 27 pounds a year later. It struck the still lower level of 23 pounds in 1890 and 1891 and recovered to 31 pounds by July 1, 1893, and retained this price, which is the highest in fifteen years, down to January 1, 1895. The course of Russian hemp has been somewhat similar. It was quoted at 25 pounds per ton on January 1, 1879, had risen to 29 pounds 10 shillings by January 1, 1884, dropped to 26 pounds on January 1, 1890 and to 18 pounds on January 1, 1892, recovering again six months later and holding most of the advance, so that on January 1, 1895, the price was 24 pounds per ton, as it had been for most of the year before. The course of Russian tallow is equally destructive of the free silver theory of prices. Its average between 1845 and 1850 was 44 shillings per hundred weight, and it was 36 shillings and 6 pence on January 1, 1879, 45 shillings on January 1, 1880, 35 shillings on January 1, 1886, and 31 shillings on January 1, 1891, and by July 1, 1893, had reached 48 shillings, at which price it was still quoted on January 1, 1895. The price of timber tested by that of Canadian yellow pine in London shows what on the free silver theory is an equally inexplicable series of fluctuations. The average price per load between 1845 and 1850 was 65 to 71 shillings; on January 1, 1879, it was from 85 to 95 shillings. On January 1, 1887, the price ruled as low as 50 to 90 shillings. On January 1, 1890, it rose as high as 97 to 115 shillings, dropping again by January 1, 1891, to 75 to 110 shillings. Since that time it has gone up and down, finally reaching on January 1, 1895, the relatively high figure of 92 to 115 shillings.

### A CONTRADICTORY THEORY.

The theory that prices would advance with the appreciation of the value of silver is an obviously contradictory one. If a 53-cent dollar were to be the measure of value, the prices of merchandise would, of course, be marked up to meet the change in the standard, but the value of various commodities comprising the mass of merchandise would remain unchanged as between each other. If the bullion in the silver dollar under free coinage came to be worth 63 cents, or even 73 cents, prices measured by the rising standard would, of course, recede, and if the dream of the candidate were to be realized, and an ounce of silver came to be worth $1.29 in gold, prices would revert to the figure they hold under the present standard, subject merely to any new conditions of supply or demand that might arise in the interim. As has been well said: Whether you measure a tree with a foot-rule or with a yard-stick, the tree remains unchanged in its own height ; and a number of trees, when compared as to relative heights, bear the same proportion to each other whether their heights are expressed in feet or yards. John Stuart Mill, whom the silver men are wont by a garbled quotation to rank as an advocate of the " quantity theory " of price, sums up the political economy of the question as follows :

"The mere introduction of a particular mode of exchanging things for one another, by first exchanging a thing for money and then exchanging the money for something else, makes no difference in the essential character of the transactions. It is not with money that things are really purchased. Nobody's income (except that of the gold or silver miner) is derived from the precious metals. The pounds or shillings which a person receives weekly or yearly are not what constitutes his income. They are a sort of tickets or orders, which he can present for payment at any shop he pleases, and which entitle him to receive a certain value of any commodity that he makes choice of. The farmer pays his laborers and his landlord in these tickets as the most convenient plan for himself and them ; but their real income is their share of his corn, cattle and hay, and it makes no essential difference whether he distributes it to them directly or sells it for them and gives them the price. \* \* \* There cannot, in short, be intrinsically a more insignificant thing, in the economy of society, than money, except in the character of a contrivance for sparing time and labor. It is a machine for doing quickly and commodiously what would be done, though less quickly and commodiously, without it; and, like many other kinds of machinery, it only exerts a distinct and independent influence of its own when it gets out of order."

### THE ECONOMIC THEORY OF VALUE.

Another way of illustrating the same truth is the following lucid exposition by MacLeod :

"The value of anything is always something external to itself. Hence a single object cannot have economic value. A single object cannot be equal or distant. If an object is said to be equal or distant, we must ask, equal to what ? or, distant from what ? So if any quantity is said to have value, we must ask, value in what ? And as it is absurd to speak of absolute or intrinsic distance, or absolute or intrinsic equality, so it is equally absurd to speak of absolute or intrinsic value. It is impossible to predicate that a quantity has value without at the same time implying that it can be exchanged for something else; and, of course, everything it can be exchanged for is its value in that commodity. Hence any economic quantity has as many values as quantities it can be exchanged for, and if there is nothing for which it can be exchanged, it has no value.

"Any economic quantity may have value in terms of many other. Suppose that A is ten guineas then B may any one of the other three species of economic quantities. It may be a watch, or so much corn, or wine, or clothes, or any other material chattel. Or it may be so much labor, instruction, or amusement, or service. Or it may be a right of action, or a debt, or the funds, or a copyright, or any abstract right. Each of these species of property is of the value of ten guineas, and it follows that each of them is equal in value to the other; because things which are equal to the same thing are equal to each other. The value of the money in the pockets of the public is the products, services and rights it can purchase. The value of the goods in the warehouses of merchants and traders is the money in the pockets of the public."

"'The value of an incorporeal right is the thing promised which may be demanded. The value of a five-pound note is five sovereigns; the value of a postage stamp is the carriage of a letter; the value of a railway ticket is the journey; the value of an order to see the play is seeing the play; the value of a promise to cut a man's hair is the cutting of the hair; the value of an order for milk, bread, wine, soup, coals, etc., is the milk, bread, wine, etc. If I want a loaf of bread which costs a shilling, what difference does it make to me whether I have a shilling or the promise of the baker to give me a loaf? It is clear that in this case the shilling and the promise are of exactly the same value to me. Suppose that the price of cutting a man's hair is a shilling, what difference does it make to me whether I have a shilling or the promise of the hairdresser to cut my hair? In this case it is clear that the shilling and the promise are exactly equal value to me. In short, in the case of every product and service, the money to purchase it with and a promise to render the product or service are exactly equal value in each separate case.

"Now, what is money by the unanimous consent of economists? It is nothing but a general right or title to demand a product or service from any person who can render them, if another cannot; money has general and permanent value, while each of these promises has only particular and precarious value. Each of these separate rights then is of exactly the same nature as money, but it is of an inferior degree. But they are, each of them, economic quantities or wealth, for the very same reason that money is. It is clear that if a person had his pockets full of promises by solvent persons to render him all the products and services he might require, he would be exactly as wealthy as if he had so much money ? And he can always sell or exchange any of these orders for orders for a different thing. Hence we see the perfect justice of the doctrine of all jurists that rights are wealth."

### TWENTY YEARS OF PROGRESS.

Consideration of these economic truths will show how preposterous is the idea that the country was impoverished and the course of its progress turned backward by the formal adoption of the gold standard in 1873. The gain in wealth of the country between the census of 1870 and that of 1890 absolutely contradicts that assumption. Between 1870 and 1890 the population of New England and New York increased 31 per cent., but between 1873 and 1894 the number of depositors in savings banks increased 86 per cent., and the amount of their deposits increased 112 per cent. Between 1870 and 1890 the population of the United States increased 62 per cent., but the number of persons insured in life companies that report to the New York Insurance Department increased 104 per cent. and the amount of their policies increased 113 per cent. According to the census reports the true valuation of all real and personal property in the United States, per capita, was $780 in 1870, $870 in 1880, and $1,039 in 1890. The value of the farms in the six States, Illinois, Iowa, Minnesota, Wisconsin, Michigan and Missouri, increased 64.6 per cent. between 1870 and 1890, and deducting the population of towns of 5,000 inhabitants and over, the rest of the population in those States increased 41.3 per cent. The farm value in the six States, North and South Carolina, Georgia, Alabama, Mississippi and Louisiana, increased 74 per cent. between 1870 and 1890, and the population, including cities, increased 54 per cent. Valuations in 1870 were in depreciated currency. From 1873 to 1893 the increase in railroads constructed and in operation in the United States was 107,488 miles or about 150 per cent.

### GARBLING FACTS AND FIGURES.

The declaration of the Chicago platform that there has been since 1873 a heavy increase in the burden of taxation and of all debts is a gross and palpable misstatement. The public debt of the United States in 1873 was equivalent to a charge of $50.52 on every man, woman and child in the country, and the annual interest paid on it was equal to $2.35 per head of the population. On July 1, 1895, the burden of the debt was $12.93 and of the interest charge 42 cents per head. In other words, the reduction of the debt burden per head of the population was equal to 74 per cent. and of the interest charge 81 per cent.

The last census returns give copious details of the changes in all forms of public debt, national, State and local, between 1880 and 1890, and there is none of the great divisions of the country in which there was not a marked decrease in these ten years, both in the average rate of interest and in the amount of the annual interest charge per head of the population. The results for the whole country as to all forms of public debt were briefly these : During the ten years ending in 1890 the total national, State and local bonded debt increased $872,-517,137 or 30.86 per cent. ; the total interest charge decreased $53,610,400, or 30.10 per cent. ; the average interest rate decreased from 5.24 to 4.85 per cent., and the per capita charge decreased from $2.95 to $1.51. For every $1,000 of assessed valuation the interest charge in 1880 was $8.76 ; in 1890 it was but $3.81.

An attempt has been made by Senator Tillman and others to break the force of these figures by arguing that the progress made in the last quarter of a century has been by the East at the expense of the West and South. Among Tillman's figures are these : "There are fifteen Southern States, including Delaware and Maryland, with an area of 566,000 square miles and a population of 17,000,000 in 1890. The State of Pennsylvania has an area of 45,000 square miles and a population of 5,258,000. In the ten years between 1880 and 1890 these Southern States increased in population 2,555,000, while Pennsylvania increased 975,000 ; but in the assessed valuation of its real and and personal property Pennsylvania gained $901,000,000, while the fifteen Southern States gained only $909,000,000" This, according to Tillman, is a clear case of robbery, a demonstration of the fact that the substance of the Southern and Western people has been going to the East by reason of the financial system that has been fastened on them. The advantage of the Southern States as compared with Pennsylvania should have been $3\frac{1}{4}$ times to 1 instead of barely holding their own with it.

It is, of course, pure claptrap to institute a comparison based on territory and population between communities with a history and environment so different as those of the States of the cotton belt and the State of Pennsylvania, but if such comparison is to be attempted let it be done fairly. The census returns supply the true valuation of real and personal property, as distinguished from the assessed valuation of property taxed, in the various States and Territories, and if there is to be any discussion of the relative speed of national progress in the various sections of the country it is the former and not the latter that must be taken as the basis of comparison. In the fifteen Southern States the true valuation of real and personal property in 1880 was $7,412,000,000, while in 1890 it was $10,982,614,367—an increase of $3,570,614 367 in ten years. The true valuation of real and personal property in the State of Pennsylvania was in 1880 $4,942,000,000 and in 1890 $6,190,746,550—a gain of $1,248,746,550. In other words, the growth in wealth of the fifteen Southern States between 1880 and 1890 was equal to 48 per cent., while that of Pennsylvania was only 25 per cent. The volume of growth does not exactly come up to the standard of $3\frac{1}{4}$ to 1 demanded by Tillman, but it comes pretty near it ; and if the rate of the last ten years is kept up for the current ten the wealth of the Southern States will be found to have doubled in twenty years, while that of Pennsylvania will have increased only one-half.

#### FALSE CLAIMS TWICE THRESHED.

How utterly untrustworthy is the method of comparison by assessed valuation may be inferred by an examination of some of the other figures cited by Tillman in support of his general assertion about Southern and Western poverty and Eastern wealth. The figures have done duty before, being the basis of a similar presentation by Mr. King, of Kansas, of the grievances of what he calls the "produce district," and they are cited by Populists like Senator Allen as evidence of a fixed purpose on the part of the East "to transfer the wealth of the West from the pockets of those who produce it to the pockets of those who have had no hand in its production and no sympathy with its producers." Mr. King selects nine States from the "produce district" for comparison with the State of Massachusetts, and Senator Tillman selects six to bring out substantially the same result, which is, that while the single State of Massachusetts gained $569,000,000 in assessed valuation in ten years, the six great States gained but a few millions more. But in point of fact, while the increase of true valuation in the State of Massachusetts between 1880 and 1890 was very little over $180,000,000, the increase in the true valuation of Illinois, one of the six States compared, was ten times this amount.

The utter absurdity of making assessed valuation the basis of a comparison of State wealth is shown by looking at the returns from Illinois. According to the method of assessment there in vogue in 1880, real estate and improvements taxed were valued at $575,441,053; according to the method of 1890 the valuation was $587,442,280. That the value of taxable real estate in the State of Illinois should have increased in ten years only $12,000,000, or about one-fourth of the average annual increase of the taxable real estate of New York City, is manifestly ridiculous. It may be explained by the fact that in 1880 assessed value was 20 to 30 per cent. of the real value, while in 1890 the standard was about ten per cent.; but if this renders the figures absolutely worthless when applied to the State of their origin, they are equally so as a standard of comparison with States where a different system prevails.

#### WAGES AND COMMODITIES.

The course of wages, elsewhere treated, is the most unanswerable demonstration of the fallacy of the free silver argument. For labor is the most universal of all commodities and the one that nearly everybody has to sell. There can be no question that labor, or the services of human beings, can command more gold to-day than at any other time in the history of the world. But "if gold is becoming scarce, why should labor command an increasing share of it?" Relatively to labor there has been a fall both in gold and in goods, and labor commands more of both than before. The relation of the fall in silver to the prices of commodities is very clearly brought out in the elaborate report of the Senate Finance Committee, usually known as the Aldrich report. Here is traced the relative value of labor and products in gold from 1845 to 1860, and from that time to 1890—taking as a standard the relation between labor and products established in 1860. The Senate report gives the relative purchasing power of silver over 223 articles, and the variation up or down from the index figure of 100 indicates whether it took more or less money to buy the 223 articles than in 1860. The facts indicate that goods are 8 per cent. cheaper than in 1860, compared with gold, and silver is 50 per cent. cheaper than in 1860 as compared with gold. It now takes 31.20 ounces of silver to buy one ounce of gold, while in 1860 only 15.29 ounces would buy one ounce of gold. If more than twice as much silver is needed as before to buy one ounce of gold its commercial value has evidently fallen fully one-half. But according to the silver men silver has not fallen away from goods, the prices of commodities having kept pace with it in its downward course. In every way this has been shown to be a palpable misstatement. The tables of the Senate Committee closed with 1890 and showed that then the prices of 223 articles were only 8 per cent. cheaper than in 1860, while silver was over 50 per cent. cheaper. A comparison with the prices of to-day would show but little change in these relative conditions. The following condensed table from the Senate report indicates the general course of price before and after 1860 in the chief classes of commodities, in wages and in the price of silver bullion:

*Prices, Wages, Purchasing Power.*

|  | 1845 | 1850 | 1855 | 1860 | 1865 | 1870 | 1875 | 1880 | 1885 | 1890 |
|---|---|---|---|---|---|---|---|---|---|---|
| Meat | 79.4 | 86.6 | 104.7 | 100 | 197 | 174.3 | 140.4 | 108.6 | 107.6 | 99.6 |
| Other food | 82.8 | 80.7 | 114.5 | 100 | 240.3 | 146.3 | 135 | 116.9 | 97.2 | 103.5 |
| Cloths and clothing | 97.1 | 91.3 | 94.7 | 100 | 299.2 | 189.4 | 120.1 | 104.5 | 84.8 | 82.4 |
| Fuel and lighting | .... | 102.6 | 121.1 | 100 | 237.8 | 196.5 | 156.5 | 100.2 | 89.6 | 92.5 |
| Metals and implements | 110.8 | 114.8 | 117.8 | 100 | 191.4 | 127.8 | 117.5 | 90.3 | 77.4 | 73.2 |
| Lumber and building materials | 100.7 | 102.2 | 103.4 | 100 | 182.1 | 148.3 | 143.7 | 130.9 | 126.6 | 123.7 |
| Drugs and Chemicals | 121 | 123.6 | 129.2 | 100 | 271.6 | 149.6 | 144.2 | 113.1 | 86.9 | 87.9 |
| House furnishing | 102.3 | 125.6 | 121.1 | 100 | 181.1 | 121.6 | 95 | 85.2 | 70.1 | 69.5 |
| Miscellaneous | 114.8 | 107.7 | 115.2 | 100 | 202.8 | 148.7 | 122.9 | 109.8 | 97.5 | 89.7 |
| Average of all prices | 102.8 | 102.3 | 113.1 | 100 | 216.8 | 112.3 | 127.6 | 106.9 | 98 | 92.3 |
| Average of all wages | 86.8 | 92.7 | 98 | 100 | 143.1 | 162.2 | 158.4 | 141.5 | 150.7 | 156.9 |
| Average wages by importance | 85.7 | 90.9 | 97.5 | 100 | 148.6 | 167.1 | 158 | 143 | 155.9 | 68.2 |
| Salaries of city teachers | 74.8 | 83.8 | 91.4 | 100 | 134.7 | 186.3 | 188.1 | 182.8 | 186.3 | 86.3 |
| Paper money | 100 | 100 | 100 | 100 | 49.5 | 81.1 | 88.8 | 100 | 100 | 100 |
| Gold price of silver bullion in London | 95.3 | 97.3 | 100 | 100 | 99 | 98.2 | 92.2 | 84.7 | 78.7 | 77.4 |
| Purchasing power of wages | 84.4 | 90.6 | 86.6 | 100 | 66 | 114.1 | 124.1 | 132.3 | 162 | 172.1 |

### A HIGH PRICES BARGAIN STORE.

The absurdity of the free silver claim that high prices in themselves make prosperity, is amusingly satirized in the following burlesque hand-bill which has recently been circulated:

# GREAT BARGAINS!

### . PRICES OF ALL GOODS .

### ADVANCED FIFTY PER CENT.

## The Dearest Store in Town.

**Dry Goods, Clothing, Hats, Boots, Groceries and Hardware at Higher Prices than ever before.**

### EVERYTHING MARKED UP.

**If any line of goods is too cheap for our customers, a discount of ten per cent. will be added.**

**We guarantee that articles bought from us will cost more than the same quality can be had for elsewhere.**

A special Lot of Women's Hats, Former Price $3.50, Now Going at $7.00.
Best Sugar—Sold at Other Stores for 6 cents Per Pound, Our Price 12 cents.
One Hundred Suits Boys' Clothing, Cost $5.65 Each, Sacrificed at Only $12.
Equally Big Advance in Price of All Other Goods in Stock.

**Come Early and Avoid the Rush, as this Unparalleled Sale will only last Two Weeks.**

All persons who prefer to buy dear goods, and who favor currency schemes for raising prices, will please send their orders to the firm of

### STEWART, BLAND, ALTGELD, TELLER & CO.,

*Dealers in Cheap Money Notions, High Prices Arguments, Free Silver Nostrums and Dear Goods Theories.*

—*Weekly Hard Times Howler*, Pefferville, Calamity Co. N. G.

## LABOR AND FREE COINAGE.

All the free silver arguments as to the general fall in prices and the advance in the purchasing power of gold sustain the conclusion that labor has benefited from the process of which the silver men complain. For the average rate of wages has, from decade to decade, steadily advanced, and this advance has been accompanied by an increase in their purchasing power. In silver-using countries, the advance of wages has not kept pace with the depreciation of silver, and the rise in price of all the necessities of life has been much greater than the rise in wages. These facts are clearly understood by newspapers which speak for organized labor, and by the great body of wage-earners themselves.

That the free coinage of silver might benefit—until he had to borrow again—the debtor who is looking for an opportunity to repudiate his debts no one denies, but the assertion that it would benefit labor has yet to be proved. If there be a creditor, as distinguished from a debtor class it is composed of wage-earners. They have an interest, distinctly vital, in seeing that the dollars paid in return for their labor do not shrink in purchasing power. As Daniel Webster said in the Senate of the United States sixty-two years ago: "The very man of all others who has the deepest interest in a sound currency, and who suffers most by mischevious legislation in money matters, is the man who earns his daily bread by his daily toil."

What the working man wants is a dollar whose purchasing power either remains unimpaired or increases.

This he now has, and he is seriously asked to exchange it for one which, though almost equally hard to get, will yield him far less of the necessities and comforts of life. Herr Schippel, a Socialist member of the German Reichstag, aptly describes "this artificial forcing up of the cost of living" as "the most infamous robbery one could now-a-days undertake against the masses who work for wages." Herr Schippel's remarks are not too positive. The present standard of wages has been hardly won. It has emerged from a costly history of suffering and struggle. The workingman should be careful how he consents to any proposition for lowering it. Once sacrificed, it will be hard to get back.

### WAGES IN DEPRECIATED CURRENCY.

There can be no excuse for anybody here misapprehending the effect of a depreciated currency on the welfare of the wage-earner. The generation that lived through the paper money period and felt the effect on wages and prices of the gradual approach to and final redemption of specie payments has not yet passed away. In the report of the Senate Finance Committee in 1892-3 on wholesale prices, wages and transportation there is the most complete compilation of wages and prices which has been made in this or any other country. The comparative course of both between 1860 and 1890 is an object lesson in the effect of the kind of currency used to pay wages on their purchasing power. Taking 1860 as the starting point, at which the average of prices and of wages and the purchasing power of wages are alike represented by the figure 100, we find with the introduction of paper money a sharp and immediate divergence among the three elements of the prosperity of the wage earner. Prices shot rapidly up, wages followed at a greatly relaxed pace, and the purchasing power of wages went down. In the five years between 1860 and 1865 the average of prices rose from the index number of 100 to that of 216.8, while wages rose from 100 to .only 143.1. Thus the purchasing power of wages declined from being equal to 100 in 1860 to 66 in 1865. With the appreciation of the value of the paper dollar between 1865 and 1870 wages did not decline. On the contrary, they advanced from the equivalent of 143.1 to 162, while prices fell from 216.8 to 142.3. Thus the purchasing power of wages, which was only equal to 66 in 1865, had risen with the appreciation in value of the currency to 114.1 in 1870.

Here we see that when the depreciation in the currency standard caused a rise in both prices and wages, prices rose so much faster than wages that the wage-earner was forced to work for less and less every year, until in 1865 he was working for about two-thirds of what he had received in 1860. As Mr. McVey puts the case:

"Meanwhile, the contractor, speculator and gambler were reaping the benefits supposed to be inherent in such a money. A few of the manufacturers were growing rich, and, as there seemed to be plenty of money and apparent high wages, the idea that the North was growing rich came quite naturally. In reality the apparent prosperity was in large measure simply a display, in lavish use, of a part of the far greater sums we were borrowing and ever since have been paying, and the diversion to showy expenditure, on the part of the wealthy few, of a pitifully great and increasing proportion of what ought to have been the savings of the poor. The fellows on top made all the show and did most of the talking, while the wage-earners labored on, hoping for better things."

Mr. David A. Wells, on the strength of painstaking investigation, asserts that in New York City during the period of great inflation in the '60s the prices of food rose 90 per cent., while wages rose only 60 per cent.

## AN EXAMPLE FROM SOUTH AMERICA.

A Methodist missionary, the Rev. J. R. Wood, of Sparrow's Point, Md., who spent several years in the Argentine Republic, and made a deep study of the money market of the country whose banking and coinage systems changed several times during his residence there, makes the following statement in reference to the effect of depreciation in the currency of Argentina:

"When I arrived in South America, Argentina did not have a national banking system, but every province and state had its own banking arrangements. The principal coins used were those of Bolivia and Chili, worth in their respective countries fifty cents and one dollar. The people of Argentina, however, would not accept them for more than their bullion value, which was thirty six and seventy-two cents, respectively.

"Later a national banking system was adopted similar to the system now in use in this country. For a time this proved successful, but through bad management and a general tendency on the part of the officials to borrow from Europe, the gold reserve was tampered with and a silver standard was established.

"The paper money of this country then became irredeemable. A panic followed. The price of every commodity advanced from 100 to 300 per cent.

"The country had abundant silver, but the merchants refused to handle it, as it was depreciating daily. The wages of the poor man did not increase with the increased prices of goods, and, although doing the same amount of work, he received only about one-third of the former pay.

"Being a missionary, the condition of the poor was brought more pointedly to my notice than would have been the case had I been a merchant. I saw great suffering among those who had, under the old system, been able to live happily on the same salaries for which they were working at the time of the panic in the money market,

"A number of ladies of my party who had gone to the Republic to teach in the normal schools at $100 a month were reduced in pay to one-third of that amount, and those who had intended to return to the United States were compelled to remain in the country on account of the money panic. When they went there, the Government controlled the schools and always paid the salaries in gold, but when the silver coinage went into effect the same salaries were paid in silver. When application for passage was made at the steamship offices the price was quoted in gold, and if silver or paper was tendered a demand for three times the amount stated was made."

### WAGES IN HONEST MONEY.

In this country, since 1865, the wage-earner has received his pay in money whose purchasing power has nearly doubled, while profits on capital average scarcely half what they were. With such a history and such an experience before him, he must be a foolish man indeed who desires to lower the quality of our money. It is not meant to suggest that the wage-earner should be satisfied, or that he should not strive for even a greater share of what, in co-operation with capital, he produces. He has as good a right to plan and combine toward that end as has the capitalist to increase his profits. It is under an appreciating currency that so much has been accomplished. Does he want to change this experiment for the one which immediately preceded it, during which, after the four years 1862-65, under a depreciating currency, he found himself, though with nominally high wages, working for two-thirds the power to purchase that he had previously had.

The causes of the enhanced purchasing power of money since the early '70s have been grossly misrepresented by the silver party. They lay it to the appreciation of gold. Well-informed people know it is due rather to decreased cost of production and distribution.

Mr. David A. Wells, the distinguished economist, shows that there is no evidence that gold has appreciated in value. Not a single commodity, he says, has notedly declined in the last thirty years, in respect to which clear, abundant and specific evidence cannot be adduced in proof that the decline has been due to decreased cost of production or distribution, or to changes in supply and demand occasioned by fortuitous circumstances. Capital has been abundant and cheap since 1873, when silver was demonetized. Such being the case, the only reason why sellers have taken lower prices is either an excessive supply or a diminished demand. Gold is cheaper to-day than ever if we measure its value either by the price of labor or by the rate of interest. According to Mr. Wells' figures, measured by wages, gold, if we accept the position of the silverites that it has altered in value, has declined since 1873 in a ratio of from 100 to 88; measured by the decline in the rate of interest on gold paying securities, the fall of gold has been from 100 in 1870 to 75 in 1896.

## WHOSE THE BENEFIT?

Who will benefit by free coinage of silver in the United States at the ratio of 16 to 1? Dishonest debtors would. The owners of silver bullion also would; temporarily speculators would probably make something too. But here the enumeration ceases. No working men would be benefited, not even the mine laborers who dig the ore, for it is not probable that the mine owner would voluntarily increase the wages of the mine-workers merely because the government, through free coinage, increased the market for the mine product. Mine owners are no more generous than any other class of employers; they pay no more than current rates of wages. While the Sherman law was in operation and the price of silver very much higher than it is now, the wages of the miners were not increased by the mine owners; and it is not likely that they would be increased were the price of silver to be again advanced through Government aid. Without the bullion to take to the mint and have coined free into dollars, the laborer can have no share in whatever benefits free coinage may create. Not having any bullion himself how can he get any of the dollars which are coined free for the bullion owner, is the question which he wants answered. He is told that he will get them in payment of wages for his labor, but as only a very small percentage of the wage-earners are employed in silver mines, the bulk of the wage-earning population would not receive any wages from that source. Where, then, does their benefit come in? What the mine workers, as well as the farm laborers and all other working people need is not a change in the existing kinds and quality of money, so much as a chance to get more of the money now in use. This they cannot get as long as employers are prevented from doing business through fear of loss on their investments, by a change in the monetary system. Until the agitation of the money question has ceased and confidence in business circles has been restored, any change in the present condition of labor and business is improbable. The working men have studied this for themselves, and but few of them are now willing to accept as true the statement of interested parties that wages are low because gold is the standard, and that free and unlimited coinage of silver will produce more satisfactory conditions and wages. They have learned that since the year 1860 wages have steadily increased ; this is proved by the following table of figures compiled from the census reports and official statistics:—

AVERAGE YEARLY WAGES IN THE U. S. IN MANUFACTURING INDUSTRIES AS SHOWN BY CENSUS REPORTS.

| Year. | Population | Employees. | Total wages. | Equivalent total wages in gold. | Average Annual wages in gold. | Wages increased since previous census. |
|---|---|---|---|---|---|---|
| 1860 | 31,443,321 | 1,311,246 | $378,878,966 | $378,878,966 | $288 |  |
| 1870 | 38,558,371 | 2,053,996 | 775,584,343 | 674,421,168 | 328 | 14 per cent |
| 1880 | 50,155,783 | 2,732,595 | 947,953,795 | 947,953,795 | 347 | 5½ " |
| 1890 | 62,831,900 | 4,712,622 | 2,283,216,529 | 2,283,216,529 | 484 | 39 " |

## LABOR UNIONS AND FREE COINAGE.

Every member of a union sincerely believes that the present standard of wages has been kept up by means of labor organizations; therefore, anything likely to destroy the usefulness of these organizations should be frowned upon by him. Experience has shown that no one thing has done so much to injure labor unions as their perversion to the purposes of partisan politics. The history of the growth and decay of the Order of the Knights of Labor is a noteworthy illustration of this fact. The present political campaign will soon be over, but the labor unions will be needed in years to come. Will it pay their members to allow them to become divided and weakened in the attempt to promote the schemes of silver mine owners and the ambitions of the candidates of the free silver party? The regard of these men for the laborer will suddenly cool on the evening of election day, and the disrupted union will be left to take care of itself. Many of the men of experience in the labor movement— those who are recognized as leaders among their fellow toilers—see clearly the evil effects that would follow the participation by the labor unions as such in political campaigns, and are outspoken in their opposition to such a course. President Samuel Gompers, of the American Federation of Labor, says: "The industrial field is littered with more corpses of organizations destroyed by the damaging influence of partisan political action than from all other causes combined." There is, however, nothing to prevent working men as citizens from taking an active part in the affairs of elections, apart from their connection with labor unions. At the ballot box all citizens—whatever their calling in life may be—are on a footing of absolute equality. There, at least, it cannot be urged by the demagogue that any ' class distinction " exists. How to vote so as to best advance his own interests and those of his fellow men is the one question which interests the working man. The statement made by the silver party that the working men as a whole favor free coinage is not only insulting—it is absolutely untrue. As a matter of fact many men prominent in labor circles, who enjoy the confidence and respect of their associates, have declared that they will vote against the candidates of the silver party. Others intend to do so but don't believe in talking politics, and so keep their intentions to themselves. Many prominent working men, both in and outside of labor unions, and notably the employees of railroads, have arrayed themselves on the side of sound money. Among the first to take formal and practical action in this direction were the employees of the Fitchburg railroad system. Without regard to past political affiliations these workmen, including brakemen, engineers, firemen, conductors and other employees, formed an organization which is known as the " New England Railway Men's Non-Partisan Sound Money Club." It would cover too much space to enumerate all that is being done for sound money by employees of other railway lines.

Many of the labor papers have also taken a stand against free silver. In the *Eight-Hour Herald*, George Gunton says: "There is no aspect of the case in which wage-workers have anything to gain by the adoption of a silver standard, but they have everything to lose; they will lose in the value of all their earnings; they will lose in the purchasing power of their wages, and most of all they will lose by the enforced idleness accompanying the business disturbance and bankruptcy which a radical depreciation of our standard money would create." The *Union Record* says: "The silver mine owners are grinning and letting the fools do the shouting." The *Scranton Truth* says: "The gold standard is the financial goal for which every great nation has striven, and is the dream even of those countries that are now on a silver basis and harassed in their money policy by the fluctuations of the white metal." The *Cleveland Citizen* says: "Not the demonetization of silver, but the use of labor saving machinery which enables one man and sometimes one boy to do the work of five men or more, has caused the glut of idle labor." The *People* (Socialist) asks: "Why don't the farmers have the price of wheat fixed by law, as they raise wheat and not silver." Many other statements in a similar vein might be quoted from different labor sources, but these will suffice to disprove the assertion so frequently made by the free coinage advocates that the laboring people and the labor press are opposed to the gold standard. The position taken by so many working men and by so large a portion of the labor press against the Bryan party contradicts the assertion that the present campaign is a contest between working men and their employers, the people and the " plutocrats," the masses and the " classes." No such divisions exist, except in the distorted imaginations of the free silver politicians and chronic radicals, who, although unable to agree among themselves as to what they want, are proclaiming their intention to regulate the financial system, not only of America, but of the whole civilized world.

### THE RAILROAD MEN AND FREE COINAGE.

There certainly could come nothing but injury through the adoption of a free coinage of silver policy to those who are employed in departments of business whose revenue is in some measure regulated by the laws of the State or nation. Take the employees of steam or street railway for instance. The revenue of these companies comes from fares paid by the traveling public and from freight. In some States the fares on the steam railroads are fixed by law at a certain amount of money per mile. In nearly every city the fares upon the street railways are also fixed by law. Unlike the product of the farm or mine, the income from the fares could not possibly be increased except perhaps through increased travel. According to the free silver orators, the price of all commodities, which, of course, includes the material used in carrying on railroad business, would be increased. As many of the railroads now claim to be making no profit—some of them running even at a loss—how would it be possible for them to exist at all under an increased cost of running, except in one way: to reduce expenses in whatever direction possible. Much of the bonded indebtedness of railroads is also payable in gold. As gold would certainly go to a premium the charges on this account would be materially increased. With the expenses of insurance, rents, taxes, etc., fixed, the cost of all materials fixed, the only department of the business in which retrenchment is possible is that of labor. These reductions would be surely made, and it would be useless for the workman to strike or in any of the usual ways try to prevent these reductions. He would either have to submit to them or have no occupation at all, for all the other trades and industries which employ labor, and which would be so affected by the change in the financial policy that the working men would be idle, would offer no possible chance for discarded railway employees to get work of any kind.

### THE SILVER ADVOCATES, THEORISTS.—EXPERIENCE AGAINST THEM.

There is certainly nothing in the experience of the silver-using countries to encourage the American wage-earner to believe that his condition would be bettered by getting down to their level. On the contrary, they furnish pitiful object lessons. A table of wages paid in different employments in some of the free-silver countries compared with wages in the United States is herewith submitted. The exhibit speaks for itself. The figures, so far as foreign countries are concerned, have been taken from consular reports, and those in the United States have been taken from the report of the Senate committee appointed in 1892 for the purpose of obtaining this information from the best sources they could

## LABOR AND FREE COINAGE.

| Trades and Occupations. | U. S. | Japan. | Mexico. | Persia. | Peru. | Venez. |
|---|---|---|---|---|---|---|
| | 1891. | 1892. | 1894. | 1884. | 1884. | 1884. |
| Bricklayers | $21 18 | $2.04 | $10.00 | $2.40 | $9.00 | $9.00 |
| Hodcarriers | 13.38 | 1.14 | 3 60 | 1.90 | 5.40 | 4.63 |
| Masons | 21.00 | 2.18 | 10.80 | 1.80 | 14.76 | 9.74 |
| Tenders | 9.60 | 1.14 | 3.50 | 1.20 | 4.90 | 8.81 |
| Plasterers | 23.10 | 1.56 | 4.25 | 2.40 | 9.00 | 9.40 |
| Slaters | 21.00 | | | | | 13.20 |
| Roofers | 17.30 | 1.80 | 8.40 | 1.80 | | 8.70 |
| Plumbers | 19.00 | | | | | |
| Assistants | | | | | | 9.60 |
| Carpenters | 15.25 | 1.56 | | 2.40 | 9.00 | 9.84 |
| Gasfitters | 11.90 | | | | | 18.00 |
| Bakers | | | 7.60 | 3.72 | 3.60 | 12.00 |
| Blacksmiths | 16.02 | 1.85 | 8.00 | 3.04 | 16.30 | 12.83 |
| Bookbinders | | | 5.50 | | 13.80 | 10 25 |
| Brickmakers | | | 6.00 | 3.78 | 9.20 | 9.16 |
| Brewers | | | 6.00 | | 20.00 | |
| Butchers | | | 5.40 | 1.68 | 12.80 | 11.75 |
| Brass founders | | 3.00 | 10.00 | | | |
| Cabinetmakers | 13.32 | | 10.00 | | 14.76 | 14.45 |
| Confectioners | | | 5.00 | 2.88 | 4.20 | 10.38 |
| Cigarmakers | | | 4.50 | 1.68 | 7.50 | 12.50 |
| Coopers | 16.08 | | 7.25 | | 7.50 | |
| Cutlers | | | | | | |
| Distillers | | | 4.00 | 1.25 | | 13.50 |
| Draymen and teamsters | 10.80 | | 3.60 | | 3.50 | |
| Drivers.— | | | | | | |
|   Cab and carriage | | 1.50 | 3.60 | 1.75 | 3.50 | |
|   Street car | | | 3.00 | | 7.40 | 8.50 |
| Dyers | 9.00 | | 3.16 | 2.40 | | 10.00 |
| Furriers | | | 3.66 | | | 13.00 |
| Gardeners | 13.50 | | 3.90 | 1.48 | 5.00 | 6.50 |
| Hatters | | | 5.10 | 3.84 | 9.00 | |
| Horseshoers | | | 3.75 | 1.68 | | |
| Jewelers | | | 4.15 | 6.30 | 13.90 | |
| Laborers, porters, etc | 8.88 | 1.14 | 2.90 | 1.92 | 3.50 | 7.85 |
| Millwrights | 16.80 | | 3.30 | | | |
| Printers | 16.42 | 1.75 | 5.76 | 1.92 | 9.42 | 12.00 |
| Potters | | 1.80 | 5.76 | 3.00 | | |
| Sailmakers | | | 2.60 | | | 14.00 |
| Shoemakers | | | 2.95 | 3.84 | | 10.00 |
| Stevedores | | | 9.00 | | 4.92 | |
| Stonecutters | 21.00 | 2.18 | | | | |
| Tanners | | | 3.00 | 3.84 | 4.92 | 12.00 |
| Tailors | | 2.95 | 7.14 | 2.88 | 4.92 | 12.50 |
| Telegraph operators | | | 11.50 | | 12.10 | 11.38 |
| Tinsmiths | 14.35 | | 7.50 | 1.92 | 7.50 | 14.00 |

1.74

## JAPAN AS AN EXAMPLE.

Japan has passed through a great political and industrial revolution of late years, and is now reaping some of the advantages of her emancipation from old limitations and restrictions. Manufacturing has received a tremendous impetus, and the prices of all commodities have advanced. But wages have not advanced so rapidly nor so much as prices. In 1891 the carpenter received 15.5 cents (28 sen and 1 p.) per day, while in 1894 he received 17.25 cents (31 sen and 6 p.) per day—a gain of 11.3 per cent. in four years. If data could be secured for 1889 the advance would be still greater. The wages of the pottery maker, tea maker, foreign dressmaker, and the cotton spinner have advanced the most. The percentage of gain in the wages of the carpenter, painter, sower, farmer, and coolie have been 11 1-3, 11 1-9, 10 2-3 per cent. respectively for the four years. Policemen get from $4.50 to $8.25 per month; teachers in government primary positions from $6.50 to $19 per month; clerks in post-offices, custom house offices and similar positions receive from $4.50 to $33 per month; teachers in boys' high schools, from $8 to $40 per month. These salaries are reduced to the basis of our own money. But food products have risen faster than wages. This is especially true of rice, beans and wheat, the principal food staples of Japan. The increase in wages has been something like 14 per cent. throughout the country, while the advance of the principal staples has been 28 per cent Since 1889 rice, the principal article of food, has gone up 62 per cent., while wheat and beans have each increased 36 and 39 per cent. in their price.

## THE CASE OF CHINA.

Since there has been no great influx of silver into China, there has been little chance of any great change in the purchasing power of her silver money. Although wages, rent and taxes remain unaltered, still gold will buy more than it would before. In 1893 four shillings in gold would buy what it formerly took 6s. 6d. to purchase. In other words, $60 in gold will do what formerly required $100. Gold, however, is used in payment for imports, while silver and copper remain the money of the people. Wages are very low, skilled workmen only getting from 10 to 30 cents per day, while unskilled laborers sell their strength for 5 to 10 cents per day (as computed in silver). In the case of China the depreciation of silver has had, therefore, but little effect upon her masses. But it has not raised the nominal remuneration of wage-earners.

## THE EXPERIENCE OF INDIA.

India's development has tended to raise local prices. But notwithstanding this, she has suffered grievously by the depreciation of silver. Our silver advocates cannot deny that wages have fallen and prices risen in such a way as to make the burden of her laboring classes greater than ever before. The Indian Commission, in its report for 1892, says on page 462: "The fact that wages and all prices do not rise to the same extent enables the producer of tea, for instance, to make a temporary gain at the expense of employees and of those to whom he has to make fixed money payments. This profit is usually only temporary, since, with the depreciation of the standard, all wages and prices tend to rise, and when the rise is completed the profit disappears. If the profit should happen to be considerable, and should last a long time, it supplies an unnatural and temporary stimulus to trade which leads to overproduction and consequent reaction."

It is measurably true in India, as everywhere else, that wages and prices tend in the long run to adjust themselves to each other. But what is the immediate consequence? Given, as in India, the case of a depreciating standard, and who suffers during the years or decades of adjustment? The result proves to be the same here as elsewhere. It is labor that pays for the changes.

In this connection the recently announced opinion of the Government of India will be found interesting: "1. That a country, as a whole, makes no gain in its international trade by a depreciation of its standard, since the extra price received for its exports is balanced by the extra price paid for its imports. 2. That the producer of an article of export may make a temporary and unfair gain from depreciation of the standard, at the expense of his employees and of other persons to whom he makes fixed payments. 3. But that this gain, while not permanent, is counterbalanced by a tendency to overproduction and consequent reaction and depression, by a liability to sudden falls in prices as well as to rises, and by the check to the general increase of international trade which necessarily results from the want of a common standard of value between countries which have intimate commercial and financial relations."

### LABOR IN MEXICO.

The conditions of labor in Mexico, as set forth in the reports of foreign diplomatic officers and consuls living in that country, do not present a very attractive situation for workingmen to anticipate. Free coinage of silver amongst our neighbors across the Rio Grande has not brought any advantage to workingmen. Wages are low, while prices of the necessaries of life are abnormally high. It is difficult to maintain a respectable standard of existence.

"Labor is very cheap and abundant in Mexico," says Consul Gorman, of Matamoras, under date of January 1st, 1895, "the average farm laborer receiving $6 a month, sometimes with rations of corn only. This is equivalent, at present rates of exchange, to about 10 cents a day in American money."

The British Consul at the City of Mexico, in his report of December 5th,

1895, gives the rates of wages at a number of principal points. In the state of Sonora, Northern Mexico, they are, in Mexican currency, per day:

    Common laborers ................................................37 to 75 cents
    Miners.............................................................. 50c. to $3 00
    Factory hands (men)................................. 75c. to 2 00
    Artisans........................................................ $1 50 to 5 00

Substantially the same rates prevail in the southern part of Lower California. At Mazatlan, an important port on the Pacific coast, with three cotton factories, a soap factory and a number of small sugar mills and distilleries,

    Common laborers receive..................... 25 to 62 cents per day
    Miners................................................. $1 00 to $6 00
    Factory hands..................... ........... 62c. to 3 00
    Artisans............................................... $1 00 to 3 00

The above rates must be cut down nearly one-half to reduce them to United States equivalents, but even making this reduction the wages of skilled labor would seem to be comparatively high. This condition is attributable to the relative scarcity of skilled labor, a fact which also explains why wages paid to conductors, engineers, firemen and brakemen on Mexican railroads are also comparatively high. Few Mexicans are qualified for this work, and so trainmen have to be imported from the United States and be given an extra inducement to come.

The so called "flush times" in Mexico are not at all due to free silver, but rather an incident to the early stages of industrial development. Her skilled labor, her capital and her enterprise are drawn from other lands, chiefly our own country. She also produces certain raw materials which can be profitably marketed abroad for gold.

Behind all this nascent industrial development stands the unanswerable fact that the great bulk of her agricultural population is poor and common labor is wretchedly remunerated.

"So far from being an example of the blessings of free silver, Mexico is perhaps the most convincing illustration among all the silver using countries of the inequalities and retarding influences of a fluctuating currency."

There is the same difference in prices. Flour in Mexico was quoted at 5½ cents per pound; sugar, 19 cents; coffee, 24 cents; beans, per peck, 50 cents; rice, 8½ cents. In the United States the prices of these commodities are much less. Prices have risen in Mexico as well as wages, and, as usual, prices have advanced much faster than wages.

### THE SAVINGS OF THE PEOPLE.

It is absurd to assume that the wage earners of our own country can profit under conditions which have brought hardship everywhere else. Nor should it need any demonstration to prove that those of them who have been able to save money would be very much worse off under a debased currency. Last year there were in the United States 4,875,519 depositors in savings banks, to whom there was due $1,810,597,023, which is valuable only for its purchasing power. To the depositors it does not matter whether one-half their funds be embezzled and prices remain unchanged, or the sum remain intact and prices be doubled. The adoption of the silver standard would reduce by one-half the amount of provision made for the future by the depositors, who are mostly people of small means and largely wage-earners. The savings banks that have received gold would pay out silver, because they could not help themselves even if they desired to; the deposits are not in their vaults in the form in which it was deposited; they have been loaned in great measure to men and corporations of wealth, who have borrowed gold and would pay back silver and get rich by the operation; the banks could only pay the depositors what they could collect from those to whom they have loaned money, and the loss would fall on the depositors.

A well known Savings Bank President gives the following lucid explanation of the effect of the free coinage of silver at a ratio of 16 to 1, upon savings deposits:

"Manifestly the free coinage of silver would work evil to the man who has by dint of hard labor and economy scraped together a few hundred or a few thousand dollars and placed it in one of the 2,000 or more savings banks in this country. Every one of those 4,000,000 depositors is a capitalist, for the man who has 50 cents in a bank and all his debts paid is a capitalist to that extent, just as is the man whose deposit reaches to hundreds or thousands They represent the thrifty laboring people—the small storekeepers, the clerks, the artizans and the day laborers. The Chicago platform is an admitted attack on capital, inspired by the debtor class. The free silver agitators would lead the people to believe that it is aimed at the capitalists with millions, but as the capitalist with a million would be affected by free silver, so would a capitalist with but $10 in the savings bank. The free coinage of silver would be a blow to the 4,000,000 of thrifty persons who have deposited in the savings banks of the country almost two billions of dollars. Why?

"The depositors in the saving banks are, for the most part, men and women who have worked hard to gather together a little money for a rainy day. This they have deposited in the savings banks at a time when every dollar was worth 100 cents in gold coin, because the Government stands ready to redeem every dollar in silver with one in gold. Suppose we should have free coinage. Gold certainly would not circulate if it were undervalued by the coinage of silver at a ratio of 16 to 1. A given weight of gold, as is known, is, in the market to-day, worth over thirty times as much as an equal weight of silver. Consequently, as past experience has proved, it would either go out of the country or be hoarded. We would quickly slide to a silver basis, like China, Japan or India. Gold would go to a premium. A silver dollar would be worth just what the bullion in it is worth in the market—about 53 cents in our money to-day. So the thrifty people who deposited dollars in the savings banks when we were on a sound financial basis would, under free coinage, have their deposits dwindle to about one-half their value. Every dollar of interest that they would draw would be worth but 53 cents, according to our standard to-day. They would receive a coin called one silver dollar, but worth no more than the bullion in it, or 53 cents under our present currency system.

"I know that the majority of the officers of savings banks all over this country agree with me in my views. Whether the depositors realize the condition that confronts them, I do not know. But such a condition does confront them. The Chicago platform is an attack on their savings; it is a conspiracy against thrift. In considering the matter I have left out entirely the possibility of violent business disruption and depression. I think every savings bank depositor will see how his savings must shrink in value by reason of the inflation. That alone should bring him into the fight for honest money."

A million and three-quarters of people are shareholders in building and loan associations; nearly three-fourths of them are creditors, and a little more than one-fourth have borrowed the assets of the associations, amounting to $450,000,000 on the gold standard. On the silver standard they would repay the equivalent of $225,000,000 of gold and pocket the difference, the loss falling on the shareholders who had not borrowed  The life insurance companies doing business in the State of New York, owed two years ago $1,763,780,015 on 1,268,408 policies. The doubling of prices that would result from the introduction of the cheap dollar would reduce the provision made for widows and orphans about one-half, and the other half would not be appropriated by the companies, whose funds are loaned out; it would be made by the capitalists who have borrowed gold dollars and would repay silver dollars Many foreign-born workingmen annually make considerable remittances to their less fortunate relatives abroad. Are they prepared to pay $9.80 for a pound sterling instead of $4.90 as now ? What would be the sense of voting to bring about a condition where they would pay forty-eight cents for a German mark, and fifty cents for a French, Belgian or Swiss franc or an Italian lira, instead of the half of these sums under our present gold standard ? These things would inevitably happen under a free silver regime. We may debase our dollar, but we have no power over the pound sterling, the mark, the franc, the lira. If we choose to put ourselves in a position where, if we wish to buy foreign exchange or currency, we must pay double for it, that is our affair, but a very stupid and unprofitable affair.

There is no conceivable part of the process of reducing the currency of the country to a silver basis that would bring any benefit to the wage-earner, and there is an absolute certainty that it could bring to him, on the whole, nothing but loss.

### "THE MASSES AND THE CLASSES."

A diabolical attempt is being made to stir up social strife by telling workingmen that in this campaign the classes are arrayed against the masses. The argument is presented to them somewhat as follows:

The great oppressive forces against labor are the moneyed interests. Capitalists seek to get all they can out of labor and pay just as little as possible in return. The interests of capital and labor are and must be antagonistic. When there is such an unanimity of opinion amongst owners of capital as to the undesirability of the free coinage of silver, it is pretty safe to suppose that the workingman's interest lies in espousing the cause.

This argument is often effective to unthinking minds. The best way to dislodge it is to explain the mutuality of interests in modern industrial society. An editorial writer in the Baltimore *Sun* gives the following interesting résumé of the relations in which the members of a modern industrial community like the United States stand to one another:

"The state of such a community is best when wages are good, employment general and easy to secure, prices reasonable, and profits fair and reasonably certain. It is impossible to disturb any one of these factors without disturbing the others. If wages are reduced or employment becomes too limited, it results in forcing those who labor to a less independent and comfortable existence. But this is not all: the laborers of every kind constitute the great customers of the farmers, merchants, manufacturers and common carriers. Counting together those few in the United States who do not labor at all and those who work but do not do manual labor, their custom, or patronage, is small when compared with that of the vast multitude of laboring people. Any merchant or manufacturer or railroad officer knows this; any farmer should know it.

"It follows that whatever lowers the scale of living amongst laborers tends to force down prices and diminishs the profits of farmers, merchants, manufacturers and common carriers. This it does directly. But it also acts indirectly. The laborers, to a very large extent, own the capital of the country. They are the principal owners of the money deposited in savings banks or in beneficial and other societies—a very large proportion of the capital of the country. This capital is, directly or indirectly, invested in enterprises. To depress wages reduces these savings and curtails industrial enterprises, thus reacting to further injure labor and acting to diminish or prevent profits. Whatever depresses prices unreasonably, reduces or destroys profits, and thus paralyzes enterprise, and this, while it directly injures farmers, merchants and manufacturers, indirectly injures labor by lessening wages and the opportunities for employment. Whatever makes profits uncertain does the same thing.

"Thus it is that the industrial fabric of modern society ties us all together—we are children of one household—and what injures one injures another. Nobody is exempt from its risks. The few very rich who can live without work suffer in their incomes when the poorest suffer in their wages.

"Such being the structure of the social fabric, what sense is there in one part warring on another? There can be but one end to such wars—all must suffer. Whoever strikes another strikes himself. It is not to be denied that there is at least an apparent antagonism between some of these elements. To reduce wages too low may at times and places increase profits; but, as has been seen, this injures the greatest customer and competition will soon lower profits thus secured. To inveigh against wealth or property or reasonable profits frightens capital, hampers enterprise and restricts employment. Devilish ingenuity could contrive no better way to disturb the industrial life of the people than by agitating for the debasement of our money. This agitation destroys confidence in the future, thus paralyzing enterprise and restricting opportunities for employment, and it threatens the direct lowering of wages. Met by overwhelming opposition, it now tries to do the next worse thing it can by inciting indiscriminate hostility against those whose social function it is to plan and venture on new enterprises.

"The prosperity of the farmer depends upon the prosperity of the laboring public, and this in turn depends upon the state of industrial enterprise. By attacking capital and property one aids in the creation of alarm and uncertainty and frightens enterprise."

# PROTECTION THE PARENT OF NATIONAL DISASTER.

The free silver movement is essentially a protective movement, for just as protection by a tariff is designed to interfere with the freedom to purchase goods, so the opening of the mints to the free coinage of silver is designed to compel people to take a kind of dollar which they do not want. The financial troubles through which the country has been passing began with the tariff revision of 1890, and the extravagant appropriations of the Fifty-second Congress. Both contributed to weaken the Treasury and leave it at the end of two years practically without resources. Populism is a natural evolution of protectionism; both mean Government paternalism, and both are thus radically opposed to the principles of true Democracy.

The platform of the National Democracy declares that the demand of the Republican party for an increase in tariff taxation has its pretext in the deficiency of revenue, which has its cause in the stagnation of trade and reduced consumption due entirely to the loss of confidence that has followed the Populist threat of free coinage and depreciation of our money and the Republican practice of extravagant appropriations beyond the needs of the Government. It is the favorite claim of Republican orators that the high-water mark of prosperity was reached during the last Republican administration and that all the subsequent depression has been due to the accession of a Democratic administration to power in 1893, and to the legislation for a reduction of tariff duties which followed it. But, as has been asked, is it not more credible that the great disaster which came upon us was the outgrowth of a false system of economy which, with all our matchless resources, we were unable to longer stand? Will not future generations, when they look back to our times to draw lessons of wisdom to guide them in the direction in which they should go, rather ascribe our reverses to our follies instead of our fears? Are the advocates of a restrictive policy ready to confess that nothwithstanding our unparalleled resources, thirty years of protection had failed to establish our industries upon a foundation sufficiently firm to withstand even a proposition looking to a conservative modification of its structure?

It is matter of record that the protective system has been a fruitful source of commercial failures, of conflicts between employees and employed and of popular discontent generally. From 1873 to 1882, inclusive, the number of failures was 74,978, with liabilities aggregating $1,648,310,517. From 1883 to 1890 we were constantly on the verge of a financial crash. The Secretary of the Treasury was continually forced to purchase bonds and repay interest to check the alarm. With all, however, that could be done, we had the stringency of 1883, the panics of 1884 and 1890. The number of failures during this period, including the years 1883 and 1890, exceeded 82,000, with liabilities of more than $1,250,000,000. The failures, which numbered 6,738 in 1882, rose to 9,184 in 1883, and 10,907 in 1890, with liabilities aggregating $189.856,964. Not since the tariff revision of 1883 went into effect has the number of failures fallen below 9,000 in a single year. During this period the conflicts between employers and employees increased until riots and bloodshed became so numerous as to excite little interest except in the most extreme cases. During the years 1883, 1884, 1885 and 1886 we had 2,977 strikes in 17,271 establishments, embracing 1,039,011 employees. The number of strikes increased from 471 affecting 129,591 employees in 1881, to 1,411, affecting 499,489 employees in 1886. During the years 1882 to 1886, inclusive, lockouts occurred in 2,214 establishments, affecting 175,270 employees. The estimated wage loss to employees by reason of strikes and lockouts during these six years aggregated $59,972,440. In 1890 the McKinley law went into operation, and under the influence of this act the number of failures rose from 10,907, with liabilities aggregating $189,856,964 in 1890, to 12,273, with liabilities aggregating $189,868,693 in 1891, and the conflicts between employers and employees, which had theretofore culminated only in combats and riots, became battles between great forces armed with rifle and cannon. The number of failures in 1892 was 10,270, while in 1893 it reached the maximum height, 15,560, with liabilities aggregating $462,000,000 as against assets amounting to $262,000,000. In no country has there been such a disturbed and unsettled condition as we had. We reached a point when idleness became so common that the feats of the tramp were considered weighty demonstrations of civic unrest.

### DELUSIVE REPUBLICAN PROMISES.

Defending the course of the Republican party in 1890, Senator Dawes said: "The Republican party declared unequivocally for tariff reform, and for a reduction of the treasury receipts to those actual expenditures that a rigid economy alone justify." On this statement, Ex-Speaker, now, Secretary Carlisle made the following scornful and exhaustive comment:

"If the Senator really believes that this pledge will be redeemed in accordance with the obvious meaning of its terms, he has that kind of faith that removes mountains. Up to the present time there are certainly no indications that the revenue will be reduced as it ought to be, or that economy will be practiced in any department of the Government. On the contrary, it is evident that if the policy so far pursued is continued, the whole revenue that can be collected under the laws as they now exist will be insufficient to meet the extraordinary demands that will be made upon the Treasury. The surplus will be reduced, but taxation will be increased on many important articles. A mere enumeration of the bills now pending in Congress for the appropriation of money and for the creation of liabilities to be discharged in the future, would be sufficient to show the extravagant policy of the party in power; and it is evident that if only a small percentage of these bills should be passed, the existing surplus would be exhausted and a reduction of the revenue postponed for many years. If any considerable number of them are passed, additional taxation will be necessary, or the public debt will have to be increased."

"But whatever may be done by the present Congress in regard to pensions, subsidies, bounties and other projects now pending for the expenditure of the public money, it is safe to say that if any changes are made in the revenue laws they will increase the rates of duty wherever an increase will impose additional burdens upon consumers, and reduce the rates only in cases where reduction will not affect importations or materially diminish prices. Such a 're-adjustment of customs duties as will produce the most effective protection to American products and labor,' according to the Republican theory of protection, will necessarily reduce the revenue by prohibiting importation of dutiable goods, but it will not reduce taxation upon the people. It will in fact increase taxation, but the tribute paid by the consumers will go into the private coffers of the domestic producers, and not into the public treasury. In the end, however, it will be of no real benefit to anybody; for, while it will largely enhance the prices of finished products and thus impose upon the domestic consumer a burden he ought not to bear, it will also increase the cost of production and exclude our manufactures from all the markets of the world except our own. The Republican tariff policy as defined and advocated by Senator Dawes and the school of economists which now dominates that party, has already reduced many of our most important manufacturing industries to the verge of bankruptcy, while its disastrous effects upon the agricultural interests of the country have been so general that the wail of the farmer is heard in every part of the land. There has never been a time in our history when there was so much discontent and so little prospect of improvement as there is now among those classes that ought to be prosperous. It is not the wage-earner alone that sends his petitions and complaints to Congress and its committees. Nearly every trade, occupation and profession is organized to formulate and present its demand for relief, and the Republican party responds to their appeals by proposing to extend and strengthen the protective system of taxation under which they have been reduced to their present condition. This, and the appropriation of public money out of the Treasury for the benefit of a few favorite classes, is the only remedy it proposes. The evils resulting from thirty years of protection are to be cured by more protection, and the over-burdened taxpayers are to be relieved by having their forced contributions given away to wealthy individuals and corporations engaged in the foreign carrying trade. The farmer will continue to sell his products in a cheap market, and to buy his supplies in a dear one. He will see his competitors in South America, India, Hungary, Russia and other parts of the world constantly and rapidly encroaching upon the foreign markets in which he sells his surplus, and he will be powerless to make head against them, because the laws of his country forbid him to exchange his products for the things he needs, and to bring them here unless he pays a tax upon them equal or nearly equal to their cost abroad. The American manufacturer will find his boasted home market not merely unwilling, but unable, to take his goods at the high prices which are necessary to compensate him for the increased cost of production due to the taxes on his raw materials."

## THE RESULTS OF PROTECTION.

"While high protective duties have undoubtedly in many cases enabled the producers of the protected articles to realize enormous profits upon their investments, the mere fact that prices are higher here than abroad does not always indicate that large profits are being made. Under our system, high prices, or comparatively high prices, are absolutely necessary in order to enable our manufacturers to carry on their business, because their material costs them more than it costs any other producers in the world; and as long as it is taxed as it now is, this will continue to be the case. It is not the wages of labor in this country that increases the cost of production, for all the reliable evidence upon the subject goes to show that, although wages by the day or week, as the case may be, are higher here than abroad, yet the actual cost of the labor to the employer, compared with the amount and value of its products is less in the United States than elsewhere. What the laboring man most needs is steady employment, and this protection cannot give him. That policy which encourages trade, facilitates the exchange of commodities and opens the markets of the world to his products, is the best policy for him, because it widens the area of consumption and increases the demand for his labor. Unless a small market is better than a large one, the restrictive policy of the Republican party cannot permanently be beneficial either to the capitalists engaged in productive industries or to their employees. It is not an American policy, but a Chinese policy, that Senator Dawes and his party are advocating; and its real character and purpose cannot be concealed by reiterating the charge that its opponents propose to give to foreigners "the possession of our markets and the control of our labor." If partial commercial isolation is good for the country, total isolation must be better; and the Republican party, with complete control of the Government in all its departments, performs less than its whole duty, according to its own theory, when it stops short of absolute prohibition of international trade. There are very few, if any, articles of necessity that cannot be produced here, if a sufficient amount of money is expended in their growth or manufacture; and as protection is supposed to help everybody, including even the consumer who is compelled to pay the increased cost of production, why should we not be required to provide for all our wants regardless of the expense?

## THE HARRISON ADMINISTRATION.

It is unquestionably true that the whole administration of Mr. Harrison, with the exception of the first year, which was in some respects prosperous, as a result of the great impetus given to it by the four preceding years of sound economical administration, was that of falling revenues, increasing expenditures and a heavy flow of gold from the country. Any of these was calculated to excite apprehension, but the three combined were sufficient to and did destroy private confidence as well as the public credit. The sound financial condition of the Treasury at the time Mr. Cleveland delivered his trust to Mr. Harrison, enabled the latter to glide smoothly through the first year of his administration, but when he returned it to the hands from whence he received it there was nothing but impaired credit and an empty purse.

At the very beginning of Mr. Harrison's administration a feeling of unrest and insecurity began to show itself in financial centres and continued, with slight intervals, to the end of his term. During the year 1890 the financial stringency became so great that Secretary Windom was compelled to purchase government bonds to the amount of $73,694,850, for which he paid premiums amounting to $21,222,894. During the last months of Mr. Harrison's administration all sorts of rumors were in circulation. The report was current that an issue of bonds had been contracted by Secretary Foster in order to protect the gold reserve in the Treasury, and, but for the assistance of the New York bankers, such a transaction certainly would have been necessary. He had, in fact, given orders for the preparation of the plates upon which the bonds were to be printed.

It was only by a change in the form of the statement and a juggling with the funds that Secretary Foster was able to show an apparent balance at the end of his term. Under the provisions of an act passed by the Fifty-first Congress, the fund in the Treasury for the redemption of the national bank notes was made an asset instead of a liability. The surplus in the Treasury was in this way inflated by the transfer of $54,207,975 from one side of the ledger to the other. Not a single cent was by this change added to the assets nor a single penny taken from the liabilities, yet there was an apparent increase of the surplus of more than fifty millions of dollars.

The subsidiary silver coins, being a legal tender for sums not exceeding five dollars, had been considered, prior to Mr. Harrison's administration, as unavailable for the payment of the obligations of the Government, and, therefore, had not been counted as an available asset. This was likewise transferred from the column of unavailable to the column of the available assets, and the surplus was again augmented without the addition of a farthing. Had this system of stating the accounts been in use at the end of Mr. Cleveland's term, the surplus in the Treasury, including the reserve, would have been $183,827,190, instead of $148,096,158. Whatever, therefore, of these two funds was on hand at the end of Mr. Harrison's administration should have been deducted from the surplus as stated in order to arrive at the true balance. The amount of the National Bank Redemption Fund on hand March 1, 1893, was $22,272,061, and of fractional silver, $10,971,875, the aggregate of the two being $33,243,936. Deducting these sums from the balance of March 1, 1893, to wit, $24,128,087, and there was a real deficiency of $9,115,849.

This was the condition when Secretary Carlisle took charge. The surplus had been squandered; our gold was being transported to Europe at the rate of $12,000,000 a month; the expenditures had increased more than $60,000,000 a year, while the revenues had fallen off $18,000,000, and yet he was expected, and Republicans affected to be surprised that he was not able, to at once fully restore public confidence and give prosperity and financial stability to every industry and enterprise throughout the country.

### FALSE CLAIMS PUNCTURED.

The pretext that high protective duties have been the foundation of our national prosperity is very thoroughly riddled in the following extracts from a speech delivered by Senator Mills, of Texas, in the United States Senate on April 24, 1894.

Did not the Democratic Convention at Chicago hit the nail on the head when they branded protection as a fraud? In the name of the working people, thousands of whom they have turned out of employment and into the streets, they have plundered the country to build up a plutocracy; and now here in the midst of the widespread distress which they have sown from their hands they have the effrontery to still defend the monumental robbery in the name of the poor workingman. * * * I give here a list of articles which show from the census returns what wages are paid and from the tariff what protection is voted for our workmen.

In one ton of steel rails the labor cost is $3; the tariff is $13.44.

In $100 worth of cutlery the labor cost is $44.24; the tariff is $80.11.

In $100 worth of mats and matting the labor cost is $34.90; the tariff is $68.59.

In $100 worth of silk piece goods the labor cost is $22.54; the tariff is $60.

In $100 worth of cigars and cigarettes the labor cost it $34.51; the tariff is $125.36.

In $100 worth of woolen or worsted cloths the labor cost is $20.85; the tariff is $100.02.

In $100 worth of pottery the labor cost is $45.96; the tariff is $60.

In $100 worth of pearl buttons the labor cost is $39.60; the tariff is $143.61.

In $100 worth of tannin the labor cost is $16.34; the tariff is $119.47.

In $100 worth of coal the labor cost is from $40 to $50; the tariff is $75.
In $100 worth of cotton goods the labor cost is $24.24; the tariff is $57.08.
In $100 worth of linen the labor cost is $32.92; the tariff is $50.
In $100 worth of common window glass the labor cost is $53.09; the tariff is $98.30.
In one ton of pig iron the labor cost is $1.50; the tariff is $6.72.
In one ton of bar iron the labor cost is $4.57; the tariff is $52.98.

The only way that the laborer can receive any benefit is by the law of nature, that gives him constant employment, that gives him employment with a constant demand for his work. That is only done when we increase the consumption of the things upon which labor is expended, and we increase the consumption of the product of labor when we reduce the cost of making them —the labor cost and every other. Now, machinery does that, and so does the reduction of taxes. Then we must reduce the cost of reaching market and remove obstacles out of the way so that we may get there. We must increase the demand for employment, and as the demand for the employment of labor increases by the increased consumption of the things that labor makes, so wages will increase and employment will be constant.

### THE TRUE CAUSES OF LOWER PRICES.

Our friends contend that because prices have been falling here in the United States since they have had a tariff, that the tariff is the cause of the lowering of prices, and they are constantly pointing to us the fact that the price of a certain thing was so much thirty years ago, and it is so much less now. My distinguished and venerable friend across the way (Mr. Morrill) told us the other day in his speech that two-ply ingrain carpet was worth $1 a yard thirty years ago, and that it is now worth 50 cents a yard. Behold the tariff! The tariff did all this thing! He did not tell us that the labor cost of that yard of ingrain carpet is now 6 cents a yard, and the tariff on it is over 60 per cent. to protect it against competition, when the labor cost of that amount of goods in Great Britain is 7 cents. How does my friend or how does any other man account for the fact that prices have been falling in free-trade England as well as in the United States for the last thirty years? It will not do to say that the tariff reduces prices in the United States and free trade reduces prices in Great Britain. The same cause, under the same circumstances, ought to produce the same result. They tell us it will; but here we have prices brought down by free trade in Great Britain and under a protective tariff in the United States. Prices have been brought down by improved production, by machinery, by invention, increasing the amount of product in a given time, and lowering the cost of the product. I have here some figures that will give an illustration of the fact.

## PROTECTION THE PARENT OF NATIONAL DISASTER.

A long time ago when we were boys, when our mothers were spinning with the old hand wheel—

| | |
|---|---:|
| One thousand persons in one week spun 3,000 pounds of cotton yarn, No. 10, at $1.50 each | $1,500 00 |
| One person now spins 3,000 pounds of cotton yarn, No. 10, and receives for wages | 6 00 |
| Reduction in labor lost | $1,494 00 |

Our friends point to it and say a protective tariff did that, not the spinning jenny—not the skill and genius of the man who worked the machine and the man who invented it, but a protective tariff; and you levy 50 per cent. duty on cotton yarn and say that duty did that.

Let us follow that up a little further:

| | |
|---|---:|
| The cost price of 3,000 pounds of yarn then, at 75 cents per pound | $2,250 00 |
| The cost price of 3,000 pounds of No. 10 cotton yarn now, at 15 cents per pound | 450 00 |
| Reduction | $1,800 00 |

By a protective tariff:

| | |
|---|---:|
| Labor cost of 247 hand weavers required to weave 3,000 pounds of yarn into 11,100 yards of sheeting, each weaving 45 yards per week and receiving $3 per week as wages, was | $741 00 |
| Labor cost now of 8 weavers weave that amount in one week and receive $6 per week as wages | 48 00 |
| Reduction in weaving | $693 00 |
| Cost of cloth made by hand spinning and weaving, at 40 cents per yard | $4,440 00 |
| Cost of cloth now, at 7 cents per yard, by machinery | 777 00 |
| Reduction in cost | $3,663 00 |

And they say a protective tariff did it—not the spinning jenny and the power loom, but the protective tariff that levies 50 per cent. duty on cotton yarn and 57 per cent. on cotton goods.

Adam Smith tells of the immense benefits that come by the division of labor in making pins, from which I have gathered these figures:

| | |
|---|---:|
| Labor cost of 521 persons required to make 2,500,000 pins in one day, at one cent per hundred, was | $250 00 |
| Labor cost of one person, who now makes 2,500,000 pins in one day, and receives as wages $1 | 1 00 |
| Reduction | $249 00 |

That is done by a pin machine. Yet our friends stand here and tell us that is done by a protective tariff, and put no more duty in the interest of the poor workingman, and get him to believe that a protective tariff benefits him. Adam Smith stuck pins in the protective tariff in Great Britain till it was dead, and the common school-house and the school-master in this country are sticking pins in it now, and will continue to stick pins in it till it is as dead in this country as it is in Great Britain.

It would have required 58 persons, working one week, each making 12,000 eight-penny nails to make 704,000, now made by one, and the wages of the 58, at $6 each, was...................... $348 00
They are now made by one hand at $5 per day, six days..... ..... 30 00

        Reduction..... ................................. $318 00

It is not taxing that reduces the price of a thing. Adding to the cost never reduces the price. That cannot be done. Adding to the cost of a thing increases the price of a thing, or mathematics is a lie. It is taking from the cost of a thing that reduces the price of it. That is what machinery does, what a revenue tax does, and that is what free trade does still better. There can be no justification on earth, either in politics or common justice, to tax the products of human labor except to support the administration of government."

# THE QUESTION OF LAW AND ORDER.

While there are honest differences of opinion about the rights and wrongs of the great railroad strike of 1894, there can be no dispute about the necessity of upholding the supremacy of the law. The use of the physical arm of the Government to uphold the law is an incident of sovereignty, and to deny the existence of any such right is to reduce the Government to helplessness. From the interpretation of the law adopted by the Circuit Court an appeal was taken to the Supreme Court of the United States and by an absolutely unanimous vote, the decision of the Circuit Court was affirmed. To defy the law thus applied and thus affirmed is to assert that there is no authoritative exposition of law to be found in the country, and that a party convention may place its judgment above that of a unanimous Supreme Court.

The Chicago platform denounces "Arbitrary interference by Federal authorities in local affairs as a violation of the Constitution of the United States and a crime against free institutions." This either means something or nothing, and its authors have only themselves to blame that it is considered a defense of anarchy, when it is notorious that the most urgent support of this plank came from those whose acts upon a late occasion led to riot and from a Governor who had failed to enforce the laws of his own State against it. No one seriously questions the power and the duty of the United States, not merely upon a State's request to assist it to maintain order within its territory, but of its own motion to protect United States property and enforce Federal law. Faced with conditions which called for the exercise of this constitutional power a President can no more inquire into the merits of the controversy from which the violation of Federal law or the danger to Federal property has originated than could a policeman decline to protect a citizen against assault until he had satisfied himself whether or not the aggressor had cause for indignation. Such matters are for the courts, not for the Executive. Not merely is the courage of a President who did not dare do otherwise than promptly enforce the law admirable in itself, but the principle thus vindicated is of the greatest possible importance to our wage-earners and humbler citizens. It is to protect them against arbitrary misrule in the interest of wealth and power that laws are made; and every concession to them by connivance at their breaking of law is in the end paid for by them tenfold in the advantage always taken by wealth and power of any disposition on the part of courts to strain the law on behalf of favored suitors.

The great Chicago railroad strike of 1894 was anything but a "local affair." It involved the railroad employees of fifteen States and was, incidentally, the cause of violence and rioting which almost amounted to open insurrection. There were public rights and interests invaded. Interstate commerce was obstructed. The stoppage of mail trains deprived the people of the means of friendly communication and assistance. The United States Government, conducting the mail service as an agent of the people, was hindered and restrained from the performance of this duty. The question was presented: Ought not the government to have and exercise the power to summarily remove all obstructions to the performance of duties which it owes to the whole people?

### THE USE OF THE TROOPS.

According to the report of the Strike Commission, the President ordered the troops to Chicago for the following purposes:

(1) To protect Federal property.
(2) To prevent obstruction in the carrying of the mails.
(3) To prevent interference with the interstate commerce.
(4) To enforce the decrees and mandates of the Federal Courts.

The constitutional power of the President to issue such an order is not doubtful. As Mr. E. A. Bancroft of the Chicago bar, in a monograph upon this subject, puts it: "The President of the United States, when Congress is not in session, controls the physical arm of the United States—its military and naval forces. He is clothed by the Constitution with authority to use that power upon his own initiative and judgment to resist physical assaults upon the life, authority or property of the United States. These assaults must be directed, however, against its sovereignty. Resistance merely to its control of its property or to its assertion of its power, and not intended to question its sovereignty, would not warrant the exercise of this perogative by the President without specific authority from Congress. That authority has been given to resist interference, and to protect Government property and the rights of the people under the Constitution.

Whenever insurrection, domestic violence, unlawful combinations or conspiracies in any State so obstruct or hinder the execution of the laws * * * as to deprive any person of any rights, privileges or immunities or protection named in the Constitution * * * and the constituted authorities of such State * * * fail in or refuse protection of the people in such rights; * * * or whenever any such insurrection, violence, unlawful combination or conspiracy opposes or disturbs the laws of the United States, or the due execution thereof or impedes or obstructs the due course of justice under the same."—U. S. R. S., sections 5, 299, Act of April 20, 1871.

The President's authority and duty to take such action in view of the facts arose from the necessary power of the nation to vindicate through the President its sovereignty over the subjects named, as well as from the statute already quoted. As was said by the Supreme Court (in *ex parte* Siebold, 100 U. S., 371, 395):

"We hold it to be an incontrovertible principle that the Government of the United States may by means of physical force exercised through its official agents execute on every foot of American soil the powers and functions that belong to it. * * * The Government must execute its powers, or it is no Government."

### ATTORNEY-GENERAL HARMON'S STATEMENT.

Attorney-General Judson Harmon thus states the legal relations of the action of the President :

"I have concluded to give a public answer to the many inquiries made of me upon a subject of great moment to which general attention is now directed.

Mr. Bryan, in his letter accepting the nomination for President by the convention at Chicago, amplifies the protest which that convention made in its platform against Federal interference in local affairs, which, strangely enough, is not found in the platforms of the other two conventions which have also nominated him.

As nothing else has been done or proposed to which they can possibly apply, these protests were intended and are understood to be directed against the recent action of the President in forcibly suppressing riotous disturbances which had stopped the carriage of the mails and interstate commerce and were defying the civil officers of the United States.

The President took this action not only without the request, but in some instances against the protest, of the authorities of the States in which the riots occurred, and Mr. Bryan, taking section 4 of Article IV. of the Constitution to be the law on the subject, pledges himself against any repetition of the violation thereof which his letter necessary charges. He vindicates the wisdom of the framers of the Constitution by declaring that the local authorities " are better qualified to judge of the necessity of Federal assistance."

This, in my judgment, is a far more serious matter than the money question, or any of the other questions now before the people, grave as they all are. Our form of government may survive a wrong decision of those questions, and the people may endure for a time the evils which result from false systems of finance and taxation, but if the President has deliberately disregarded the instrument upon which the Union is founded, by supplanting the authority of a sovereign State by armed force, a precedent has been made which threatens our form of government; while, if a candidate for President may properly pledge himself in advance, as Mr. Bryan has done, to do nothing to protect the property, maintain the authority, and enforce the laws of the United States unless and until the officers of another government request or consent, then we really have no Federal Government. For a government which is not entirely free to use force to protect and maintain itself in the discharge of its own proper functions is no government at all.

The section of the Constitution to which Mr. Bryan refers is as follows :

The United States shall guarantee to every State in this Union a republican form of government, and shall protect each of them against invasion and, on application of the Legislature or the Executive (when the Legislature cannot be convened) against domestic violence.

This section plainly refers merely to the protection of the States against interference with their authority, laws or property by domestic violence, and they are wisely made solely the judges whether or when they need such protection. Mr. Bryan displays a consciousness of the limited operation of this provision in the expression 'Federal assistance,' in the clause I have quoted.

But by the express terms of the Constitution, a State has nothing to do with the maintenance of the authority or the execution of the laws of the United States within the territory of the State. The prevention and punishment of offenses connected with the mails, with interstate commerce, and with the administration of justice in the Federal courts are committed to the General Government, and to it alone. Such offenses in no wise menace the government of the State within which they are committed. Therefore the State cannot require protection against them. The State has no duties to discharge in these matters. Therefore, it can require no 'Federal assistance' with respect to them.

Of course, domestic violence often, as in the recent riots, is directed against both State and Federal authority indiscriminately, and either or both may suppress it. And in such cases the action of each in maintaining its own authority over the subjects committed to it tends to aid the other. But in such cases each is acting in its own independent right as a sovereign government, and on its own behalf. It would be as absurd to claim that the United States must neglect its own interests because in protecting them those of a State may be incidentally protected, as to claim that a State must let riot run free because it happens to be directed against Federal rights or officers as well as its own. This would limit and belittle the sovereignty of both governments. *Imperium in imperio* would be false.

According to Mr. Bryan there is somewhere implied in the Constitution—for it is nowhere expressed—a prohibition of the use of force by the United States against persons who, within the limits of a State, may be successfully resisting its officers and completely paralyzing all its operations as a government, unless the local authorities shall first make request or give consent.

This is contrary to the settled principle that, while the Federal Government is one whose operation is confined to certain subjects, it has, as to those subjects, all the attributes of sovereignty, and one of these is always and everywhere within the territory of the States which compose it, to suppress and punish those who in any wise interfere with the exercise of its lawful powers. The fact that there are within that territory other governments exercising sovereignty over all matters not so committed to it can make no difference under our double form of Government, the essential principle of which is a partition of powers to be exercised independently over the same territory.

The sovereign right of the United States necessarily follows its officers and agents everywhere they go, protecting and maintaining them in the discharge of their duties. Congress has accordingly, by Section 5297 of the Revised Statutes, authorized the President to use the armed forces of the Government in aid of the State authorities when requested by them, as provided in the Constitution, and has also, by the following section, 5298, authorized him to employ such forces, upon his own judgment alone, against 'unlawful obstructions, combinations, or assemblages of persons,' 'in whatever State or Territory thereof the laws of the United States may be forcibly opposed or the execution thereof obstructed.'

It was under the power conferred by this last section that the late rebellion was suppressed. Mr. Bryan's doctrine that this law is unconstitutional is more dangerous than that of secession. The latter, at least, left the Government some power and authority in the territory of States which should choose to remain. Mr. Bryan's would reduce it to the idle mimicry of the stage.

It was no more intended to make the General Government dependent upon the States with respect to the matters committed to it than to make the States subject to the General Government with respect to the rights reserved to them. As the General Government is authorized to maintain a regular army and navy which the States cannot do, and as the militia of all the States is subject to the direct call of the President, it was natural that the States should be made to call on it for aid against violence, but there was no reason why it would call or wait on them for protection to itself.

What I have said is well known to lawyers and students of the Constitution. It is chiefly intended for the people at large before whom the subject has now been brought.

I will recall in this connection the following resolution proposed by the Hon. John W. Daniel, of Virginia, who was president of the convention which nominated Mr. Bryan, which was passed by the Senate July 12, 1894, Congressional Record, page 8663, without apparent dissent:

'*Resolved*, That the Senate indorses the prompt and vigorous measures adopted by the President of the United States and the members of his Administration to repulse and repress by military force the interference of lawless men with the due process of laws of the United States and with the transportation of the mails of the United States and with commerce among the States.

'The action of the President and his Administration has the full sympathy and support of the law-abiding masses of the people of the United States, and he will be supported by all departments of the Government and by the power and resources of the entire nation.'

It must be that Mr. Bryan, amid the many demands of his time and attention, has fallen into an inadvertence. I cannot believe that he really thinks the

President has no power under the Constitution and laws to maintain the Government intrusted to his charge.

Nor can I believe that Mr. Bryan means to promise or to make or to permit others to think he has promised not to interfere if he should be elected and the situation of the riots of 1894 should arise during his term. I will not lightly question either his knowledge as a lawyer or his sincerity as public man. Certainly his letter is generally misunderstood, unless it means either that Mr. Bryan thinks the President has no power, or that he would himself not use it if elected."

### TWO OTHER VIEWS.

In regard to this same question, a well-known labor leader recently said in a public speech: "The men engaged in that strike, who belonged to the American Railway Union, were dismayed to see that violence had been resorted to, and they earnestly endeavored to put an end to it. They tendered their services in aid of law and order; it was their wish that peace should be preserved. Had not the Government of Illinois been in the hands of fear-stricken politicians not a blow would have been struck, not a dollar's worth of property would have been destroyed. It was a lack of appreciation of the just demands of labor and a fear of losing votes in the future which prevented them from doing their duty by labor and the State in checking violence the moment it began. 'Government by injunction' would never be known in the United States had government by incompetency not preceded it."

And Gov. Palmer, in his speech of acceptance, said manfully: "When Governor of my adopted State, while I opposed and by peaceful means successfully resisted the interference of the United States by its military forces in the purely local concerns of the State, I distinctly conceded the right, and asserted the duty, of that Government to enforce within the States or elsewhere its own laws by its own agencies."

### "GOVERNMENT BY INJUNCTION.

The Chicago platform continues: "We especially object to government by injunction as a new and highly dangerous form of oppression." Here again it would have been more honest as well as more intelligible if, instead of leaving to inference the special wrong complained of, it had been plainly stated. No one believes in "government by injunction." As worded, therefore, the protest is meaningless, unless a covert attack is thereby aimed against the power of the Federal Courts to use a most efficient branch of its equity power.

The bill filed by the United States on July 2 alleged that the American Railway Union and its officers, naming them, had entered into a combination and conspiracy embracing a great number of persons, members of that organization and others whose names were unknown, to tie up and paralyze certain specified lines of railroad, twenty-two in number, and to prevent them from performing their usual duties as common carriers of interstate commerce and from transporting the United States mails; that the conspirators, many thousands in number, to accomplish such unlawful purpose, by threats, intimidation, force and violence against the employees of said railroad companies engaged in said business, and by spiking switches, derailing cars and the like, had already seriously interfered with their business of transporting freight and passengers between the States and of carrying the United States mails, and in many instances had completely checked the same. That the conspirators had gathered in large mobs upon the lines of said railroads, and were endeavoring by violence, intimidation, threats and persuasion to induce the employees of such railroads to disobey the orders of their employers and to refuse to perform their accustomed duties, and to quit the service in such business of interstate transportation and the carrying of the mails; and by like means were preventing and attempting to prevent other persons desirous of entering such service from doing so, and were threatening to still further interfere by the means aforesaid with the operation of trains and cars by said companies engaged in interstate transportation until they should completely tie up and paralyze the same.

## THE ORDER OF INJUNCTION.

An injunction was prayed against the American Railway Union and its officers, naming them, and thirteen other persons, naming them, and all other persons whomsoever, combining or conspiring with the defendants named, commanding them to refrain from all acts and doings complained of and threatened. As Mr. E. A. Bancroft, has remarked: "The real scope of this order has been generally misstated and misunderstood, and the error has been emphasized by dubbing it an 'omnibus' injunction. An examination of the order shows that it consists of two parts, though they are not separated. The first portion enumerates the particular things which the defendants may not do, and those things are all in themselves unlawful and injurious. But among them the persuading of employees to quit the service of the railroad is not included; the only use of the word 'persuade' is in the clause forbidding the defendants to induce employees in the service of said railroads to refuse to perform their duties as employees of said railroads engaged in interstate commerce or the carriage of the United States mails. It does not forbid them to use persuasion to induce employees to quit the service."

"The second portion of the order, embracing the last two clauses, forbids the doing of any act—even though it be lawful in itself—in furtherance of any conspiracy or combination to restrain either of the railroads from freely controlling and handling interstate commerce, and also forbids the ordering, directing, aiding or abetting any person to commit any or either of the acts aforesaid."

"Whether the Government could properly file a bill for such relief is one with the question whether the United States Circuit Court could properly grant the injunction upon such a bill."

The Supreme Court of the United States has passed affirmatively, and without a dissenting vote, on each of these propositions. It took up the contention that it is outside of the jurisdiction of a court of equity to enjoin the commission of crimes, and admitted its truth, but it held that when there is interference, actual or threatened, with property or rights of a pecuniary nature, the jurisdiction of a court of equity arises, and is not destroyed by the fact that such interference is accompanied by or is itself a violation of the criminal law.

### THE LESSON OF THE STRIKE.

If the railroad strike of 1894 brought home one lesson more strongly than another, it was that anarchy is not a cure for defective legislation and that no private or public interest can be so great as to warrant a compromise with violators of law. There is much in the strike and in the position of those who condemn the suppression of its violence to suggest Lyman Abbott's judgment of Napoleon:

"He was an embodiment of the spirit of the French Revolution, in which some of the noblest sentiments of love and liberty ever framed into eloquent words stand in strange contrast with some of the blackest and bloodiest crimes ever written in tragic deeds. And both serve as a warning to the philosophy which in our time confounds liberty and lawlessness, which conceives a man to be good because he has good impulses, or a state to be secure because it has noble ideas; which forgets that the lawless will of a multitude is no better than the lawless will of an individual, and fondly imagines that a people may know no law higher than their own inclinations, and yet the voice of the people be the voice of God."

The merits of the strike are not the question at issue, it is whether the law as applied by the Circuit Court with the unanimous approval of the Supreme Court of the United States, should be accepted and respected as the law of the land. Our system of government knows no higher sanction than this, and the party which makes this kind of authoritative exposition of the law the subject of rancorous denunciation, ranges itself on the side of disorder and proclaims itself the propagandist of revolution.

That there have been abuses in the administration as well as in the enactment of Federal law; that in this connection there have been real wrongs which ought to be redressed, as well as fancied ones, which have been sincerely felt, no one will deny. And, whether or not those are such as might now fitly be made an issue of our politics, the framers of the Chicago platform might have rendered a real service by directly stating them and proposing a remedy. With a depravity which, instead of stating wrong in order that it may be amended, criticises law only as an invitation to law-breaking, an order-loving people can make no compromise. For any effective remedy of defects that may exist in the administration of justice by the Federal Courts, the first essential is that laws once made shall be obeyed. To complain of wrong and in the same breath to suggest violation of law is to obstruct the only remedy possible among a civilized people.

# RECORD OF THE DEMOCRATIC ADMINISTRATION.

The just way to judge an administration is by its fidelity to the interests of the people, to the pledges of the platform upon which a President is elected, and to the promises of its chief. Three promises were contained in the Democratic Platform of 1892. They relate to the currency, the tariff, and to the civil service.

## I. THE CURRENCY.

The platform of 1892 denounced the Sherman Silver Purchase Act of 1890 as a "cowardly makeshift, fraught with possibilities of danger in the future," and demanded its speedy repeal. Very soon after President Cleveland's second inauguration the menace of the Sherman Act culminated in the panic of 1893. A special session of Congress was called, and the act itself was repealed.

The platform then went on to pledge the party to "insure the maintenance of the parity of the two metals, and the equal power of every dollar at all times in the markets and in payment of debts, and we demand that all paper currency shall be kept at par with and redeemable in such coin. We insist upon this policy as especially necessary for the protection of the farmers and laboring classes, the first and most defenseless victims of unstable money and a fluctuating currency."

During the war, and the ten years that followed, this country had full experience of the evils thus pointed out in the platform. The paper currency was not kept at par with and redeemable in coin. Its value fluctuated and the farmers and the laboring classes suffered. No man when he made a bargain to work for another, or when he planned for a crop, could tell what the dollar in which he was to be paid would be worth or what it would buy. Prices varied as the currency varied, and the people of this country determined to recur to the well-established Democratic policy of redeeming all paper currency in gold, or in silver kept on a parity with gold. In order to provide for this redemption it became necessary to accumulate gold in the Treasury, and accordingly the Resumption Act of January 14, 1875, authorized the Secretary of the Treasury to purchase gold and to issue, sell and dispose of bonds for that purpose. This was done. A stock of gold was accumulated in the Treasury, and on the first of January, 1879, we resumed gold payments. Meanwhile the owners of silver mines, the value of whose product had been diminished by the greatly increased production of silver, endeavored to get a market for the silver which they produced from the Government, and the Act of February 28, 1878, was passed, directing the purchase of two million dollars' worth of silver bullion per month and the coinage of the same into silver dollars. Silver certificates were authorized to be issued by the Treasury upon the deposit of these silver dollars.

These purchases did not, however, maintain the market price of silver. But the silver-producing States had votes, and there were enough politicians in both parties to seek to secure those votes, and accordingly, in 1890, the Sherman Act was passed, which provided for the purchase of four million five hundred thousand ounces of silver per month and the issuing of government notes in payment, which were made redeemable in coin. This was supposed by many to be the total production of silver in this country. There were those who honestly believed that the purchase of this vast amount of silver by the Government would raise the price. It turned out, however, that the quantity of silver in the world was practically unlimited, that the purchases by the Government could not maintain the price, which was settled by fixed laws of supply and demand that no government can control, and though this artificial market raised silver in 1890 to $1.02 an ounce, yet it steadily fell from that time until 1894, when it sold for as low as 64 cents per ounce.

Meanwhile the agitation for the unlimited coinage of silver was kept up, and business men, both in this country and abroad, began to realize the danger of still further concessions to the owners of silver mines, and to the honest but misguided men whom they had persuaded to co-operate with them. It was very well understood that the free coinage of silver—the supply of silver being unlimited—would reduce the value of the American dollar to the value of the silver contained in it, and that it would be perfectly impossible for the Government, with free coinage, to maintain the parity of the two metals. Naturally, therefore, many who feared that the Government would not be able to keep the pledge of the Democratic platform already quoted, began to draw gold from the treasury. The debtors of the Government ceased paying gold into the treasury, and paid all their debts in paper and silver, as debtors always will if the option is given them. The creditors of the Government, on the other hand, demanded from the government gold, as creditors always will if the option is given them. The result was a steady drain upon the treasury,[1] until, on the 12th of February, 1895, the gold coin in the treasury was only $51,392,583, while the outstanding gold certificates were $52,578,529.[2]

At this time, therefore, there was not gold coin enough in the treasury to pay the outstanding gold certificates and we had none at all with which to pay the United States notes, amounting to $347,681,016, not to speak of the coin notes, amounting to $152,584,417, issued under the Act of 1890.[3]

---

[1] The gold coin and bullion in the Treasury April 30, 1889, was $328,203,901. September 30, 1894, it was only $123,665,776. (Treasury Report for 1894, pages 29, 30). During the same time the silver coin and bullion increased from $307,057,392 to $509,814,353. *Ibid*, p. 32.

[2] See Treasury Report of that date, published in leading Chicago and New York papers of the next day.

[3] Treasury Report, 1894, p. 65. Of these United States notes there were counted as available cash in the Treasury, February 12, 1895, $51,143,314.42 See Report for that day.

The gold bullion in the treasury was $42,526,127, making a net gold reserve against four hundred and fifty millions of paper payable on demand of only $41,340,181. During the ten weeks previous to this date our own people had drawn out in gold from the Treasury of the Government, exclusive of that which was exported, $43,933,913. The rate at which gold was being drawn out was rapidly increasing, and if something had not been done to prevent the draft, the whole amount in the Treasury would have disappeared within a month, and the Government would have had nothing with which to pay its ordinary debts but silver dollars. These certainly are legal tender for all debts not expressed to be paid in gold, but their intrinsic value is only about fifty cents. The Government now keeps up the credit of the silver dollar by redeeming all coin notes in gold. But the moment the Government ceases to do this, and pays its obligations only in silver, that moment the silver dollar will be taken only according to its actual commercial value, and we shall have two standards, just as we had during the war. The Government then was compelled to pay, and did pay, all its current debts in paper, and this paper at one time during the war was worth less than forty cents on the dollar, measured by the gold standard.

The fear of a return to this condition was general among creditors and investors during 1893 and 1894. It was this fear that palsied the manufacturer, and that cut down the profits of the farmer. It was this fear that closed factories and threw men out of employment.

In this emergency, the President of the United States and the Secretary of the Treasury, with a courage worthy of all praise, made the contract with the great bankers of New York and London by which not only did they agree to furnish gold for the present needs of the Government to the amount of sixty-five million dollars, but agreed that they would "bear all the expenses and inevitable loss of bringing gold from Europe, hereunder, and, as far as lies in their power, will exert all financial influence and will make all legitimate efforts to protect the Treasury of the United States against the withdrawals of gold, pending the complete performance of this contract."

Had it not been for this act, the Government would have had nothing to pay its debts with but the silver coin and bullion in the treasury, and it would have been compelled to pay all its salaries and contracts in silver and silver notes. This means distinctly that we should have gone into national bankruptcy, and paid our debts at fifty cents on the dollar. Our credit, individual and national, would have received a blow from which it would not have recovered for years. The greatest sufferers would have been laboring men, wage-earners, pensioners, depositors in savings banks, and the like.

The Administration has been censured by the advocates of silver coinage for the issue of these bonds, and for a subsequent issue which was made necessary by the subsequent reduction of the gold in the treasury. In what the Administration has done it was not only carrying out the pledges of the platform, but the pledge of two statutes of the United States:

"It being the established policy of the United States to maintain the two metals on a parity with each other upon the present legal ratio, or such ratio as may be provided by law." Act of July 14, 1890 (26 United States Stat. at Large, 89).

This pledge was repeated by the Act of November, 1893 (27 *ibid.* p. 4):

" And it is hereby declared to be the policy of the United States to continue the use of both gold and silver as standard money, and to coin both gold and silver into money of equal intrinsic and exchangable value, such equality to be secured through international agreement, or by such safeguards of legislation as will insure the maintenance of the parity in value of the coins of the two metals, and the equal power of every dollar at all times in the markets and in the payment of debts. And it is hereby further declared that the efforts of the Government should be steadily directed to the establishment of such a safe system of bi-metallism as will maintain at all times the equal power of every dollar coined or issued by the United States, in the markets and in the payment of debts."

What was meant by the issue of bonds for the purchase of gold is simply this: The Government had solemnly pledged itself "to maintain at all times the equal power of every dollar coined or issued by the United States in the markets and in payment of debts." To be false to this pledge would have made every paper dollar issued by the United States redeemable only in silver dollars. These silver dollars were worth only about fifty cents. As long as the Government keeps them on a par with the gold dollar by redeeming its paper in gold at the option of the holder, so long one dollar has purchasing power equal to that of the other. But the moment that this act of the Government ceases, that moment the silver dollar becomes worth just what the silver in it is worth, and no more. That would have meant that every pension, every laboring man, every farmer, every business man in the country, when paid for what he sold or for his work, would have been paid in dollars worth only half what they were when the bargain was made. Mr. Cleveland was the only person in the country who had the power to save our people from this disgrace and loss. To do it he made a contract by which those who had gold sold it to the Government and received in payment government bonds.

In this same agreement the offer was distinctly made to Congress that they might save the people sixteen million dollars if they would authorize payment for the gold thus bought in three per cent. bonds, containing an express agreement to pay the principal and interest in United States gold coin of the present standard of weight and fineness. This offer Congress refused. The bonds were paid for in the four per cent. bonds authorized by previous statutes, which are payable in coin, but not "specifically in gold coin." Thus the free-silver agitation cost us sixteen million dollars at one stroke. If this lesson should teach our people that a fixed standard for the payment of debts is the best policy, it will be worth all it cost.

In other words, when the Chicago platform condemns the issue of bonds in time of peace, it means that instead of taking money from those who are able to lend it to the Government in order to enable the Government to pay its debts and keep its promise, it would disgrace the Government by violating its promise, and ruin the people by compelling them to accept in payment dollars really only worth fifty cents.

When this platform speaks of a syndicate of bankers it simply means men who have money to sell. The Government needed money and naturally went to those who had it to sell. If it needed wheat it would go to the dealers in wheat. If it needed beef it would go to the dealers in beef. When it needed money it naturally went to those who had money. The money which it got was for the benefit of every American citizen, and more for that of the poor than of the rich, because they needed it most.

## II. THE TARIFF.

The Democratic platform of 1892 demanded that the collection of tariff taxes "shall be limited to the necessities of the Government as honestly and economically administered." Mr. Cleveland's ringing message of 1887 had not been forgotten. The Democratic party in the House of Representatives, acting in full co-operation with the Administration, passed a bill which responded to this pledge of the platform. A small coterie of Democrats in the Senate, some of whom are now supporters of Bryan, compelled an amendment of this bill which diminished its value. The House was compelled to submit, but the bill as passed was a great improvement on the McKinley tariff. It reduced or repealed the taxes on raw material, and in this way diminished the cost of the necessaries of life and increased the market for American manufactured products, both at home and abroad. The charge is often made against this bill that it did not produce sufficient income. The answer to this is twofold:

1. The income tax which it did contain would have produced sufficient income, even for the large expenditure which has since been voted by Congress. This was declared unconstitutional by the United States Supreme Court. The Republican party made this a pretext in the present Congress for increasing protective taxes, and refused to impose revenue taxes which would have met the deficiency in revenue. Failing to do this, their plain duty was to reduce expenditure so as to keep within the government income. Instead of this they passed an extravagant River and Harbor Bill, which was vetoed by the President, but which they succeeded in passing over his veto. It would be absurd for a man who had an income of over ten thousand dollars a year, but

who extravagantly spent fifteen thousand, to complain of the smallness of his income. The honest thing for him to do would be to reduce expenses and keep within his means. The failure to do this is not the fault of the Democratic Administration. That did all that an administration could to keep down the expenses of the Government. But Congress alone has power to make appropriations, and it is Congress that has run the nation in debt by expenditures far beyond its income.

### III. THE CIVIL SERVICE.

The Democratic platform of 1892 declared "public office is a public trust." It reaffirmed the "declaration of the Democratic National Convention of 1876 for the reform of the Civil Service" and called for "the honest enforcement of all the laws regulating the same." It pledged the Democratic party to reform "abuses which threatened individual liberty and local self-government." This pledge the President has amply kept. Early in the administration he brought within the operation of the Civil Service laws the Agricultural Department and the Mint, and greatly extended their application to the Indian service and in the Customs service. By more recent orders he has extended the operation of these laws in all branches of the service, and has thrown open to public competition many of the most important places in the Government. What all this means is simply this:

That the appointment to about eighty-five thousand two hundred offices of the U. S. Government shall henceforward be made, not for partisan service, but for merit, and that those who serve the Government faithfully shall have an opportunity to be promoted instead of seeing persons of no experience in the public service appointed over their head. This offers a public career to every American citizen, however humble his birth, who is competent to serve his country, and gives him security of tenure by taking away the temptation to remove him and appoint somebody else in his place for political reasons.

The Chicago platform declares, "We are opposed to life tenure in the public service," and also declares for "fixed terms of office." These phrases can only mean "a clean sweep" at the end of every four years. It is obvious that the partisans of Bryan, who falsely called themselves Democrats, are hungry for the spoils of office. The same selfishness that leads the silver-mine owners to demand a market for their product from the Government which is given to no one else, leads their other leaders to demand the turning out of the faithful servants of the Government and the appointment of themselves.

It must be plain, therefore, to every impartial observer, that the present Administration has loyally kept the pledges of the platform upon which Grover Cleveland was elected, and that the Chicago platform, as expounded by its candidate, betrays them all. It is true that this platform contains a tariff-reform plank, but it is equally true that Mr. Bryan declares that the question of the tariff is not involved in the present election, and that its reform is no concern of his. It demands the free coinage of silver which would inevitably bring the country to a single standard, with a dollar worth only about fifty cents. This would not only violate the provisions of the U. S. statutes already quoted, but the pledges of the Democratic party. It is plain, therefore, that the Bryan party is no more entitled to the name of Democrat than pirates would be to the title of honest mariners who had stolen a ship and hoisted its flag at the peak. The true Democrats of the party must be loyal to the principles of their party and preserve it for the lasting welfare of the American people.

# THE NATIONAL FINANCES, 1888-1896.

The claim has been made that the revenue yielded by the McKinley tariff act was sufficient for all the expenses of the Government, and that it was only after the enactment of the Wilson act that a deficit began to appear. In point of fact, the immediate effect of the McKinley act was a great reduction of revenue. The return it yielded became year by year less and less adequate to produce a surplus, and the last year of the operation showed a large deficit.

During the fiscal year 1888—ended June 30, 1888—the revenues of the government were $111,341,273 in excess of its expenditures.

During the fiscal year 1889—ended June 30, 1889—the revenues were $87,761,080 in excess of the expenditures.

During the fiscal year 1890—ended June 30, 1890—the revenues were $85,040,271 in excess of the expenditures.

The so-called McKinley Tariff Act took effect on the 6th day of October, 1890, and during the fiscal year 1891—ended June 30, 1891—the revenues were $26,838,541 in excess of the expenditures.

During the fiscal year 1892—ended June 30, 1892—the revenues were $9,914,453 in excess of the expenditures.

During the fiscal year 1893—ended June 30, 1893—the revenues were $2,341,674 in excess of the expenditures.

During the fiscal year 1894—ended June 30, 1894—the expenditures exceeded the revenue to the amount of $69,803,260.58, notwithstanding the fact that the expenditures of the Government were $15,952,674 less than in the preceding year. The McKinley Bill was in force during the whole of the fiscal year 1894.

The so-called Wilson Tariff Act took effect on the 28th day of August, 1894, and the revenues for the fiscal year 1895—ended June 30, 1895—were $42,805,223.18 less than the expenditures; and during the fiscal year 1896—ended June 30, 1896—the revenues were $25,203,245.70 less than the expenditures.

*Receipts from Customs and Total Receipts from All Sources Under McKinley Act*

|  | CUSTOMS. | ALL SOURCES. |
|---|---|---|
| Twelve months ending Sept. 30, 1891.. | $196,794,357 89 | $371,932,536 81 |
| Twelve months ending Sept. 30, 1892.. | 185,838,859 19 | 364,847,501 72 |
| Twelve months ending Sept. 30, 1893.. | 189,182,905 46 | 365,534,609 55 |
| Eleven months ending Aug. 31, 1894.. | 112,590,939 77 | 292,078,342 91 |

*Receipts from Customs and Total Receipts from All Sources Under Wilson Act.*

|  | CUSTOMS. | ALL SOURCES. |
|---|---|---|
| Twelve months ending Aug. 31, 1895.. | $161,201,169 35 | $295,061,022 16 |
| Twelve months ending Aug. 31, 1896.. | 154,218,813 94 | 321,726,319 37 |

### CONDITION OF THE TREASURY MARCH 1, 1889, AND MARCH 1, 1893.

There has been a copious amount of misrepresentation as to the condition of the United States Treasury in the four years between the end of President Cleveland's first term and the beginning of his second. The following figures show how serious was the depletion of available funds which took place during that time.

On the 1st day of March, 1889, the beginning of President Harrison's administration, the available funds in the Treasury, exclusive of the $100,000,000 gold reserve, were as follows:

| Agency account............................................. | $64,502,445 02 |
|---|---|
| Net balance in Treasury................................ | 165,846,471 10 |
| Total....................................................... | $230,348,916 12 |

On the 1st day of March, 1893, the beginning of the present administration, the available funds in the Treasury, exclusive of the $100,000,000 gold reserve, were as follows:

| Agency account........................................... | $38,365,832 90 |
|---|---|
| Net balance in Treasury................................ | 24,084,742 28 |
| Total ..................................................... | $62,450,575 18 |

In addition to the ordinary revenues received during President Harrison's administration, there was covered into the Treasury $54,207,975.75, which had been held in trust under the law as a fund for the redemption of national bank notes. This proceeding was authorized by the Act of July 14, 1890, commonly known as the Sherman Act.

### PUBLIC DEBT PAID BY THE TWO ADMINISTRATIONS.

The following may serve as a corrective to current misstatements in regard to the share borne by a Democratic administration in the reduction of the public debt.

From the 1st day of March, 1885, the beginning of Mr. Cleveland's first administration, to March 1, 1889, the public debt was reduced $341,448,449.20; and from March 1, 1889, the beginning of Mr. Harrison's administration, to March 1, 1893, the reduction of the public debt was $236,527,666.10.

The amount of free gold in the Treasury on the 7th day of March, 1893, when the present Secretary took charge of the Department, was $100,982.410.

## VALUES OF IMPORTS AND EXPORTS.

The claim has been made that one result of the operation of the Wilson Tariff Act has been an enormous increase of imports and a great shrinkage of exports. How little ground there is for such a statement may be seen from the following statement:

|  | Imports. | Exports, Dom. and Foreign. |
|---|---|---|
| Oct. 1, 1890, to Sept. 30, 1891 | $824,716,842 | $923,362,015 |
| Oct. 1, 1891, to Sept. 30, 1892 | 837,280,798 | 998,226,775 |
| Oct. 1, 1892, to Sept. 30, 1893 | 830,150,318 | 876,332,434 |
| * Oct. 1, 1893, to Aug. 31, 1894 | 603,865,896 | 790,706,509 |

*Values of Imports and Exports of Merchandise Under the Wilson Tariff Act.*

| | | |
|---|---|---|
| Sept. 1, 1894, to Aug. 31, 1895 | $759,108,416 | $806,670,050 |
| * Sept. 1, 1895, to July 31, 1896 | 687,695,637 | 837,802,519 |

*Excess of Exports of Merchandise alone, and of Merchandise and Silver, Under McKinley Act.*

|  | Merchandise. | Merchandise and Silver. |
|---|---|---|
| Oct. 1, 1890, to Sept. 30, 1891 | $98,645,173 | $103,537,310 |
| Oct. 1, 1891, to Sept. 30, 1892 | 160,945,977 | 175,091,707 |
| Oct. 1, 1892, to Sept. 30, 1893 | 46,182,116 | 68,672,811 |
| * Oct. 1, 1893, to Aug. 31, 1894 | 186,840,613 | 219,546,927 |

*Excess of Exports of Merchandise alone, and of Merchandise and Silver, Under Wilson Act.*

|  | Merchandise. | Merchandise and Silver. |
|---|---|---|
| Sept. 1, 1894, to Aug. 31, 1895 | $47,561,634 | $86,960,538 |
| * Sept. 1, 1895, to July 31, 1896 | 150,106,882 | 194,435,730 |

*Annual Average Excess of Exports of Merchandise Alone.*

| | |
|---|---|
| Under McKinley Act of 1890 | $123,153,470 |
| Under Wilson Act of 1894 | 98,834,258 |

*Annual Average Excess of Exports of Merchandise and Silver.*

| | |
|---|---|
| Under McKinley Act of 1890 | $141,712,189 |
| Under Wilson Act of 1894 | 140,698,134 |

* Eleven months.

## Commercial ratio of silver and gold each year 1687-1895.

[NOTE—From 1687 to 1832 the ratios are taken from Dr. A. Soetbeer; from 1833 to 1878 from Pixley and Abell's tables, and from 1879 to 1894 from daily cablegrams from London to the Bureau of the Mint.]

| Year. | Ratio. | Year. | Ratio. | Year. | Ratio. | Year. | Ratio. | Year. | Ratio. | Year. | Ratio. |
|---|---|---|---|---|---|---|---|---|---|---|---|
| 1687... | 14.94 | 1723.. | 15.20 | 1759.. | 14.15 | 1795.. | 15.55 | 1831.. | 15.72 | 1867... | 15.57 |
| 1688... | 14.94 | 1724.. | 15.11 | 1760.. | 14.14 | 1796.. | 15.65 | 1832.. | 15.73 | 1868... | 15.59 |
| 1689... | 15.02 | 1725.. | 15.11 | 1761.. | 14.54 | 1797.. | 15.41 | 1833.. | 15.93 | 1869... | 15.60 |
| 1690... | 15.02 | 1726.. | 15.15 | 1762.. | 15.27 | 1798.. | 15.59 | 1834.. | 15.73 | 1870.. | 15.57 |
| 1691... | 14.98 | 1727.. | 15.24 | 1763.. | 14.99 | 1799.. | 15.74 | 1835.. | 15.80 | 1871... | 15.57 |
| 1692... | 14.92 | 1728.. | 15.11 | 1764. | 14.70 | 1800.. | 15.68 | 1836.. | 15.72 | 1872... | 15.63 |
| 1693... | 14.83 | 1729. | 14.92 | 1765.. | 14.83 | 1801.. | 15.46 | 1837 | 15.83 | 1873... | 15.92 |
| 1694... | 14.87 | 1730.. | 14.81 | 1766.. | 14.80 | 1802.. | 15.26 | 1838.. | 15.85 | 1874.. | 16.17 |
| 1695... | 15.02 | 1731.. | 14.94 | 1767.. | 14.85 | 1803.. | 15.41 | 1839.. | 15.62 | 1875... | 16.59 |
| 1696... | 15.00 | 1732.. | 15.09 | 1768.. | 14.80 | 1804.. | 15.41 | 1840.. | 15.62 | 1876... | 17.88 |
| 1697..  | 15.20 | 1733.. | 15.18 | 1769.. | 14.72 | 1805.. | 15.79 | 1841.. | 15.70 | 1877... | 17.22 |
| 1698... | 15.07 | 1734.. | 15.39 | 1770.. | 14.62 | 1806.. | 15.52 | 1842.. | 15.87 | 1878.. | 17.94 |
| 1699... | 14.94 | 1735.. | 15.41 | 1771.. | 14.66 | 1807.. | 15.43 | 1843. | 15.93 | 1879... | 18.40 |
| 1700... | 14.81 | 1736.. | 15.18 | 1772.. | 14.52 | 1808.. | 16.08 | 1844.. | 15.85 | 1880... | 18.05 |
| 1701... | 15.07 | 1737.. | 15.02 | 1773.. | 14.62 | 1809.. | 15.96 | 1845.. | 15.92 | 1881... | 18.16 |
| 1702... | 15.52 | 1738.. | 14.91 | 1774.. | 14.62 | 1810.. | 15.77 | 1846.. | 15.90 | 1882... | 18.19 |
| 1703... | 15.17 | 1739.. | 14.91 | 1775.. | 14.72 | 1811.. | 15.53 | 1847.. | 15.80 | 1883... | 18.64 |
| 1704... | 15.22 | 1740.. | 14.94 | 1776.. | 14.55 | 1812.. | 16.11 | 1848.. | 15.85 | 1884... | 18.57 |
| 1705... | 15.11 | 1741.. | 14.92 | 1777.. | 14.54 | 1813.. | 16.25 | 1849.. | 15.78 | 1885... | 19.41 |
| 1706... | 15.27 | 1742.. | 14.85 | 1778.. | 14.68 | 1814.. | 15.04 | 1850.. | 15.70 | 1886... | 20.78 |
| 1707... | 15.44 | 1743.. | 14.85 | 1779.. | 14.80 | 1815.. | 15.26 | 1851.. | 15.46 | 1887... | 21.13 |
| 1708... | 15.41 | 1744.. | 14.87 | 1780.. | 14.72 | 1816.. | 15.28 | 1852.. | 15.59 | 1888... | 21.99 |
| 1709... | 15.31 | 1745.. | 14.98 | 1781.. | 14.78 | 1817.. | 15.11 | 1853.. | 15.33 | 1889.. | 22.10 |
| 1710... | 15.22 | 1746.. | 15.13 | 1782.. | 14.42 | 1818.. | 15.35 | 1854.. | 15.33 | 1890... | 19.76 |
| 1711... | 15.29 | 1747.. | 15.26 | 1783.. | 14.48 | 1819.. | 15.33 | 1855.. | 15.33 | 1891... | 20.92 |
| 1712... | 15.31 | 1748.. | 15.11 | 1784.. | 14.70 | 1820.. | 15.62 | 1856.. | 15.38 | 1892... | 23.72 |
| 1713... | 15.24 | 1749.. | 14.80 | 1785.. | 14.92 | 1821.. | 15.95 | 1857.. | 15.27 | 1893... | 26.49 |
| 1714... | 15.13 | 1750.. | 14.55 | 1786.. | 14.96 | 1822.. | 15.80 | 1858.. | 15.38 | 1894.. | 32.56 |
| 1715... | 15.11 | 1751.. | 14.39 | 1787.. | 14.92 | 1823.. | 15.84 | 1859.. | 15.19 | 1895... | 31.60 |
| 1716... | 15.09 | 1752.. | 14.54 | 1788.. | 14.65 | 1824. | 15.82 | 1860.. | 15.29 | 1896 (6 months) | 30.32 |
| 1717... | 15.13 | 1753.. | 14.54 | 1789.. | 14.75 | 1825. | 15.70 | 1861.. | 15.50 | | |
| 1718... | 15.11 | 1754.. | 14.48 | 1790.. | 15.04 | 1826.. | 15.76 | 1862.. | 15.35 | | |
| 1719... | 15.09 | 1755.. | 14.68 | 1791.. | 15.05 | 1827.. | 15.74 | 1863.. | 15.37 | | |
| 1720... | 15.04 | 1756.. | 14.94 | 1792.. | 15.17 | 1828 . | 15.78 | 1864 . | 15.37 | | |
| 1721... | 15.05 | 1757.. | 14.87 | 1793. | 15.00 | 1829.. | 15.78 | 1865.. | 15.44 | | |
| 1722... | 15.17 | 1758.. | 14.85 | 1794.. | 15.37 | 1830.. | 15.82 | 1866.. | 15.43 | | |

## "16 TO 1."—MINT DIRECTOR PRESTON'S EXPLANATION.

Director of the Mint Preston has issued the following statement of the coinage ratio between gold and silver:

"All standard silver dollars coined by the mints of the United States since the passage of the act of January 18, 1837, have been coined in the ratio of 1 to 15.9884—generally called the ratio of 1 to 16, 15.9884 being very nearly 16. Still, to reach accurate results, the former and not the latter figure must be used in calculation. The ratio is obtained in this way: The silver dollar contains 371.25 grains of pure silver, and the gold dollar 23.22 grains of pure gold. If you divide 371.25 by 23.22 you will get the ratio of weight between a gold dollar and a silver dollar—that is, 15.9884.

It is true that to be on a par with gold silver would (at our ratio) be worth $1.2929. The reason is this: A gold dollar contains 23.22 grains of pure gold. In an ounce, or 480 grains, of gold, there are as many dollars as 23.22 is contained times in 480 grains. If you divide 480 by 23.22 you get $20.67, the number of dollars that can be coined out of an ounce of pure gold; in other words, the money equivalent of one ounce of gold or of 15.9884 ounces of silver at the ratio of 1 to 15.9884. Now, if 15.9884 ounces of silver be worth $20.67, one ounce will be worth $1.2929, as you can prove by simple division. The same result is obtained by dividing 480 grains, or one ounce, of silver by 371.25, the number of grains of pure silver in a standard silver dollar, at the ratio of 1 to 15.9884, which gives $1.2929.

Sixteen ounces of pure silver will coin a little more than one ounce of gold; 15.9884 ounces of silver will coin exactly the same amount of money as one ounce of gold—that is, $20.67. You can prove this by dividing 15.9884 ounces by 371.25 grains. The operation is as follows: 15.9884 multiplied by 480, divided by 371.25, equals $20.674. It is not true that sixteen ounces of silver will coin only $16.80 at the ratio of 1 to 16.

As will be seen above, one ounce of silver will coin $1.2929. Multiplying $1.2929 by 16 gives $20.68. You can make the same result in another way: Sixteen ounces troy, or 7,680 grains, divided by 371.25 gives the number of silver dollars that can be coined out of sixteen ounces of silver; 7,680 divided by 371.25 equals $20.68."

# A FREE COINAGE CATECHISM.*

THE purpose of this series of questions and answers is to put, in simple form, the problems raised by the free-coinage controversy, with a plain answer to each. All statistical facts given are transcribed from official publications.

### THE MONEY SUPPLY.

Q. What is the fundamental claim of the free-coinage advocates? A. They claim that the amount of money in circulation has been decreasing since the demonetization of silver, and that this decrease has caused a general fall in prices.

Q. Is it true that the money supply has been decreasing? A. it is not.

Q. What are the facts? A. So far as the United States is concerned, there has been an enormous increase. In 1860 the money in circulation in this country was $442,102,477; in 1872 it was $738,309,549; by the Treasury bulletin at the opening of July, 1896, it was $1,509,725,200.

Q. Can you give the details? A. Certainly. Here they are:

*Money in Circulation July 1, 1872.*

| | |
|---|---|
| State bank notes | $1,700,935 |
| Fractional currency | 36,402,929 |
| United States notes | 346,168,680 |
| National bank notes | 329,037,005 |
| | $713,309,549 |
| Add specie in circulation on the Pacific Coast | 25,000,000 |
| | $738,309,549 |

*Money in Circulation July 1, 1896.*

| | |
|---|---|
| Gold coin | $456,128,483 |
| Silver dollars | 52,175,908 |
| Small silver | 59,999,805 |
| Gold certificates | 42,320,759 |
| Silver certificates | 331,259,509 |
| Treasury notes of 1890 | 95,217,361 |
| United States notes | 225,451,358 |
| Currency certificates | 31,840,000 |
| National bank notes | 215,331,927 |
| | $1,509,725,200 |

* Revised and enlarged edition, reprinted by permission from "The Evening Post." Copies in envelope size can be had at 2 cents a copy (postage 1 cent for 2 copies), by addressing Evening Post Publishing Co., 206–210 Broadway, New York.

Q. What does this show? A. It shows that our money supply has increased 240 per cent. as compared with 1860, and 104 per cent. as compared with 1872.

Q. Has the money supply increased faster than the population? A. Very much faster.

Q. How do you prove this? A. By dividing the total money in circulation at each date by the total population of the country at the same date, and thus finding the circulation per capita.

Q. What does such a process show? A. The per capita circulation of the the United States on July 1, 1860, was $14.06; on July 1, 1872, it was $18.70; at the opening of July, 1896, it was $21.15.

Q. But has not the money supply of the world at large been decreasing? A. On the contrary, it has been increasing rapidly.

Q. How is this proved? A. By the statistics of new gold production.

Q. How large has this production been? A. The reports of the Director of the Mint, which are acknowledged authority, show that from 1873 to 1894, inclusive, the world's total new gold production has been $2,526,834 900.

Q. Is this new product of gold increasing or decreasing? A. It is increasing with enormous rapidity.

Q. Give the figures. A. In 1873 the world's gold production was $96,200,000; in 1880 it was $106,436,800. In the year 1890 it was $118,849,000. In 1894 it was $180,626,100. For 1895 it was $203,000,000, and the mint estimate for 1896 is $220,000,000.

Q. What does this mean? A. It means that the amount of gold annually added to the world's money supply has more than doubled in the last twenty-three years.

Q. Is not this annual rate of production liable to decrease? A. On the contrary, all experts in the American, Australian, and South African gold fields look for a further and very heavy increase over the present rate of production.

Q. But has not the disuse of silver with full coinage facilities cut down the total annual addition to the world's metallic money supply? A. It has not.

Q. Why? A. In 1873 the world's gold production was $96,200,000; its silver production, $81,800,000; total, $178,000,000. Last year the production of *gold alone* was $203,000,000.

Q. Was not the combined annual production of gold and silver larger than this at the time of the Californian and Australian gold discoveries? A. It was not.

Q. What was the highest record of that period? A. Between 1856 and 1860, the world's average annual production of gold was $134,083,000; of silver, $37,618,000; total, $171,701,000; or less, by $31,800,000, than last year's production of gold alone.

Q. What are we to say, then, of the argument that the money supply, since silver free coinage was abandoned, has been contracting? A. That it is utterly false as applied to the world at large, and especially so as applied to the United States.

### THE FALL IN PRICES.

Q. Is it true, nevertheless, that the prices of wheat and many other farm products have fallen heavily? A. It is.

Q. How are such declines, in wheat for instance, to be explained? A. By the enormously rapid increase in grain-growing area throughout the world.

Q. Has this increase been especially rapid since 1872? A. The increase in grain-growing area in this period, especially in North America, South America, and Asia, has never been approached in any equal period in the history of the world.

Q. How do we judge of actual competition in the sale of wheat? A. By the supplies thrown annually on the world's great distributing markets.

Q. What market in particular? A. England, where most of the buying nations go to purchase their grain.

Q. What are the figures? A. As recently as 1880 Great Britain imported, for consumption and reëxport, 55,261,924 hundredweight of wheat—a large increase over the preceding annual average. In 1895 it imported 81,749,955 hundredweight.

Q. What has made possible this remarkable increase in wheat production? A. The exceedingly rapid development of transportation facilities in newly cultivated grain countries; among them India, Russia, and the Argentine Republic.

Q. Has there been an increase in the United States itself? A. An enormous increase.

Q. How large? A. In 1875 there were 26,381,512 acres of wheat cultivated in this country; in 1891 there were 39,916,897, an increase of 50 per cent. The yield in 1875 was 292,136,000 bushels, a heavy increase over preceding years. In 1891 the yield was 611,780,000. Even last year, with a greatly reduced acreage and a partial crop failure, the yield was 467,100,000 bushels.

Q. Has the yield of other crops increased correspondingly? A. It has.

Q. Give instances. A. The cultivated area of corn in the United States in 1871 was 34,091,137 acres; in 1891 it was 76,204,515; increase, 124 per cent. The yield of corn last year was more than double that of any year prior to 1875. Both the acreage and the average annual yield of oats have doubled since 1871. Our cotton crop in 1894 was 50 per cent. greater than in any year prior to 1887.

Q. Was a decline in grain and cotton prices, under such conditions, inevitable? A. As inevitable as a decline in the price of clothing, or furniture, or books, or steel rails, or pins, when competition in their manufacture has extended enormously.

Q. Would free coinage help the producers of grain to a larger profit, under such conditions? A. Not in the least.

Q. Why not? A. Because if the nominal price of grain were to rise through inflation of the currency, the price of everything else would rise also, and the farmer would be relatively no better off than he was before.

Q. Do the free-coinage advocates use in their speeches these statistical facts which we have examined? A. They do not.

Q. Can the subject be understood without examining them? A. It cannot; the whole question rests on these facts regarding money and production.

Q. Why do the free-coinage speakers not use these facts and figures? A. Because the facts and figures are against them.

Q. Is there any dispute over the truth of the figures quoted in these answers? A. They are undisputed, even by free-coinage men. They are taken from the reports of the United States Treasury, of the Department of Agriculture, of the Director of the United States Mint, of the United States Bureau of Statistics, and of the British Board of Trade; each of them, in its respective sphere, the highest known authority.

### FREE COINAGE AND WAGES.

Q. What have we proved by examining the statistics of money supply and production? A. Three facts: (1) that the money supply of this country and of the world at large is not contracting, but increasing rapidly; (2) that the low price of farm products is caused by increased production, not by contraction of the currency; and (3) that the farmer's condition would not be at all improved by free coinage of silver.

Q. Do not many of our fellow citizens, however, believe that free coinage will make them prosperous? A. They do.

Q. Why not try the experiment, then, and satisfy these people? A. Because the experiment would involve general ruin and distress.

Q. Would the rich suffer most from such an experiment? A. They would suffer least of all.

Q. Who would chiefly suffer? A. All wage-earners, all employees at fixed salaries, all depositors in savings banks, all holders of life insurance policies, all veterans receiving government pensions, and finally all purchasers of food, clothing, and other necessaries of life.

Q. Why would free coinage harm the wage-earners? A. Because their income would remain unchanged, or would change but slightly, while their living expenses would increase enormously.

8.04

Q. Why would their expenses increase under free coinage? A. Because of the violent, general, and permanent rise of prices.

Q. Would such a rise in prices be inevitable? A. It would necessarily follow the lowering of the money standard.

Q. Would everything which a wage-earner buys advance in price? A. Everything; there could be no exception.

Q. But would not wages and salaries advance correspondingly? A. All of the world's experience in currency inflation proves that they would not.

Q. Has this country had any experience in the results of such currency experiments? A. It has.

Q. When? A. Between 1860 and 1865, when the gold standard was abandoned and the currency inflated with paper money.

Q. Did prices in that period rise faster than incomes? A. Very much faster.

Q. Give the figures. A. Between 1860 and 1865 the inflation of the currency caused an increase, in the average price of all articles in this country, of 116 per cent.

Q. What was the increase in wages? A. During the same period wages increased on the average 43 per cent., against the increase of 116 per cent. in prices.

Q. What did this mean? A. It meant that the cost of living increased nearly three times as fast as wages and salaries.

Q. Where are these figures obtained? A. From an expert investigation made in 1892, by order of the United States Senate. This investigation covered actual market prices of all articles for a series of years, and actual wages in all employments. Its report is standard authority.

Q. Is the United States Senate's report our only witness to the high prices of 1865? A. Its figures are confirmed by the newspapers of the period, which may be consulted at any large public library.

Q. Give some of the actual prices. A. A barrel of flour in 1860 cost $8.25, in 1866 it cost $16.25. A pound of butter cost 17 cents in 1860, in 1865 it cost 55 cents. In 1860 a pound of coffee cost 11½ cents, in 1864 it cost 43 cents. A Brussels carpet cost $1.20 per yard in 1860, in 1864 the cost per yard was $3.50. A ton of coal cost $4 in 1860, in 1865 it cost $10. These are only wholesale prices; retail prices rose even faster.

Q. Give some actual comparisons of wages. A Day-laborers' wages in the mechanical trades of cities rose, on the average, only from $1 a day in 1860 to $1.50 in 1865. Average compositors' wages rose only from $1.66 to $2.50. Locomotive engineers in the East averaged $2.30 a day in 1860, $2.88 in 1865.

Q. What was the result, with such people as these, of the abandonment of the gold standard? A. Inability to live as they had lived before, and in many cases suffering and want.

Q. What other classes of people suffered? A. People with small salaries: clerks, bookkeepers, teachers, clergymen, store salesmen, railway employees. Few of such salaries increased as much as 50 per cent., but the cost of living doubled.

Q. Who else experienced hardship? A. All families living on an insurance fund left at the death of a husband or father. All people drawing interest on savings-bank deposits. All government pensioners. The income of these people did not increase at all, but prices of what they had to buy went up 116 per cent.

Q. Would the experience of all such people be the same under free silver coinage? A. There could be no other result.

Q. Might not wages and salaries rise faster now, under currency inflation, than they did after 1860? A. They could not rise as fast.

Q. Why? A. Because in those years the army enlistment of laborers and salaried employees had made the home demand for labor abnormally active.

Q. What, then, do the free-coinage leaders ask of the wage-earner, the salaried man, and the savings-bank depositor? A. His vote to increase the cost of living.

Q. Is this a reasonable request? A. As reasonable as if they asked him to vote for lower wages.

### ARE LOWER PRICES AN EVIL?

Q. Has the decline in prices during this generation been a misfortune to the American people? A. It has not.

Q. Why not? A. Because people whose earnings are small can now enjoy comforts such as never before in the history of the world were within their reach.

Q. But have not wages fallen since 1872, along with prices? A. They have not; in the great majority of cases they are higher.

Q. How is it possible that producers and manufacturers should pay higher wages, when prices of their products have declined? A. Prices declined because of great improvements and economies in production; the laborers' share was therefore increased.

Q. Is this true with grain production? A. Even with grain.

Q. What has been the chief result of the decline in the price of grain? A. Plenty of food within reach of everybody.

Q. Was this true before the recent enormous increase in the world's grain product? A. It was not.

Q. What was one familiar incident of the earlier part of this century? A. Famine.

Q. Caused by what? A. Frequent scarcity and high prices for food.

Q. When was the last destructive and fatal famine? A. In Russia, in 1891.

Q. What followed that famine? A. Cultivation of new grain country all over the world, immense additions to the grain in storehouses, and a great decline in the price of wheat.

Q. Is the world likely, under these new conditions, again to witness widespread famine? A. Probably never again.

Q. Is not this a gain to civilization? A. Combined with the cheapened cost of clothing, it is one of the greatest blessings of modern history.

Q. Do the free-coinage advocates describe this cheapening of food and clothing as a blessing? A. They denounce it as a curse.

Q. Where, for instance, is it so denounced? A. In last June's address of the silver leaders to the American people.

Q. Is it the purpose of these leaders to put an end to these low prices? A. Their words leave no doubt on that point.

Q. Can such an attempt be successful? A. Only when the wage-earners of the United States vote to substitute poverty for comfort, want for plenty.

Q. Are the wage-earners likely to do this? A. Not if they retain possession of their senses.

### WHAT IS MEANT BY 16 TO 1?

Q. What is the meaning of free coinage at 16 to 1? A. It means that sixteen ounces of silver shall have the same debt-paying power in this country as one ounce of gold.

Q. Does this mean silver produced in the United States only? A. It means all the silver in the world, in whatever form it may exist.

Q. What is the present market value of silver as compared with gold? A. Sixty-eight and three-quarter cents per ounce.

Q. What ratio between the two metals does that price correspond to? A. About 30 to 1.

Q. What would the silver dollar be worth under free coinage, as compared with the gold dollar? A. About 53 cents.

Q. What would be the effect of free coinage at 16 to 1 on the prices of commodities? A. The prices of all imported and exported commodities would immediately rise in the proportion of 53 to 100. That is, every such article which can now be obtained for 53 cents would cost $1. Other articles would rise eventually in the same proportion, but more slowly.

Q. What would be the effect on wages? A. The first effect would be great confusion, because all business would be disarranged. Many employers would fail, and many workmen would be out of a job in consequence. Since wages do not rise spontaneously, the workingmen would at first lose 47 per cent. of their pay; that is, they would nominally receive their present wages, but it would be worth only 53 cents on the dollar in the purchase of commodities.

Q. How could they recoup themselves? A. Only by successful strikes or by voluntary concessions of their employers.

### WHAT MONEY OUGHT TO BE.

Q. What is the indispensable quality and first requisite of money? A. That it should be universally acceptable.

Q. Is there any kind of money universally acceptable but gold? A. There is not.

Q. Would not silver be equally acceptable if it were equally legal tender? A. Silver dollars are legal tender. Give any man the option of taking one hundred of these pieces or ten gold pieces of $10 each and he will choose the latter. Therefore they are not equally acceptable.

Q. Is the difference in weight the only reason why gold is more acceptable than silver? A. It was the only reason when civilized nations made their choice between the two.

Q. What reasons exist now that did not exist then? A. A variation of 50 per cent. has taken place in the value of the two metals. In addition to being sixteen times as heavy, silver has lost one-half of its value during the interval.

Q. Have you mentioned all the reasons why gold is acceptable as money and silver is not? A. The most decisive reason is that the civilized world has adjusted itself to the gold standard during a long period of time. All business is bottomed on it. It is an accomplished fact co-extensive with the commercial world. To change to another standard would be literally turning the commercial world upside down.

Q. Is the preference for gold universal? A. It is universal among civilized men. Even the silver advocates in the United States prefer gold in their business affairs. Senator Stewart of Nevada makes his mortgages payable in gold. When he was reproved for this bad example, he said that he merely followed the universal custom on the Pacific Coast, where he lives. So we have his authority for the statement that in the section of the Union where the demand for silver is most vociferous everybody prefers gold in his private business.

Q. Can you give any other examples? A. Gov. Altgeld, the chief of the free-silver movement in Illinois, is a gold man in his private business. He is the president and largest stockholder of the Unity Building Co. in Chicago. All the rents of this building are made payable " in standard gold coin of the United States." The New York *Herald* published a fac-simile of one of these leases in its issue of July 15.

Q. Can you give any other examples? A. The Territory of Arizona brought a bill before Congress two or three years ago, asking authority to issue bonds payable specifically in gold, on the ground that the money could be borrowed at a considerably lower rate of interest than if they were payable in dollars without specifying the kind of dollars. The State of Utah last June negotiated a specific gold loan for the same reason. Yet both Arizona and Utah are politically for silver.

Q. What do these acts signify? A. Two things: First, that gold is preferable to silver in the general estimation of mankind; second, that payment in gold is an advantage to borrowers.

### GOLD STANDARD AND THE POOR.

Q. What do the free-coinage leaders especially charge against the gold standard? A. They declare that it has helped the rich, and has caused distress and loss to everybody else.

Q. Is this statement true? A. It is not.

Q. Suppose the gold standard had worked injury to every one except the rich; how should we know the fact? A. People with small incomes would have been growing steadily poorer since the gold standard was adopted.

Q. Have such people been growing poorer? A. On the contrary, their prosperity, since this country returned to the gold standard in 1879, has increased in an unprecedented degree.

Q. What proof have you of this? A. The increase in savings-banks deposits.

Q. By whom are such deposits made? A. They consist almost entirely of the surplus income of tradesmen, wage-earners, and small producers.

Q. What are the figures of these deposits? A. In 1879, the total savings-bank deposits in the United States were $802,490,298; in 1895 they were $1,844,357,798; increase, $1,041,867,500, or 129 per cent.

Q. What is your authority for these figures? A. The official statements of the savings banks to the United States government, published in the reports of the Comptroller of the Currency.

Q. What do the figures show? A. They show that during the seventeen years since this country's return to the single gold standard the savings of its poorer people have been a thousand million dollars larger than they were in any preceding period.

Q. Are the savings-bank deposits our only proof that the people have prospered under the gold standard? A. The building and loan associations are another striking proof.

Q. Who are the depositors with building and loan associations? A. Chiefly wage-earners, tradesmen, and people with small salaries.

Q. What do the reports of these associations show? A. Twelve years ago the deposits with such associations were comparatively insignificant. In 1892 the returns of the United States Department of Labor showed the aggregate to be $500,000,000. To-day the total of these deposits in this country is estimated at $750,000,000.

Q. How do all these figures compare with savings-bank deposits and with building and loan association accounts in countries now on a silver standard? A. Such countries have neither savings banks nor building and loan associations.

Q. Why? A. Presumably because the wage-earners in those countries have no savings to deposit

### GOLD STANDARD AND LIVING EXPENSES.

Q. How do you explain so enormous an amount in the savings of our people? A. Wages have increased since the return to the gold standard. Great improvements and extension of production have lowered prices and reduced the cost of living. This has necessarily increased the people's savings.

Q. What is your authority for stating that wages have increased since our adoption of the gold standard? A. The highest known authority, the United States Senate report of 1892, already referred to in this Catechism.

Q. How much does this report show average wages to have increased since the resumption of specie payments? A. Up to the latest date covered by the report, they had increased 20¾ per cent. In many industries the increase had been much larger.

Q. Then the average wage-earner's income has increased under the gold standard, while living expenses have decreased for everybody? A. Such are the facts.

Q. Would this advantage continue under free silver coinage? A. It could not. We have already shown that wages would not increase spontaneously if at all, while prices for necessaries of life would rise rapidly.

Q. Do the free coinage leaders admit this certain rise in prices? A. They do; they declare that all prices are now too low, and that free coinage will raise them.

Q. But do not these people claim that high prices for food, clothing and household necessaries will cause general contentment and prosperity? A. They do.

Q. How can we be sure that they are not right? A. Read up the record of years when currency inflation had caused high prices in this country. Look into the condition of other countries where prices now are high under a silver standard.

Q. When were prices and living expenses highest in this country? A. In 1865 and 1866.

Q. What did the American people of that time think of the high prices? A. They complained bitterly.

Q. Where can we find any record of such complaint? A. Go to a public library and read the newspapers of those years.

Q. Give some illustrations. A. In 1865 the New York papers seriously advised people to stop eating meat, in order to check the high prices. Letters from readers published in these papers complained that milk, butter, coal and ice were almost beyond the poor man's reach. One letter, in the New York *Times* of June 29, 1835, deserves to be quoted: "All last winter," the writer says, "I could hardly afford to buy any meat. The little bits of beef and mutton that we poor people buy cost so much that my wife says it is like eating money." You can readily consult all these published letters.

Q. Would people object to high prices now as much as they did then? A. Every head of a family and housekeeper is competent to answer this question.

Q. If prices advanced under free coinage, would not the employer of labor be able to pay very much higher wages? A. His own living expenses would increase as fast as his income, his business would be thrown into confusion, and all his profits would become a matter of speculation.

Q. Was this his experience when prices rose before 1865? A. It was emphatically his experience.

Q. But surely, if the money supply increased, the wage-earner would get his share? A. He could get no more than his employer paid him.

Q. But might not his employer advance wages simply because the money supply had increased? A. We leave the answer to this question to the wage-earner himself.

### GOLD STANDARD AND THE FARMER.

Q. What do the free-coinage advocates commonly answer when they are confronted with the facts already stated in this Catechism? A. They reply that whether the gold standard of currency has helped the wage-earner or not, it has seriously hurt the farmer.

Q. What do they allege to be the average farmer's condition? A. They declare that as a result of the gold standard the farmers of this country have fallen into a desperate state of poverty.

Q. Is this true? A. It is not.

Q. How can you prove that it is not true? A. By the fact that farmers have been buying more farm land under the gold standard of currency and raising more crops. By the fact that farmers in many Western states are paying off their mortgages. By the fact that in the grain country, outside of parts of Kansas and Nebraska, farm lands are selling for much more than they brought half a dozen years ago. Finally, by the personal testimony of experts.

Q. How do you know that the farmers are buying more land? A. By the increase in acreage planted.

Q. Give the figures. A. In 1872 the combined acreage of wheat, corn, oats, barley and buckwheat in the United States was 65,428,119; in 1894 it was 128,428,092; increase nearly 100 per cent. This year's acreage is not greatly changed from 1894.

Q. Would this increase have been possible if farming had been a losing enterprise? A. Certainly not. When people find that they are losing money in a business they are apt to stop that business altogether. The last thing they do is to extend the same business to double its former magnitude.

Q. How do you know that farmers are paying off their mortgages? A. By the best of authority, the statements of the loan and mortgage companies which lent the money.

Q. Can you give any instance? A. One company, the New England Loan and Trust, lately published, in an official statement to its security-holders, the fact that $198,944 in farm mortgages were paid off during last March alone. Of this amount $92,044 was paid before the principal was due.

Q. How do you know that farm lands have risen in value? A. In Iowa particularly we base our information on numerous deeds of sale made within the last year or two, showing advances of 10 to 20 per cent., within four to ten years, in the value of land sold.

Q. Have all farm lands risen in value? A. Not all.

Q. Where are the chief exceptions? A. In parts of Kansas, where the uncertain climate has made the original purchase a bad investment; in parts of Nebraska, where the rainfall is uncertain, and where the opening of Oklahoma lowered the price of all neighboring farm country. These were the unlucky experiments, such as are found in every trade.

Q. What personal testimony have you as to farming conditions generally? A. Mr. Prime, the well-known crop expert, and a thoroughly unbiased authority, lately said in a published interview: "The farmers in the West were never so well off as they are to day. They never had so much to eat and drink, or better clothes to wear, or owed so little."

Q. But is it not true that almost all the farmers are heavily in debt? A. It is not.

Q. How do you know they are not? A. By the statistics of the United States census.

Q. What do these statistics show? A. By the census of 1890 there were in the six states of Iowa, Kansas, Nebraska, Minnesota, North Dakota and South Dakota 720,479 families cultivating farms. Of this number 248,750 families had mortgages on their farms, 230,728 owned their farms free, while 241,001 rented their farms, and therefore had nothing to do with mortgages.

Q. What does this signify? A. It signifies that in six representative far Western grain states hardly one-third of the cultivators of farms have on their land any mortgages whatever.

Q. But are not the farmers in the South more heavily in debt than this?
A. The proportion of Southern farmers under a mortgage is wholly insignificant.

Q. Give some figures. A. By the 1890 census families owning farms free in Kentucky numbered 118,080; families owning mortgaged farms numbered 4,991. In Tennessee farms owned outright were 103,346; mortgaged farms, 3,431. In Alabama the proportion was 68,798 to 3,131; in Georgia it was 71,116 to 2,491; in North Carolina, 101,321 to 5,202.

Q. Would not free silver coinage help the farmers to a larger export trade?
A. Not unless they sold their grain abroad for a lower price than they sell it now, because they must sell in competition with all the world.

Q. But if gold was at a premium would it not be a profit to the farmer to sell his grain abroad for gold, and then sell his gold here for depreciated silver? A. Everything he wished to buy with depreciated silver—clothing, carpets, furniture, farm implements—would rise exactly as much.

Q. Would not the country's export trade be helped by free silver coinage?
A. Our export trade has increased since the demonetization of silver and since our adoption of the gold standard more rapidly than ever before.

Q. How large was this increase? A. Since 1872 the annual exports of the United States have increased 134 per cent.

Q. In what products was this export increase largest? A. In products of the farm.

Q. Comprising what? A. Grain, cotton, tobacco, meat, live cattle, sheep and hogs.

Q. What was the increase in these products? A. In 1872 we exported $354,906,637 worth; in 1878, $515,955,203; in 1892, $754,480,843.

Q. What do you conclude from all these facts? A. That in spite of occasional set-backs, occasional poor harvests and occasional mistakes in farm land investment the farmer in the United States has prospered under the gold standard, and will prosper under its continuance, and that all the "racket" to the contrary is made by the few who have failed and by noisy demagogues.

### PROSPERITY UNDER A GOLD STANDARD.

Q. Does the gold now produced by the world go freely into money circulation? A. It does.

Q. How can you prove that fact? A. By the annual coinage statements of the leading gold-producing and gold-importing nations, all of which show a steady increase. By the amount of gold in the world's great depository banks, which has increased with equal rapidity. These are perfectly trustworthy signs.

Q. Is it not true that most of the new supply is "cornered" by the Rothschilds? A. There is not the slightest reason for supposing such a thing.

' Q. But if the world's gold supply has been increasing so rapidly, and is not "cornered," why has it grown harder every year for our government to maintain its own gold reserve? A. Because of the free silver coinage movement in this country.

Q. How can that movement affect our gold reserve? A. First, by forcing so much new silver and paper money into circulation that nobody pays gold any longer to the government. Second, by the threat that the free-coinage party will redeem the government notes and bonds in silver only, which causes holders of the notes to present them now for gold.

Q. Why should such holders present their government notes for redemption now? A. For the same reason that made people, in the good old state bank days, rush in for redemption the notes of a bank which was likely to stop payment.

Q. Are there not other nations than our own whose currency requires a large gold resrve? A. There are.

Q. What nations, for instance? A. Germany, France, England.

Q. Do not these countries have the same trouble with their gold reserve as our Treasury does? A. Not in the least. The gold reserve in each of these three countries is larger than necessary, and is constantly increasing.

Q. Why is their situation so different from ours? A. Because there has been no doubt of the money standard in Germany, France or England.

Q. But has not the United States always had especial trouble in getting gold for its currency? A. It has not.

Q. When did it get gold easily? A. It was in 1834, when the gold standard was adopted, and in 1861, when paper money was substituted and the gold standard abandoned.

Q. Did gold flow in readily at any other period? A. It did.

Q. When? A. After the resumption of specie payments by the United States in 1879, which was accepted by the world as our readoption of the gold standard.

Q. What followed that resumption of specie payments? A. Within two years, $174,000.000 gold was sent to us from Europe.

Q. But surely this gold did not go into the Treasury? A. More of it than the Treasury needed went in.

Q. How do you know that? A. As early as September 19, 1879 the Secretary of the Treasury announced that "gold coin, beyond the needs of the government, had accumulated in the Treasury," and authorized the use of gold in regular Treasury expenditures.

Q. Were those two years a period of prosperity? A. For this country, a period of unparalleled prosperity.

Q. How long did this prosperity last? A. Until the silver-coinage movement was again threatening our maintenance of the gold standard.

## A FREE COINAGE CATECHISM.

Q. What happened then? A. Gold payments into the Treasury almost ceased, and gold withdrawals through redemption of government notes grew larger.

Q. Suppose all the gold in the Treasury reserve were to be used up; what would happen? A. The government could not pay gold coin to the holders of its notes.

Q. What difference would that make to a holder of a government note—say of a dollar bill—who did not care to use gold? A. His dollar bill would depreciate along with all other government notes. Since it no longer could exchange for a dollar in gold, it would no longer buy what a dollar in gold would buy.

Q. How would such depreciation show itself? A. By an artificial and general rise in prices, without a rise in wages and salaries.

Q. Has this ever actually happened? A. During our civil war, when the gold standard was abandoned, the government paper money depreciated to 50 per cent. of its gold value, the gold premium rose above 100, and there was a frightful advance in prices.

B. Then would suspension of gold payment on government notes injure all holders of such notes? A. Sooner or later, it would cheat every man with a dollar bill in his pocket.

## PRINCIPLES OF MONEY AND BANKING.*

### THE NATURE AND USE OF MONEY.

Everybody wants to "make money," and few think they need any instruction as to its "use." But in this sense the word money is used in a loose way instead of the word wealth, and a great deal of harm has come from this confusion of terms. From it, indeed, came the notion that a country grows wealthy in proportion as money is kept from going out of it, and the belief that government can make wealth by coining money or issuing paper as a substitute for money. Money is simply that kind of wealth commonly current in exchange, and whose terms are used for valuations. It is peculiarly useful as a medium of exchange and as a measure of value, but otherwise and for itself it may be one of the least desirable forms of wealth.

Just as a boy contrives "pin-money" to help out his "swaps," so the early nations contrived money to get rid of inconveniences in direct barter. The shoemaker does not often want a hat just when the hatter wants a pair of shoes, nor can the hatter conveniently take one shoe for his hat or the shoemaker take two hats for his pair of shoes. Money, as a common medium of exchange, enables us to do away with the "double coincidence of wants and possessions," for which barter waits. We accomplish half our exchange—that is, the shoemaker sells his shoes, and holds the purchasing power in suspense—that is, the shoemaker keeps the money till he wants a hat or something else. Or, if the shoemaker sells on credit, he uses the terms of money to record the indebtedness of the buyer in his books. The use of money, instead of barter, is one of the great steps of progress; the seller can now buy when, where, and as he desires.

The first use of money, then, is as the *common medium* of exchange; any one will take it anywhere for any goods, and it enables one to buy as much or as little as he wants. It is the highway of exchange, enabling any producer to deal with any consumer, and so fulfilling the first condition of wealth, of getting most for least labor. Second, money becomes in this way a *common measure* of value, or common "value-denominator" by which the values of all other things are compared. A price-current in money is understood by all, and a hundred articles are priced in a hundred items, instead of in the 4950 it would take if we priced each article in terms of every other. This furnishes a universal language of trade. Third, money is a *standard* of values, or measure for deferred payments. This is the use in "credit," which is purchase in which

---

\* Chapters reprinted from Bowker's "Economics for the People," (copyright, 1886, 1892, by R. R. Bowker), revised by the author to date, by permission of Messrs. Harper & Brothers.

payment is put off. The word comes from the Latin word *credo*, "I believe," for it is given in the belief that the debtor will pay. A promise to pay at a future time is expressed in terms of money in preference to other commodities, because people understand this term and because they look upon money as of staple value. Fourth, money becomes thus a convenient *storer* of values, so that men can buy when they desire, now or in the future, to best advantage, There are here two distinct kinds of use—one direct, as the common medium in actual use in exchange ; the other indirect, as a common measure, standard, and storer of values, in which not money itself but its terms are used.

These two kinds of use—the use of the thing and the use of the name, or the direct use and the representative use of money—must be kept very clearly in mind. A farmer who says to his boy, "Go to the wheat-bin and get me a bushel," may mean a bushel of wheat or a bushel-measure : it is important for the boy to find out which. The word money or the word dollar admits of this same double sense. There is the same difference between a dollar which represents cost of production, or labor-value, and a dollar which is simply a name printed on a piece of paper, that there is between a "bushel" of wheat and a "bushel" measure. The one is good in itself; the other is useless except so far as it is generally accepted to measure real products.

Different nations have used different kinds of wealth as the common medium of exchange, which was the use for which money came into being. Our word "capital" comes from the Latin *caput*, a head, as does the word "cattle," and like "pecuniary," coming from the Latin *pecunia*, wealth, *pecus,* a herd, *pecu*, cattle, points to the early use of cattle and sheep as money by the Greeks, Romans and Germans. But these, though they could be driven about, could not be easily carried or divided ; and wheat was also used by the old nations as soon as they became farmers as well as herdsmen, doubtless partly as "small change." Most of the barbarous nations selected that kind of wealth most current (whence our word currency), most easy to carry and most easy to handle in small as well as large quantities. Dates were used by some African tribes, rock salt by the Abyssinians, olive oil by the Ionian islanders, tea compressed in small cakes by the Russians, tobacco by the early American planters. The fees of the Clerk of the Supreme Court of the United States, in cases where the Government is a party, were long reckoned, following old Maryland customs, in pounds of tobacco, and settled according to an old legal valuation of tobacco. All these kinds of money recognize that the sound basis for money-value is wealth—something which has cost proportionate labor.

In the progress of civilization it was found that the metals were the most convenient kind of wealth to use as money. Iron was used by the Spartans, lead by the early Romans and early English, tin by Swedes, Mexicans and other people, copper or bronze by almost all nations. All of these, of course, cost a certain amount of labor to mine them. At last it became settled that the two "precious metals," gold and silver, were most convenient of all. A third, platinum, was used for a little time in Russia. The two precious metals meet every condition for good money: they cost such an amount of labor as to make them convenient to handle within the common range of buying and selling; they have utility as ornaments and in many industrial arts; they are thus easily transferable and universally acceptable; they are almost imperishable, not wasting greatly either by handling, or rust, or conversion into coin and back again, and their fusibility and ductility render them accurately divisible. These, with copper or an equivalent as "small change" or token currency, are the money of the trading world; and as gold possesses most of the qualities named in even greater degree than silver, there is evident a tendency toward the use of that metal as the one final standard among the most civilized nations. The nature of "paper-money," so called, or substitute-money, we have yet to consider.

### GOLD AND SILVER AS STANDARD MONEY.

"And Abraham weighed to Ephron the silver . . . four hundred shekels of silver, current money with the merchant" (Genesis xxiii. 16). This first record of a business transaction shows clearly the origin of metal money—it was so much weight of metal. "Shekel" meant a "weight" (about half an ounce Troy), just as the English "pound" was at first a pound weight of silver. The shekel, later on (Exodus xxxviii. 24), was measured "after the shekel of the sanctuary," probably a standard of weight kept in the temple, like the standard weights now kept by each nation, by which its coinage is regulated. But the "shekel of gold" came to mean less weight than the "shekel of silver," so that a standard was kept for each—probably a result of just such changes in the value of the two kinds of money as we see in later times.

Gold and silver have been found in almost all countries, and they were early used as money. Men soon found that it was easier to count than to weigh with scales. This led to coinage, the making of pieces of metal of fixed weight and fineness, whose value is shown by the stamp. The rude Abyssinians make their rock-salt into bars a foot long and three inches square, which serve the same purpose. In the early days, when all trading was a matter of honor, sealed bags of gold-dust passed at a fixed value. When public opinion made a dishonored man a social outcast, there was little cheating. Rings and the Chinese "cash" (dating to 2500 B. C.) were early forms of metal-money. Our modern coin, the round, flat piece, stamped on both sides, is traced back to the Greek Pheidon, king in Argos, about 750 B. C. The old coins were of irregular edge, which could be easily clipped or filed; the edge is now "milled" by a machine invented in 1685, so that modern coins are protected against all loss but wear. To make this as little as possible, an "alloy" of harder metal is mixed with gold or silver—in the United States coins one-tenth copper alloy to nine-tenths fine metal, in the English coins one-twelfth—but only the precious metal is reckoned in valuing the coin. In old times a coigne, or wedge, like the printer's quoin, was used in stamping, whence our word "coin." The Roman coins were made in the Temple of Juno Moneta, whence our word mint, the factory where money is coined, as well as the word money itself.

Gold and silver are used as money partly because they last longer, so that each year's product adds but a small proportion to the existing stock, and vary less in value than almost any other things. Nevertheless, they have varied in value, according to supply and demand; at one period both together, when all prices, or values of other things in money, rose as they fell, in recent times silver falling greatly relatively to gold. Silver had been of equal value with gold in some barbarous countries. In Japan, when it was opened to foreigners, it took but four times the weight in silver to equal in value the same weight in gold; among the Greeks, before Xenophon, it took $13\frac{1}{3}$; later, and among the Romans, 12 times, though it is said only 9 to $7\frac{1}{2}$ times the weight of silver equaled gold after the return of Julius Cæsar. During the Christian era the rate has varied in different times and in different countries at the same time, being in the early centuries about $12\frac{1}{2}$; later on as high for silver as $9\frac{3}{8}$ in England (1262), and $10\frac{1}{10}$ in Spain (1500); in 1641, about 12 in Germany, $13\frac{1}{4}$ in England, $13\frac{1}{2}$ in France; in 1724, $14\frac{1}{4}$ in France, $15\frac{1}{2}$ in England; in the present French coinage $15\frac{1}{2}$ and in the English $14\frac{1}{2}$, while the market rate for silver bullion has of recent years ruled much below $15\frac{1}{2}$, and has been as low as 32 weights of silver for the same weight in gold.

It is agreed on all sides that steady money is most important for sound business. "Mono-metallists" assert that only one kind of metal can properly be used as a standard, by preference gold, because silver must always have "ups and downs" in relation to gold, and first one and then the other would be used in business according to which was cheapest, if both were "standards." "Bi-metallists" assert that the world needs both gold and silver for standard money, and say that if civilized countries would unite in coining silver at a fixed rate of $15\frac{1}{2}$ or 16 to 1 gold, there would be no serious derangement. Most economists favor the single gold standard. The question has been made a political one, and two international conferences have been held, without reaching results. Great Britain and its Australian and American colonies, Germany, Scandinavia and Chili are the chief gold-standard countries, using silver as "legal tender" only for small sums; Russia, India, China and Japan, Mexico and Central America use a single standard of silver. The double standard is maintained by France, Italy, Belgium, Switzerland and Greece, which are bound into the "Latin Union," by Spain, and by the United States. Silver, which up to the fourteenth century was chiefly used for coinage, seems to remain the money of the less civilized countries; the general tendency seems to be in favor of a single standard, and that gold.

But the two metals, used as money, have also had their "ups and downs" together. There was in circulation in the Roman empire in the time of Christ (so Mr. Jacobs estimates) about $1,790,000,000 gold and silver. With the decline of the empire and the invasion of the Goths mining practically stopped, and the loss and wear of coined money reduced the stock in Europe by the year 800 to less than $168,000,000, a point at which it was kept, by the revival of mining, until the discovery of America in 1492. Meanwhile money had greatly risen in value; it required only £3 10s. weekly ($17.50) for the subsistence of King Henry VI. and ten retainers while prisoners (1470) of Edward IV. The discovery of America began a new chapter in the history of money; after the opening of the great silver mines of Potosi in 1545, and the invention by a Mexican miner of the process of amalgamating silver with mercury, over $10,000,000 yearly was sent to Europe. Money fell rapidly; the price of corn rose in England from 2s. to 6s. and 8s. per quarter; prices generally rose fourfold; debts were made almost nothing; and to the ensuing derangement and distress historians trace the beginning of English pauperism, and those money troubles of Charles I. which led to the great rebellion.

About 1809 Europe had $1,900,000,000 metal money in circulation, but the Spanish-American revolutions reduced the silver supply, and the product of the Ural gold-mines, opened in 1823, did not make good the loss, so that in 1829 the stock was down to $1,566,000,000. The discoveries of gold in California (1848) and Australia (1851) again changed the face of things. The annual yield of gold and silver, over two-thirds gold, while before it had been two-thirds silver, rose to $190,000,000 and over; and economists, who had feared a disastrous rise in prices, now began to fear as disastrous a fall. It is estimated that the commercial countries had in 1895 about $8,000,000,000 coin and bullion, about half gold, of which the United States has $618,000,000 gold and $625,000,000 silver; France, $850,000,000 gold and $487,000,000 silver; Great Britain $580,000,000 gold and $115,000,000 silver; and Germany, $625,000,000 gold and $215,000,000 silver. The opening of the Nevada and Colorado mines has increased the relative production of silver; out of the world's product (1895) of $203,000,000 gold and $226,000,000 silver (U. S. coinage value), the United States supplied $46,000,000 gold and $72,000,000 silver, or one-third. Silver in the London market has fallen as low as 32 to 1. But the great increase in money seems to have been offset by the increased productive activity brought about by machinery and by other causes.

Variations in prices from period to period have led economists, and particularly Professor Jevons, to urge the use of a "tabular or multiple standard of value" to reckon payments which are to be made many years off. Some of the long English leases of land, fixed centuries ago in money, are now ridiculously small. On the other hand, the colleges of Oxford, Cambridge and Eton, receiving "corn rents," according to a law of Queen Elizabeth's time, are much better off, but the value of the rentals varies greatly from year to year. The "multiple standard," it is claimed, would avoid both these difficulties; the price of given quantities of a number of articles of common use, such as corn, potatoes, beef, wool, coal, etc., would be added together each year, and the total declared in terms of money by the Government. If it took $80 or $120 to buy what cost $100 at the first, then the payment would be $80 or $120 in money instead of $100, but it would buy exactly the same amount of goods. This is really deferred barter, so that the same equivalent in things may be paid back, without reference to the prices of the things or their value in money.

## United States Money.

During our war, when metal-money, and particularly "change," was very scarce—so that we used postage-stamps and afterward "postal currency," representing five or ten or twenty-five or fifty cents' worth of postage-stamps— a good many shopkeepers issued copper tokens "good for one cent," which passed current as money. Many of them were not good for a cent, and were never redeemed by the issuers. Probably in the early days of coinage, private people thus made coins. But now only nations do so, for "the public faith" is the best surety that coins contain so much metal of such a fineness, or will be good for the money's worth, and coinage is, as Jefferson said, "peculiarly an attribute of sovereignty." Counterfeiting was once punished in England as treason, by death; it is punishable in this country, in the case of United States notes, by fifteen years' imprisonment. It is recognized as one of the most serious crimes against property, because it undermines the very foundations of sound business, honesty in weights and measures. Even were good metal used, coining by individuals is by law a misdemeanor.

The Constitution gives to Congress the power "to coin money, regulate the value thereof and of foreign coin, and fix the standard of weights and measures," and denies to the States power to "coin money; emit bills of credit; make anything but gold and silver coin a tender in payment of debts." A clause giving Congress the power to "emit bills on the credit of the United States" was struck out in the debates, to avoid, as was said in the debates, even a "pretext for a paper currency, and particularly for making the bills a tender either for public or private debts." The Continental Congress in 1785 unanimously adopted as the money unit the "dollar," the name coming through the Spanish "dollar" from the German "thaler," or "Joachimsthaler," the Joachim thal or dale being the seat of great silver-mines where ounce-pieces were coined. The law establishing the mint, 1792, provided for a silver dollar unit of 416 grains, $371\frac{1}{4}$ grains of it fine metal, and a gold "eagle" or ten-dollar piece of 270 grains, $247\frac{1}{4}$ grains fine ("the proportionate value of gold and silver" being defined "as 15 to 1, according to quantity in weight"), besides other gold, silver, and copper coins. In 1834 and 1837, changes were made, the later law providing for coin 9-10 fine, the silver dollar weighing $412\frac{1}{2}$ grains and the gold eagle 258 grains. The present coins are: of gold, the double-eagle ($20), eagle ($10), half-eagle ($5), and quarter-eagle ($2½), the gold dollar (not coined since 1890) being the money unit with a standard weight of 25.8 grains; of silver, the dollar, half-dollar, quarter-dollar, and dime; of base metal, the five and one cent pieces. The law of 1853 provided that half dollars and other subsidiary silver coins should contain but 384 grains gross weight to the dollar, and made a seignorage charge of $\frac{1}{2}$ of one per cent. —afterwards reduced. From 1873 to 1878 the silver "trade-dollar" of 420 grains (378 fine metal) was struck, chiefly for foreign trading. It was a legal-tender, by an oversight in the law, up to five dollars, till 1876, when its legal-tender character was repealed. In 1883 Government declined to receive it at full value, people began to realize that it did not contain a dollar's worth of silver, and it fell to about 85 cents. In 1873, the gold dollar, of 25.8 grains gross weight was made "the unit of value." In 1878 Congress passed over the veto of President Hayes the Bland-Allison Act, providing for a "standard silver dollar" of $412\frac{1}{2}$ grains as an unlimited "legal tender," and the coinage of $2,000,000 to $4,000,000 of these per month, and in 1887 these were made exchangeable for the "trade dollar." The "Sherman Act" of 1890 provided for the purchase at market price of 4,500,000 ounces of silver each month, of which 2,000,000 ounces, or enough to provide for the redemption of "silver certificates," should be coined monthly, the profit or seigniorage going into the Treasury. This act was repealed in 1893, to stem the panic of that year.

The Government declares what money shall be "legal-tender" among its citizens, that is, what kind of money when tendered by a debtor shall make a legal offer to discharge a debt. If you offer to pay rent in any other kind of money than legal-tender the landlord can refuse to accept it, and can get a court to put you out as though you had refused to pay. The gold coins of the United States and the "standard silver dollar" are legal-tender for all sums; the small silver for sums not exceeding ten dollars; and the nickels or the old copper cents for sums not exceeding twenty-five cents in any one payment. The small silver and nickels issued for "change," make no pretense to full value, and are a "token money," to be redeemed by the Government. They are purposely under-weighted, so that they shall not be melted down or carried out of the country.

The word legal-tender is commonly used to signify the "United States notes" or "greenbacks," issued under the Acts of February 25, 1862, and March 3, 1863, which say on the back: "This note is a legal-tender at its face value for all debts, public and private, except duties on imports and interest on the public debt," both of which are payable in metal-money. The law signed by President Lincoln February 25, 1862, was the first making anything but gold and silver coin a legal discharge of debts, although the Continental Congress, January 4, 1777, passed a resolution asking the States to declare its bills-of-credit legal-tender, which was done by eight States. The Law of 1862 was passed as a "war measure," and included "all debts within the United States." In December, 1869, the United States Supreme Court declared that the legal-tender clause was "unnecessary and improper," that its application to pre-existing debts impaired the obligation of contracts, and that the law was therefore unconstitutional. In 1870 two vacancies on the bench were filled by President Grant; on a new case a rehearing was had, and in January, 1872, the decision was overruled, and it was held that "Congress has power to enact that the Government's promises to pay money shall be, for the time being, equivalent in value to the representation of value determined by the coinage acts." "There are times," added Justice Bradley, "when the exigencies of the State rightly absorb all subordinate considerations." This decision justified the issue of legal-tenders as a war measure; but a third decision, in March, 1884, went further, and declared, only one judge dissenting, that Congress has power at any time to authorize the issue of legal-tender notes, on the ground that this is an attribute of sovereignty not reserved or denied by the Constitution. The decision is regarded by most economists as dangerous, and it is believed that even the war could have been carried on at less final cost if other financial measures had been used.

Of course, in making metal-money it costs something to test the metal and stamp it into coins. This cost may be paid for as a general expense of the Government out of taxes, and the full weight, or face value, of metal put into the coin. This is "gratuitous coinage," and is the English practice. Some economists object that it leads jewelers to melt up new coins instead of assaying for themselves, and makes the Government pay for a "perpetual motion" of coinage. Or, this cost may be paid by deducting enough metal before making the coin. This deduction is "seigniorage," the pay of the seignior or sovereign. Up to 1853 the United States had gratuitous coinage, but in that year a seigniorage of one-half of one per cent. was established for gold coins and silver dollars, reduced in 1873 to one-fifth. Since 1875, gold coinage has been gratuitous. Both England and the United States now have "free coinage" for gold, that is, any citizen can have gold bullion (uncoined metal) made into coin by the mint on the same terms as the Government. The coinage of standard silver dollars is now determined in the United States by the redemption of "silver certificates," and is practically discontinued because of the great number in the Treasury vaults. The amount of "change" coined depends upon the public need, as determined here by the Treasury, in England by the Bank of England.

The trouble with seigniorage is, that it makes it easier for a government to debase its own coins, either by putting in less metal or by mixing in a cheaper metal. Up to 1300 (Edward I.) a "pound" really meant a pound's weight of silver, and a shilling a twentieth of that. But the coinage was again and again reduced in weight, so that for generations, it is now supposed, the English people actually weighed out their coins in settling payments. The steadiness of prices in face of a known debasement of coinage cannot otherwise be explained. Sixty-six shillings now make up a pound of silver, so that the pound sterling is but three-tenths of a pound's weight of silver. Several English monarchs, notably Henry VIII., also debased their coinage secretly by alloy. One of the Spanish gold coins, a maravedi, was debased in quality till it became only copper. People, however, may go on taking this debased money, and calling it by the old name for a long time, and one of the great economists, Ricardo, sets it down as a law of seigniorage that a debasement of coins does not itself produce depreciation of currency, so long as no more is issued than the people really need in their exchanges. This is true so long as the people are willing to take the poor money as good, either because they cannot get better, or because they do not know better, or because of habit, or because the law tells them to. But when they begin to get afraid of the debased money, and prices start up, so that a dollar in wages does not buy in cheap money what it did, and they take to barter or modify or limit their production, then come "bad times." The people who earn wages, and the small shopkeepers, feel the effect worst. This happened in 1883, when our "trade dollar" stopped circulating; the poor people and country stores could buy only 85 cents' worth with the dollar they had taken for a hundred cents.

PAPER AS MONEY.

Even the precious metals weigh a good deal, and, in large amounts, are inconvenient to carry or to keep. If, therefore, a government, or a bank, or a trustworthy person, will keep the coin for the owner, and give him paper certificates that it is held by them, he likes these better, though they are only pieces of paper, worth nothing in themselves. They are like the title-deeds of a house. The "gold certificates" and "silver certificates" of the United States are of this sort. Such paper is "representative money" in the strictest sense, since each "dollar" represents an actual dollar in metal-money, and it is "convertible" at any moment into metal-money. The metal remains unused, while the paper passes current from hand to hand in its place, as currency.

Now, a banker finds that this unused money is not called for by its real owners all at the same time. If they permit him to use or loan part of the metal, he can make a profit for them or for himself or for both by getting interest for it, keeping enough "reserve" of metal to pay the demands presented each day. The Bank of Sweden, founded in 1657, early issued "bank money," or notes undertaking to pay to the bearer at sight a certain amount of metal-money. So long as such money can actually be had on demand for the paper, this kind of paper currency is also "convertible."

If, however, the bank managers make a mistake, and do not keep enough reserve, the holders of notes may become frightened and make a "run" on the bank to get their part of the metal out before other depositors use up the supply. The bank may then have to "suspend payment" until it can "realize" on the securities it has taken for loans; that is, get real money for them. If enough people are scared to make a general "panic," it will be very hard to get the real money even by selling the securities at a loss. Thus notes which were called "convertible" become "inconvertible," because you cannot on demand convert them into the metal-money for which they are supposed to stand. Their power-in-exchange, or value, will be no longer "as good as gold," but will depend on the confidence people have in the ability of the issuer to pay by-and-by.

During the war our Government, not having enough money for its needs, said to the soldiers and the shopkeepers : "We cannot pay you money now, but we will some time; meanwhile these pieces of paper are evidences of debt, which other citizens must accept from you as money." These were the "legal-tenders," a paper currency inconvertible at the time of its issue, but which became convertible when the United States "resumed" specie payment, January 1, 1879. It was a mortgage on the earnings of the people, to be collected by future taxes. Other governments, when hard up, have done the same thing, but usually their currency has not been made good. The assignats of the French Revolution assigned to the holders the lands seized by the State, but few holders got the lands or saw their money again; our Continental currency in like manner became worth nothing. Inconvertible currency of this sort is not representative of wealth, but evidence of debt : it is promises-to-pay, or credit-money. A government may use its authority to force a loan and give such currency compulsory circulation, but its power-in-exchange, like that of inconvertible bank money, depends at once on the confidence in its being made good. In the dark days of the war greenback dollars bought less than forty cents gold would buy; and when the Government tried to prevent their further fall by prohibiting dealings in gold, people only lost confidence all the more, and greenbacks bought still less.

The economist Ricardo points out that government inconvertible currency is like a coinage debased its entire value, for the cost of printing is almost nothing. According to his "law of seigniorage," such a debased currency does not necessarily depreciate or buy less than its face-value, if no more of it is put in circulation than the public need. But usually people become afraid that it is not worth its face-value ; it falls—*i. e.*, buys less ; more is needed to make the same amount of purchases; and thus depreciation, inflation of prices, speculation, and all their train of ills set in. There have been very few cases where an inconvertible currency has kept at par (of equal value) with gold. The Bank of England notes from 1797 to 1808 (after which date they fell), and those of the Bank of France in 1848 and after 1871, are almost the only instances.

We cannot, in short, speak of "paper money" as though it were all of one kind or one quality—all good or all bad. We must discriminate, as we would between a 2.40 trotter and a tread-mill sack-of-bones, though each is called a horse. Economists dispute fiercely as to whether paper can or can not be "money," but this is really a quarrel about words. "Money is that money does," says one economist. Some use the word "money" to cover any substitute, others only for the metal or other value-money itself. The last is the original meaning and does not mislead, and paper is more accurately called substitute-money or currency. As a common medium of exchange, paper is more convenient than metal; it costs less to print it than to make coins. If paper is worn, or lost, or destroyed, in transit, no wealth is lost; without it the great volume of modern trade could scarcely have developed, and the lack of circulating medium would have greatly disturbed prices. It has accordingly been used for many centuries; Marco Polo found a paper currency of mulberry-bark in China before 1300. Adam Smith likens it to a highway in the air, leaving the old roads for crops. But as a common measure of value, it really depends on its own relations to metal-money, and as a standard of deferred payments and a storer of values it may prove ruinously treacherous. When "greenbacks" fell to 40 per cent., all who owed debts gained, for the moment; when they rose, all who owed lost—in neither case by their own doings. An inconvertible paper currency is usually costly in the long run. We honor the "blood-stained greenback" for its help in the war; but if our financiers could have avoided paper currency—as Napoleon, after the paper collapse of France, did throughout his great wars—we might have been saved the enormous loss of paying out at forty cents and redeeming at a hundred. Steadfastness is the great safeguard of sober industry, and paper currency has been called "the alcohol of commerce" and "mock money." "In the land of Mendacity," says an Italian writer, "they use only paper money."

Paper currency lacks also the final quality of real money—universality, for it is "good" only within the bounds of the credit of the country which issues it. Metal-money helps trade to regulate itself. If sugar is cheap in the West Indies, i. e., money dear, or if a great wheat-crop has brought us an excess of metal (which the United States produces and usually exports) i. e., money is cheap, money flows from us to the West Indies and we get our sugar cheap. But if we have a debased money, the natural course of trade is checked and we lose the profit.

Also, when full-value and debased currency are circulating together with the same purchasing power, "bad money," as stated by what is called Gresham's law, "always drives out good money," which people hoard or send away where they cannot use the bad money. When bad money thus checks exchange with other countries, it acts at home to check production, raise prices, produce inflation, and wreak ruin. It shuts out a country from the benefit of the world's trade, and makes buyers fewer. Thus "cheap money" is dear in the end.

There could not be a greater misfortune to every honest worker—farmer, shopkeeper or mechanic—in the United States than the issue of so-called "fiat money" (Latin, *fiat*, let it be created) as a means of creating wealth. You cannot make nothing good for something by printing on paper "good for one dollar, on the credit of the United States," without the intention of ever paying the dollar. This would not be credit money, because credit means belief in final payment. It would have no "labor-value," nor any value, because it would neither cost labor, nor represent labor stored as wealth, nor be a promise to pay labor. The Government could circulate it only by paying it out for work, or for existing debts, or by loaning it, or by giving it away. If it were given away either everybody could get it alike, so that no one would need to sell real things for it, or a few in the ring would get it at the expense of the many. If it were loaned, the borrowers would some day have to pay back, probably with a more costly currency after the "fiat money" had disappeared from sight, so that a mortgage would eat up the farm or the house. If it were paid out for work, that is, in wages, a laborer getting three "dollars" a day in place of one would be no better off, because the farmer would require three dollars instead of one for the wheat which cost him a day's work. Prices would rise, but a day's work would not buy more. Dishonest men who owed debts would gain by forcing such a legal-tender on the people they owed ; but new dealings would be on special contracts to pay in real money, as in the time when greenbacks were lowest, for no law can make a man sell what he prefers to keep. As times grew harder, "more money" would be the cry, as the drunkard cries for more rum, and the currency would be worth less and less. When the sham came to its end, the worthless paper would be not in the bank and the merchant's safe, but in the pocket of the worker and the till of the small shop keeper. This happened in the case of the silver trade-dollar also, and a like thing would happen if the under-weight silver dollar drove out gold. All this is true as to all "cheap money," that is, money in which the coins have not full value or full weight in fine metal. "Repudiation" is the most foolish crime of States, for it prevents all credit ; "fiat money" is a repudiation in advance. "A disordered currency," said Daniel Webster, is "the most effectual of inventions to fertilize the rich man's fields by the sweat of the poor man's brow."

## BANKS AND BANKING.

The little rills up on the hillsides do not count for much, but when they fill the mill-pond the farmer can grind his grist and the woodman can saw his logs by their help. A bank is just such a reservoir of money stored for use. The depositors add their dollars to the capital of the stockholders, and this money is then let out when and where it is needed for business. These loans are often made to governments, either directly or by buying government issues. This was, in fact, the purpose of the first public banks, started in Italy probably before 1200. The Greeks had their trapezites or bankers, so called from the table (*trapeza*) on which they counted out the money ; and when banking was revived by the Jewish money-lenders of Italy in the Middle Ages, each had his *banca*, or bench, which was broken (*rotta* or *rupta*) when he failed to pay as he promised, so he was said to become bankrupt.

Beside loaning to governments or to corporations—that is, buying their "bonds" or "securities"—banks loan their money to private persons, such as merchants, whose promises-to-pay are called notes-of-hand or mercantile paper. The use of money is paid for by adding an extra sum called interest at the end of the time, say $106 for $100 at the end of a year, or by deducting a like sum as discount, the borrower receiving but $94 instead of the $100 he promises to pay a year hence. If money is scarce or times risky, or the man doubtful, so that his credit (the belief in him) is poor, he will have to pay greater interest or discount; if the money market is "easy," less. The bank may trust him simply on his note, or he may give it collateral—that is, securities alongside with his own promise. This loaning is the first way in which a bank does service and makes profit.

A bank usually permits its depositors to draw on it orders to pay money, called checks, a word which comes from Exchequer, the name given to the British Treasury because it formerly used a checkered table like a chess-board for convenience in counting. This enables men to pay debts without carrying about money. The great "clearing-houses" in New York and London do this service for the banks themselves, clearing up at the close of each day transactions of millions by receiving orders on banks which owe from banks which are owed, and transferring any small balance from a debtor bank to a creditor bank. This canceling of indebtedness is a second service of banking.

A bank also, by the help of banks in other places, collects distant debts. A creditor—that is, some one to whom money is owed—"draws" upon the debtor who owes him; the *draft*, or order-to-pay, is sent by a bank in New York to its correspondent bank in Chicago, which sends out a runner to collect it from the Chicago debtor. Or it may be the debtor's own note which is sent on for collection. If he does not pay, the bank protests, and returns the draft or note with an affidavit called a *protest*. When drafts are drawn upon people in other countries they are called "foreign exchange." The bank sells to a man in New York the right to receive or transfer in London, for instance, money due by some other Englishman to some other American. This saves the risk and cost of sending specie, *i.e.*, gold or silver money or bullion; and the charge for this service—that is, the rate of exchange—varies, within the limits of the cost of shipping specie as freight, according to whether more or less money is due in London than there are debts to be paid there. It costs a little over half a cent to get a gold dollar safely to London; the value of the English pound, in which London settlements are made, is reckoned by our mint at $4.86$\frac{69}{100}$; the rate-of-exchange brings a bill-of-exchange perhaps to $4.90, above which point it pays better to ship gold. This collection of debts is a third service of banking.

A bank dealing in money knows how much foreign or debased coins are really worth, and buys them for that much current money. Where there is mixed money this is very important; it was the origin of the great Bank of Amsterdam and of much of the mediæval Jewish banking. This is a fourth service.

A bank is also a place of safe deposit for valuables, and English banking grew out of the business of the goldsmiths, who took valuables for safe-keeping, and got in the habit of advancing money on them. Many of the Crusaders thus borrowed money of the Jews. This is a fifth service of banking, though now "safe deposit companies" have taken much of this business.

Here, then, are five kinds of service which a bank performs, and for which it rightly earns money, without touching what most people think is the chief work of a bank, the issue of paper-money. The earliest "bank of issue" was probably that of Sweden, founded in 1657. Like each of the other five named, this service may or may not be a feature of a true bank: the "issue department" and the "banking department" of the great Bank of England are virtually two separate banks, doing different things. The issue of paper-money, if wisely done, is a sixth service, but it includes the greatest danger of the banking business. In England only the Bank of England, which is the financial representative of the Government, can issue bank-notes, and, above £15,750,000 represented by securities (of which the £11,000,000 owed by the Government to the bank is the greater part), it must keep a pound in gold in its vaults for each pound-note issued. This is the result of Sir Robert Peel's famous Bank Act of 1844, in which the advocates of the "banking principle" upheld by Thomas Tooke, who argued that so long as you can actually get gold for your bank-note there is no need of limiting issues by law, were defeated by those who held to the "currency principle," led by Lord Overstone, who argued that without such limitation currency is almost sure to be over-issued and so inflate prices by its depreciation. Our "National currency," issued by the National Banks, is protected by a deposit with the United States Treasury of Government bonds, against which only ninety per cent. of their face-value can be issued in currency, and by the Government guaranty of receiving it for all dues except interest on the public debt. These banks also keep a gold reserve, usually about 12 per cent. of their notes.

The one purpose of all these branches of the banking business is to make the most of the existing stock of capital. Safely done, this helps everybody. Careless banking, on the contrary, cripples all business. The need of banks wherever people do business is shown by the fact that when a little place starts up in the West, the keeper of the country store becomes virtually banker for the place until a public bank is started. The "wild-cat" banks before the war at the West, nevertheless, did a great deal of harm: they issued great quantities of paper-money, kept as little as two per cent. of specie, and failed to pay their notes. The country was cursed with paper-money, much counterfeited, from hundreds of banks of all shades of credit, which no one would take until he could look up the facts in the "Bank-note Detector," issued monthly in those days. This system of banks chartered by the States was largely superseded, early in the war, by the system of National Banks, under acts of February 25, 1863, and June 3, 1864. The greatest amount of notes authorized was $354,000,000, which was never quite reached. These notes were covered by the deposit of United States bonds, and gave a safe and convenient currency, similar to the "greenbacks." The profit of interest and on lost notes, as in the case of State-bank notes, is made by the banks, and not, as in the case of "greenbacks," by the Government; but this is perhaps compensated for by the service done by the banks, and the regulation of the currency by the needs of business instead of by arbitrary law. The present problem of banking is what securities can be used as a basis of National-bank notes, as the Government pays its debt and withdraws its bonds.

In 1895, there were 3,712 National Banks, with $657,000,000 capital, $1,715,000,000 deposits, and $182,000,000 circulation; there were also reported 1,017 savings-banks, with $1,844,500,000 deposits; and 5,086 State and private banks and trust companies, with $392,500,000 capital, and $1,340,800,-000 deposits—these being but partial returns; so that we have over 9,800 banks, with probably $1,050,000,000 capital, and nearly $5,000,000,000,000 deposits.

Savings-banks are confined usually to receiving deposits in small sums, and pay the depositors, in interest and dividends, the whole profit from the loaning of this money. They are governed by trustees representing the depositors, only a few having separate capital and stockholders, and they are restricted by law from loaning except on specified security. In England the Post-office Department is a great savings-bank, receiving savings in postage-stamps or money at each post-office, and loaning the total to Government by investing it in Government bonds.

Banks, we have seen, are really stores which deal in money, collecting it and letting it out much as a grocer buys and sells groceries. They give credit for money just as a grocer would give credit for goods. But because money is the general medium of exchange, and banks are usually public institutions, the bank reports, showing the "reserve" held by them, show the commercial condition of the community much as a steam-gauge shows the pressure in a steam-engine. When money is "scarce" and much wanted, or when times are risky, bankers charge a greater rate of interest or discount; and as London is the great banking centre, the rate made from week to week by the governors of the Bank of England, usually varying between 3 and 4 per cent., is an indication of the state of trade in the whole world. Bankers need to be very wise in these matters, else the community may be tempted into over-speculation by too free loans or frightened into panics by over-caution. Thus the usefulness of any bank, and of the whole banking system, depends upon the honesty and good judgment of the men conducting it. No law can prevent foolish people from putting money into swindles which call themselves "banks" or "bankers," and such people must pay the penalty in loss. But a system of sound branch banks throughout the country, like that in Scotland, is a great boon to a people.

# THE DEMOCRATIC PARTY—ITS HISTORY AND PRINCIPLES.*

It is just about one hundred years ago that the Democratic party in the United States was born of the theoretical and philosophical temper which pervaded Europe and America in the latter years of the last century, and the practical fruit of which had been the destruction of monarchical institutions in America and France. Instead of dealing, as typical Anglo-Saxons would have dealt, as probably Hamilton and John Adams would have dealt, only with the particular wrongs and inconveniences of British oppression, the genius of Thomas Jefferson had, in the Declaration of Independence fifteen or twenty years before, made the thirteen colonies define the whole reason and framework of government. Much of what he said now seems truism. It was the supreme merit of his career that he turned truths into truisms. He declared the theoretical rights—what he called the "inalienable rights"—of man; he declared the justification of government to be its ability to secure those rights; he declared respect or obedience to be due government solely as in actual practice it secured those rights. Whenever government ceased to perform this practical work, it was only prudence, and never awe, which should restrain citizens, if they were to be restrained at all, from overthrowing it. Divinity was no longer to hedge it around.

Very soon after the end of the American Revolution Jefferson went to Paris, where he lived during several years of the intellectual ferment which preceded the cataclysm of the French Revolution. After our Constitution was formed and Washington's administration was well under way, Jefferson, returning home, was still, or perhaps more zealously, an apostle of the rights of man—a thoroughgoing iconoclast toward every image of government as an earthly deity. To his influence we probably owe the first ten amendments of the Federal Constitution—that bill of rights which has been so largely copied into the constitutions of the American States. They form a series of declarations of jealousy of government, or rather of the bodies of men who from time to time compose government. Their meaning is that the price of liberty is eternal vigilance toward rulers—not less toward rulers elected by the people than toward those set over the people by the once useful but now absurd system of primogeniture. While he was the nominal head of Washington's Cabinet, Jefferson and his friends viewed with intense dislike the effort of Hamilton and his friends to form into a governing class the citizens who had property, the citizens who, through a dangerous slip, were called the "well-born," and their

---

* Condensed and revised from an Address by Edward M. Shepard, Brooklyn, 1892.

effort to lodge in the Federal Government the chief political powers of every State. Hamilton had proposed life-tenure for the President and Senators, and the appointment of the Governors of the States by Federal authority, with the power to every Governor of an absolute veto upon the legislation of his State. In our admiration for his great powers, and our gratitude for his splendid services in setting up the framework of our Government, it is sometimes forgotten that the Federal Constitution is a radically different thing from what Hamilton would have had it; that but little of it is his handiwork; that it represents quite as much, to say the least, the Democratic view as the Federalist view of American politics. In private Hamilton declared it to be a "frail and worthless fabric." Democracy—and by that he meant the eager jealous participation of all citizens in the government, as well those whom he deemed unimportant and incompetent as those who held responsible places in the community and were skilled in affairs—Democracy he declared, just before his death, to be a "virulent poison."

From the time of Jefferson's return to America and his appointment as Secretary of State in 1790 until his inauguration as President in 1801, the Democratic party was in its first stage; and in that stage it tended toward extreme opposition to the Hamiltonian views. In the formation of lasting popular opinion, in permanently molding the political instincts and institutions of America, and in setting up ideals which have in our land grown stronger and stronger with the lapse of time, the genius of Jefferson was, with the possible exception of that of Franklin, the most fruitful which our country has known. Within twelve years after our present Government began he had gathered a majority of the people of the United States into an organization then called the Republican, afterward called the Democratic-Republican, and finally, and until the present time, called the Democratic party. During that period the principles of the party were well settled. They appear in Jefferson's political papers, in his incessant correspondence, in the Virginia and Kentucky resolutions, for both of which, doubtless, Jefferson and Madison were largely responsible, and in a great wealth of political and party literature more or less *doctrinaire*.

The Democratic principles were in substance these: *First*, just government is a mere instrument for accomplishing certain useful and practical purposes which citizens in their other relations can not accomplish, and primarily, and chiefly, to protect men as, without trespass upon others, they pursue happiness in their own way. Every effort, by ceremonial or otherwise, to ascribe to government virtue or intelligence, or invite to it honor, not belonging to the men who compose it, is an effort against the public welfare. *Second*, the less government does, the more it leaves to individual citizens to do, the better. Every grant of power to government ought, therefore, to be strictly and jealously construed as impairing to some extent the natural rights of men.

*Third*, there should be the maximum of local self-government. Where it is doubtful between the Federal Government and a State, or between a State and a lesser community, which should exercise a power, the doubt ought to be solved in favor of the government nearer the home, and more closely under the eye of the individual citizen. *Fourth*, it follows that the expenditure of money by the Government ought to be the least possible; the collection and disbursement by public officials of money earned by other men tends to corruption, not only in the jobbery and thievery more or less attending irresponsible expenditure of money, but perhaps more seriously in its tendency to create in the minds of citizens a sense of dependence upon government. And *fifth*, to sum up all the rest, the Government should make the least possible demand upon the citizen, and the citizen the least possible demand upon the Government. The citizen should never suppose that he can be made virtuous by law, or that he ought to be helped to wealth or ease by those of his fellows who happen to hold the offices, and for that reason to be collectively called "the Government."

Such was the Democratic creed at its beginning; and, in spite of many lapses, such the creed, at least as a creed, has remained until the present time. Certain constructive functions, like the post-office in the Federal administration, or the care of streets in municipal administration, it is admitted—it was then admitted—must be performed by the Government. Those constructive functions, with the increase in wealth and complexity of modern life, tend to increase in number and importance. But, as to each one of them, the burden is upon those who would have the Government assume it, to show that government is fit for it; and by government is always meant the men actually making up the administration, with all the limitations upon their intelligence and integrity, and with all the disadvantages incident to the performance of business by those who bear but an insignificant part of its burdens. It is with ample regard to these considerations that we should determine as to each constructive work, whether it ought to be done by some division of the Government. The main purpose and justification of government is, in every response of the Democratic litany, and with ceaseless iteration, declared to be the protection of the individual citizen in best and most freely exercising his calling and in living his life without trespass upon the like freedom of his neighbor. Long before the birth of Herbert Spencer the best of the propositions of Social Statics was an axiom of the Democratic party. The creed is to many neither warm nor inspiring. It declares that equal justice to all men is the only generosity which government should promote. It says: "Let each man take care of himself. Let no man, through the power of popular majorities, shift his burdens upon other men."

Out of the triumph of this creed, which the first year of our century brought, and incidental to that triumph, have come many things unpleasant to well-ordered citizens. The refusal to recognize public men as a class possessing esoteric knowledge, the admiration for the plain, simple man, has not infrequently led the American people to put incompetence and stupidity into official place. The dislike of forms, the determination to deal with realities, has sometimes led to the neglect of forms necessary to thoroughness, precision and convenience. Whatever were, whatever still are, the blemishes of its fruits, such was the Democratic creed when Jefferson entered the White House.

From 1801 until 1825 the Democratic party was in control of the machinery of government. At the end of that time there was no opposition. When the presidential election of 1824 took place each candidate was declared by his supporters to be the best Republican of them all. John Quincy Adams and Henry Clay, quite as much as Andrew Jackson and William H. Crawford, were supposed to be followers of Jefferson and Madison. So utterly destroyed was the Federal party that its traditions have since that time played no practical part in the development of the United States. The career, for instance, of Abraham Lincoln is quite as far away from Federalist ideals as the career of Andrew Jackson. Both careers were made possible by the surrender of the land to the political ideas of the philosophers who were our Presidents during the first sixteen years of the century. Not, however, that all the Democrats were mere theorists. There were among the Democratic statesmen of the time several able administrators. Gallatin, for instance, was one of the greatest executives our country has known. The Clintons, and, among the younger men, Van Buren, were highly competent in the efficient transaction of the business of government. Never have our national finances been better cared for.

When John Quincy Adams became President he determined, although without recurrence to the ceremonial features of Federalism, to make the Washington Government a firmer, abler institution, to start it in the way of constructive work, to make it open the great highways through the country, to make it influential abroad. Joined, as Adams was, by the attractive abilities and character of Henry Clay, the Whig party was formed during this administration; and from the election of 1828, in which Adams was defeated for re-election, until 1844, the Democratic theories of government were ably and patriotically attacked by some of the most famous Americans. Under Jackson and Van Buren the Democratic party dissolved the close alliance between the Federal Government and the banks. The Federal Government was not, directly or indirectly, to loan money to its citizens, for that was the proposition substantially maintained by the Whigs in the bank controversy. Since then Government has indeed deposited moneys with banks, but only as a mere convenience, and never under a general policy of helping bankers or merchants. Under Jackson and Van Buren the Democratic party showed genuine energy and ability of the first order in the executive administration of affairs. The United States has never known more forcible administrations than theirs.

From 1800 to 1844 the Democratic party, being almost continually in possession of the Government, had almost lost sight of, or grown lukewarm toward, its Kentucky and Virginia resolutions and its State Rights predilections. It was a thoroughly Union party; it was *the* Union party. The disunionists were for some years chiefly New England Federalists. In 1833 there was the later outbreak of disunion in South Carolina under Calhoun and other seceders from the Democratic party, in suppressing which the Democratic administration used emphatic language of intense and peremptory devotion to the Union which would not have ill-fitted an original Federalist. Indeed, if one will apply to politics the elementary rules of human conduct, he will perceive it to be no very wonderful thing that the party in possession of the Federal administration is always a Union party, or that disunionists are always men out of the control of the central administration.

In Van Buren's presidency occurred the memorable financial crisis of 1837 and 1838; and his resolute and unpopular application of the principle that citizens in pecuniary trouble must not look to the Federal Government for loans of credit or other help, but must work out their own salvation, was one of the finest exhibitions of patriotic and far-seeing wisdom known to American history. In my opinion, the Democratic party did not again reach an equal height until December, 1887.

About 1844 the slavery question definitely entered party politics. Slavery existed only in the Southern States; and in those agricultural communities the Democratic party, standing for low duties on imports, had come to be strongest. Its strength there was, however, quite unrelated to its opinions on the slavery question. But later, under the threats of interference with slavery in the States, the South more and more drifted to the Democratic party because of its strict doctrine of non-interference with the domestic affairs of the States. And when the slave-owners wished, as they soon after did, not only to protect the institution in the States, but to extend it into new territory, they carried the Democratic party far away from its creed.

Among the Democrats there was—there had always been—a large anti-slavery feeling. Jefferson had been almost an abolitionist; out of the Democratic party there later came to the Republican party many abolitionists, among them John P. Hale, Salmon P. Chase and David Wilmot. The Southern Democrats, after a struggle, captured the ogranization of their party, and refused Van Buren the nomination of 1844 because he was opposed to the annexation of Texas and to the extension of slavery which it meant. From that time until the election of Lincoln the Democratic party organization promoted, or at least, did not resist, the demand of the South. It was still a Union party; in the opinion of many of its members at the North, its Unionism was too strong. It so far believed in the Union that it was willing, as they thought, to sacrifice its own principles of liberty and local self-government in order to preserve the Union.

The motives of the chief Democratic leaders of this period were patriotic to a high degree. Disunion seemed to them to be the greatest of evils; and they believed, and rightly, that disunion must come, unless concession after concession should be made to the slave-holding South. The Whig party was no better. It had become contemptible long before it fell to pieces on the rise of the present Republican party. The Dred Scott decision, declaring that the Federal Constitution, of its own force, carried slavery into all the territories, out-federalized the Federalists. Van Buren, in his history of political parties, quite justly rejoiced to point out that Buchanan had been originally a Federalist and that in his old age he had returned to Federalism; that Taney, the Chief Justice who had pronounced the Dred Scott decision, had likewise been originally a Federalist and had in his old age returned to Federalism.

The present Republican party was founded in 1854 upon the proposition that there should be no further extension of slavery. It was not an anti-slavery party so far as concerned the States and Territories in which slavery already existed. Until it was chosen to power, it was not a Unionist party. On the contrary, its leaders, and notably Lincoln and Seward and Chase, before the presidential election of 1860, speeches, set the "higher law" above the Union. The Democratic party being at last turned out of power in 1861, all the Democrats of the South and a few of those at the North became disunionists. The Republican party, however, immediately upon its triumph in 1860, began to turn from the "higher law"; it became in its turn a Union party. Its leaders voted for extreme pro-slavery measures, designed to conciliate the South.

It is one of the amazing facts of our political history that after the presidential campaign of 1860, in which the Republican party urged as its chief claim to power its determination that slavery should be excluded from the Territories, the Republican party helped in the early-months of 1861, even Charles Sumner not opposing, to pass laws bringing in the new Territories of Colorado, Nevada, and Dakota without that exclusion of slavery for which alone they had come to power. This party of the higher law, not panoplied, but weighted, with executive power. also yielded to the slave-holders for the sake of the Union. For that they were ready to occupy the position which the Democrats had occupied from 1844 until 1860. Lincoln, though not a bold leader, was a wise man. Though he would, as he himself very explicitly said let his black fellow-men remain in slavery for the sake of the Union, he was rejoiced when, to the North, Union at last came to mean abolition. And he showed incomparable skill in dealing with this sentiment, now leading, now following it.

During the war and the days of reconstruction the Democratic party was the usual party in opposition. I can not pause to describe its career from its defeat in 1860 until the revival of its traditional policy in 1874. I must say, however, that very insufficient justice has been done to the patriotism of the great mass of Democrats during the Civil War. The Union could never have been restored but for their general and effective loyalty. If during the war there had been no constitutional opposition from that party, if in its ranks there had not been at least two-fifths of the loyal people of the North, the Union would have been restored shorn of some of its chief merits, and with a framework very different from that which had been set up by the fathers, and which so wonderfully survived the flame and destruction of our great struggle.

In 1874 the Democratic party was taken firmly in hand by Samuel J. Tilden and his coadjutors. Gov. Tilden was deeply imbued with the traditional principles of his party. He had been an admiring pupil of Van Buren, who had himself been a disciple of Jefferson. He had joined Van Buren in the Free-Soil revolt of 1848 against the dictation of the slave holders. When that revolt had failed he had returned to the party, and there stayed during the unionist period of the Democratic party which I have described. He was elected Governor of New York in 1874 upon a platform whose distinctly and tersely drawn propositions were completely Jeffersonian. The Federal Government must not issue fiat paper; it must not promote manufactures or any kind of business at the expense of those not engaged in it; it must not meddle with the affairs of the several States ; a civil service law must destroy those evils of patronage which, however much practiced by Democrats, had been among the most flagrant violations of Democratic principles. With Tilden's success there came into the administration of the Democratic party a body of younger men, of superior intelligence, of great sincerity, and warmly devoted to the traditions of the party. Indeed their devotion was one of the most honorable and effective tributes paid him. After the electoral controversy of 1877, and his failure—through a scandalous and criminal perversion of the popular will—to actually reach the White House, reaction from a steadfast course set in, as it had more than once before. In 1880 the Democratic party, shrinking from its own principles and abandoning its own leader, met a defeat not altogether undeserved. When at last, in March, 1885, it secured the Presidency, the business and practical requirements of administration of a great machine of Government long set up were so great, and the temper of Mr. Cleveland and his associates was rightly so practical, that considerable time elapsed before Democratic theories could be put in practice or even very distinctly enunciated. In a series of veto messages, however, in the latter part of his administration, and especially in his famous tariff messages of 1887, and in his annual message of 1888, after his defeat, there was clear and definite return to the traditional principles of the Democratic party. He enunciated, in a phrase of his own, the sum of them all, when he said that it was for the citizen to support the Government, and not for the Government to support the citizen.

The great parties of the United States have never differed as to the duty of the Federal Government to coin money. So that the mere question whether or not silver shall be as freely coined as gold does not involve the great difference of principle between the two parties. But we know that few people are interested in the abstract question of bimetallism dealt with by the economists. If the free coinage of silver could take place only at a rate which would make a silver dollar equal to the existing gold dollar, there would be no agitation for free silver. The reason which influences the masses of people—outside of the few silver-producing States, who demand free coinage—is the fact, perfectly realized, that the silver dollar proposed to be coined would be intrinsically worth far less than a gold dollar, and that, when coinage becomes free, the only circulating dollar would be a silver dollar worth far less than the present dollar, a dollar to be obtained for far less labor—that is to say, at far less cost. This is the very motive which underlay the paper-money mania after the war. The Government at Washington seems to the citizen who does not observe the real springs of power to be illimitably powerful; it can by law create a dollar of one hundred cents out of a bit of paper or out of seventy cents' worth of silver. So the pressed and worried planter or farmer is tempted by the illusion against which the Democratic party, whenever loyal to its own principles, will firmly protest—to appeal to the mysterious but imaginary deity who sits enshrined under the dome on that Capitoline Hill which overlooks the Potomac.

No strength of Government, no efficiency of administration, no conscientious care by rulers for the citizens under them, will, in the long run, bring to the welfare and happiness of the country a tithe of what will come from the independent character of the citizen himself, from his pride in his self-support, from his jealousy of interference, and, to sum it all up, from his refusal, whether by device or the brute power of majorities, to cast his burden upon other men. When the citizens of a commonwealth are of this type, we need have no great concern about government. It is because effect follows cause that from such men will come sense and prudence and integrity in public business, efficiency in political action, and strength and thoroughness in administration. So long as the Democratic party in its life and practice stands for this theory of government, it will be a power for lasting public good. So long it will deserve, and I believe it will enjoy, a fitting success and honor.

# PUBLIC MEN ON SOUND MONEY.

GEORGE WASHINGTON:

"It (inflation) will not benefit the farmer or the mechanic, as it will only enable the debtor to pay his debt with a shadow instead of a substance."

ROBERT MORRIS:

It (unsound currency) has caused infinite private mischief, numberless frauds and the greatest distress.

There is a great impropriety, not to say injustice, in compelling a man to receive a part of his debt in discharge of the whole.

Arguments are unnecessary to show that the scale by which everything is to be measured ought to be as fixed as the nature of things permits of.

ALEXANDER HAMILTON:

There is scarcely any point in the economy of national affairs of greater moment than the uniform preservation of the intrinsic value of the money unit. On this the security and steady value of property essentially depend.

Gold may, perhaps, in certain senses, be said to have a greater stability than silver, as being of superior value; less liberties have been taken with it in the regulations with different countries.

Its standard has remained more uniform, and it has in other respects undergone fewer changes, as, being not so much an article of merchandise, owing to the use made of silver in the trade with the East Indies and China, it is less liable to be influenced by circumstances of commercial demand.

And if, reasoning by analogy, it could be affirmed that there is a physical probability of greater proportional increase in the quantity of silver than in that of gold, it would afford an additional reason for calculating on greater steadiness in the value of the latter.

There can hardly be a better rule in any country for the legal than the market proportion. The presumption in such case is that each metal finds its true level according to its intrinsic utility in the general system of money operation. As long as gold, either from its intrinsic superiority as a metal, from its rarity, or from the prejudices of mankind, retains so considerable a pre-eminence in value over silver as it has hitherto had, a natural consequence of this seems to be that its condition will be more stationary. The revolutions, therefore, which may take place in the comparative value of gold and silver will be changes in the state of the latter rather than in that of the former."

PRESIDENT JEFFERSON:

The real credit of the United States depends on the ability and the immutability of their will to pay their debts.

The proportion between the values of gold and silver is a mercantile problem altogether.

Just principles will lead us to disregard legal proportion altogether, to inquire into the market price of gold in the several countries with which we shall principally be connected in commerce, and to take an average from them.

I very much doubt a right now to change the value, and especially to lessen it. It would lead to so easy a mode of paying off their debts. * * * Should it be thought, however, that Congress may reduce the value of the dollar, I should be for adopting for our unit, instead of the dollar, either one ounce of pure silver or one ounce of standard silver, so as to keep the unit of money a part of the system of measures, weights and coins.

The original "demonetization of silver" was effected by the following order from Thomas Jefferson:

DEPARTMENT OF STATE,
May 1, 1806.

SIR—In consequence of a representation from the Directors of the Bank of the United States that considerable purchases have been made of dollars coined at the Mint for the purpose of exporting them, and as it is probable further purchases and exportations will be made, the President [Thomas Jefferson] directs that all silver to be coined at the Mint shall be of small denominations, so that the value of the largest pieces shall not exceed half a dollar. JAMES MADISON.

ROBERT PATTERSON, Esq.,
Director of the Mint.

PRESIDENT MADISON:

It is essential that the nation should possess a currency of equal value, credit and use wherever it may circulate.

PRESIDENT JACKSON, Message to Congress, 1834:

The progress of our gold coinage is creditable to the officers of the Mint and promises in a short period to furnish the country with a sound and portable currency.

PRESIDENT JACKSON, Message to Congress, 1835:

It is pleasing to witness the advantages which have already been derived from the recent laws regulating the value of the gold coinage.

PRESIDENT JACKSON, Message to Congress, 1836:

A depreciation of the currency, by excessive bank issues is always attended by a loss to the laboring classes. This portion of the community have neither time nor opportunity to watch the ebbs and flows of the money market.

Engaged from day to day in their useful toils, they do not perceive that although their wages are nominally the same, or even somewhat higher, they are greatly reduced in fact by the rapid increase of a spurious currency which, as it appears to make money abound, they are at first inclined to consider a blessing. It is not so with the speculator, by whom this operation is better understood and is made to contribute to his advantage. It is not until the prices of the necessaries of life become so dear that the laboring classes cannot supply their wants out of their wages that the wages rise and gradually reach a justly proportioned rate to that of the products of their labor.

SECRETARY INGHAM, first Secretary of the Treasury in the Cabinet of Andrew Jackson, May 4, 1830:

However exactly the proper equilibrium of values of gold and silver may be adjusted at the Mint, the balance is liable to be disturbed by causes which can neither be anticipated nor controlled by political power. If the regulation be founded on the most exact calculation of relative values for the time being, the vibrations of the values of gold and silver must alternately cause the expulsion of each, and where one metal is more essential to public convenience than the other, the adjustment which exposes that under any circumstances to general exportation or melting may become a greater evil than a regulation which constantly excludes from circulation the less desirable coin. * * * The proposition that there can be but one standard in fact is self-evident. * * * The history of coinage abounds with mint regulations to keep gold and silver together, and statutes prohibiting under severe penalties the exportation of either, all of which have disappointed every expectation of their projectors. The adoption of one metal as a standard measure of property is recommended by its simplicity. No change in the mint regulations can ever be required, and it removes every pretext for dishonest or unwise government to debase their coins.

CAMPBELL P. WHITE, of Committee of New York Bankers, 1832:

The committee think that the *desideratum in the monetary system is the standard of uniform value;* they cannot ascertain that both metals have ever circulated simultaneously, concurrently and indiscriminately in any country where there are banks or money-dealers, and they entertain the conviction that the nearest approach to an invariable standard is its establishment *in one metal,* which metal shall compose exclusively the currency for large payments.

DEMOCRATIC COMMITTEE OF THE HOUSE OF REPRESENTATIVES, 1834:

The committee think that the desideratum in the monetary system is a standard of uniform value. They cannot ascertain that both metals have ever circulated simultaneously, concurrently and indiscriminately in any country where there are banks or money dealers, and they entertain the conviction that the nearest approach to an invariable standard is its establishment in one metal, which metal shall compose exclusively the currency for large payments.

THOMAS H. BENTON, 1834:

It has an intrinsic value, which gives it currency all over the world to the full amount of that value without regard to law or circumstances.

It has a uniformity of value, which makes it the safest standard of the value of property which the wisdom of man has ever yet discovered.

Its portability, which makes it easy for the traveler to carry about with him.

Its indestructibility, which makes it the safest money that people can keep in their houses.

Its superiority over all other money, which gives to its possessor the choice and command of all other money.

It is a constitutional currency, and the people have a right to demand it for their currency as long as the present Constitution is permitted to exist.

JOHN C. CALHOUN, 1834:

With these convictions, and entertaining a deep conviction that an unfixed, unstable and fluctuating currency is to be ranked among the most fruitful sources of evil, whether brewed politically or in reference to the business transactions of the country, I cannot give my consent to any measure that does not place the currency on a sound foundation.

DANIEL WEBSTER, 1834:

The very man of all others who has the deepest interest in a sound currency, and who suffers most by mischievous legislation in money matters, is the man who earns his daily bread by his daily toil.

A general and universally accredited currency, therefore, is an instrument of commerce which is necessary to its just advantages, or, in other words, which is essential to its beneficial regulation.

A disordered currency is one of the greatest political evils. It undermines the virtues necessary for the support of the social system and encourages propensities destructive of its happiness.

There are some political evils which are seen as soon as they are dangerous, and which alarm at once as well the people as the Government.

Wars and invasions, therefore, are not always the most certain destroyers of national prosperity. They come in no questionable shape. They announce their own approach, and the general security is preserved by the general alarm.

Not so with the evils of a debased coin, a depreciated paper currency or a depressed and falling public credit.

These insinuate themselves in the shape of facilities, accommodation and relief. They hold out the most fallacious hope of an easy payment of debts and a lighter burden of taxation.

Credit has done more, a thousand times, to enrich nations than all the mines of all the world.

The circulating medium of a commercial community must be that which is also the circulating medium of other commercial communities, or must be capable of being converted into that medium without loss. It must be able not only to pass in payments and receipts between individuals of the same society or nation, but to adjust and discharge the balance of exchanges between different nations. It must be something which has a value abroad as well as at home, and by which foreign as well as domestic debts can be satisfied.

DANIEL WEBSTER, Speech at New York, March 15, 1837:

He who tampers with the currency robs labor of its bread. He panders indeed to greedy capital, which is keen-sighted and may shift for itself, but he beggars labor, which is honest, unsuspecting and too busy with the present to calculate for the future. The prosperity of the working classes lives, moves and has its being in established credit and a steady medium of payment. All sudden changes destroy it.

Honest industry never comes in for any part of the spoils in that scramble which takes place when the currency of a country is disordered. Did wild schemes and projects ever benefit the industrious? Did violent fluctuations ever do good to him who depends on his daily labor for his daily bread? Certainly never. All these things may gratify greediness for sudden gain, or the rashness of daring speculation, but they can bring nothing but injury and distress to the homes of patient industry and honest labor.

SAMUEL J. TILDEN, Speech at New Lebanon, October 3, 1840:

An unstable currency, producing instability in business and prices, is peculiarly injurious to the farmer. Neither his education nor his disposition accustoms him to watch the barometer of the exchange. When he has conducted his business with prudence and skill, with a familiar knowledge and sagacious estimate of all the circumstances that belong to it, he ought to be safe. He ought not to be subject to the tremendous agency of an unseen cause which may disappoint his wisest calculations and overwhelm him in sudden ruin. He ought to be secure in the tranquillity of his fireside from the curse of an unstable and fluctuating currency.

SAMUEL J. TILDEN, Governor of New York, Message to Legislature, 1875:

Nothing could be more unwise, more mischievous in its ultimate results, than to interrupt the healing process of nature by expedients which will fail of affording any real relief, and will be certain to accumulate new materials for another catastrophe. It has seemed to me fit that on this occasion the opinions of the great commonwealth we represent, which is so largely interested in these questions, should be declared on the side of sound finance, public integrity, and national honor; and in making this communication the medium of an authentic expression on the subject, I follow the example on similar occasions of several of the most illustrious of my predecessors.

HORATIO SEYMOUR, Governor of New York, Message to the Legislature, 1864:

These foreign creditors of ours are strangers, who lend us their money when we want it upon no security but our word of honor. If we do not pay them back their money to the strict letter of our bargain we incur a shame that can never be removed from us.

We deprive New York of an element of strength which heretofore has been wisely used and which its people have found profitable, to wit, its unquestioned credit. Principle and policy unite to commend the action I urge upon you. It is the only way in which the State can in truth fulfill its contract. It is the only way in which the State can keep itself in a position to go into the markets hereafter as a borrower.

President GRANT, Second Inaugural Address, March 4, 1873:

My efforts for the future will be directed to the restoration of our currency to a fixed value as compared with the world's standard of value, gold, and, if possible, to a par with it.

President GRANT, Message to Congress, 1874:

These two causes have involved us in a foreign indebtedness, contracted in good faith by borrower and lender, which should be paid in coin, and according to the bond agreed upon when the debt was contracted—gold or its equivalent. The good faith of the Government cannot be violated toward creditors without national disgrace.

BENJAMIN H. BRISTOW, Secretary of the Treasury, 1875:

It is among the first and most important functions of government to give to its people a sound and stable currency, having a fixed relation to the standard of values in general use among nations. The true matter with which government has to do is not so much a question of the volume as of soundness and stability of the currency. When it has established a currency of fixed and stable value, having a known relation to that of other powers, and furnishing a uniform medium of exchange, the volume may and should be left to be determined by the wants of trade and business. Natural causes, aided by individual effort and enterprise, will regulate the volume of currency far more wisely and with greater safety to business than acts of Congress imposing artificial limits, subject to increase or diminution at every session.

LOT M. MORRILL, Secretary of the Treasury, 1876:

It is respectfully submitted that the coin payment to which the faith of the nation was pledged in 1869 was gold and not silver, and that any other view of it, whatever technical construction the language may be susceptible of, would be regarded as of doubtful good faith and its probable effect prejudicial to the public credit.

President HAYES, Message to Congress, 1877:

All the bonds that have been issued since February 12, 1873, when gold became the only unlimited legal-tender metallic currency of the country, are justly payable in gold coin or in coin of equal value. During the time of these issues the only dollar that could be or was received by the Government in exchange for bonds was the gold dollar. To require the public creditors to take in repayment any dollar of less commercial value would be regarded by them as a repudiation of the full obligation assumed. The bonds issued prior to 1873 were issued at a time when the gold dollar was the only coin in circulation or contemplated either by the Government or the holders of the bonds as the coin in which they were to be paid. It is far better to pay these bonds in that coin than to seem to take advantage of the unforeseen fall in silver bullion to pay in a new issue of silver coin thus made so much less valuable. The power of the United States to coin money and to regulate the value thereof ought never to be exercised for the purpose of enabling the Government to pay its obligations in a coin of less value than that contemplated by the parties when the bonds were issued. Any attempt to pay the national indebtedness in a coinage of less commercial value than the money of the world would involve a violation of the public faith and work irreparable injury to the public credit.

President GARFIELD, Inaugural Address, March 4, 1881:

The chief duty of the National Government in connection with the currency of the country is to coin money and declare its value. Grave doubts have been entertained whether Congress is authorized by the Constitution to make any form of money legal tender. The present issue of United States notes has been sustained by the necessities of war, but such paper should depend for its value and currency upon its convenience in use and its prompt redemption in coin at the will of the holder, and not upon its compulsory circulation. If the holders demand it, the promise should be kept.

President ARTHUR, Message to Congress, 1884:

I concur with the Secretary of the Treasury in recommending the immediate suspension of the coinage of silver dollars and of the issuance of silver certificates. The Secretary avows his conviction that unless this coinage and the issuance of silver certificates be suspended, silver is likely at no distant day to become our sole metallic standard. The commercial disturbance and the impairment of national credit that would be thus occasioned can scarcely be overestimated.

President CLEVELAND, Message to Congress, 1885:

When the time comes that gold has been withdrawn from circulation, then will be apparent the difference between the real value of the silver dollar and a dollar in gold, and the two coins will part company. Gold, still the standard of value, and necessary in our dealings with other countries, will be at a premium over silver; banks which have substituted gold for the deposits of their customers may pay them with silver bought with such gold, thus making a handsome profit; rich speculators will sell their hoarded gold to their neighbors who need it to liquidate their foreign debts, at a ruinous premium over silver, and the laboring men and women of the land, most defenseless of all, will find that the dollar received for the wage of their toil has sadly shrunk in purchasing power. It may be said that the latter result will be but temporary, and that ultimately the price of labor will be adjusted to the change; but even if this takes place, the wage-worker cannot possibly gain ; he must inevitably lose, since the price he is compelled to pay for his living will not only be measured in a coin heavily depreciated and fluctuating and uncertain in its value, but this uncertainty in the value of the purchasing medium will be made the pretext for an advance in prices beyond that justified by actual depreciation.

President HARRISON, Message to Congress, 1891:

I am still of the opinion that the free coinage of silver under existing conditions would disastrously affect our business interests at home and abroad. We could not hope to maintain an equality in the purchasing power of the gold and silver dollar in our own markets, and in foreign trade the stamp gives no added value to the bullion contained in coins. The producers of the country, its farmers and laborers, have the highest interest that every dollar, paper or coin, issued by the Government shall be as good as any other. If there is one less valuable than another, its sure and constant errand will be to pay them for their toil and for their crops. The money-lender will protect himself by stipulating for payment in gold, but the laborer has never been able to do that. To place business upon a silver basis would mean a sudden and severe contraction of the currency, by the withdrawal of gold and gold notes, and such an unsettling of all values as would produce a commercial panic. I cannot believe that a people so strong and prosperous as ours will promote such a policy.

DANIEL MANNING, Secretary of the Treasury, 1885 :

A large proportion of our workingmen of mature years have had an instructive experience that lowering value of any so-called dollar legal tender of payment for their wages is a lowering that is compensated to everybody else before compensation reaches them. It is a lowering that lifts the prices of all commodities before it lifts the rates of their wages. A cheaper dollar for workingmen of the United States means a poorer dollar. The daily wages of our workingmen and working-women are by far the largest, by far the most important, aggregate of wealth to be affected by the degradation of the dollar, or of any legal-tender equivalent of the dollar. All other aggregates of wealth, the accumulations of capitalists, which can only obtain profitable use by being turned over daily in the wages of workmen and the employment of the captains of their industry, all other aggregates of wealth which remain unemployed in the payment of wages of the day, the month, the year, are not to be compared in their sum to this gigantic sum. It is this gigantic sum, the wages of labor, which is assailed by every policy which would make the dollar of the fathers worth less than its weight in gold. The debt of the United States, large as it is, is a wart beside that mountain.

DANIEL MANNING, Secretary of the Treasury, 1886:
But whether or not a non-equivalent of the coin dollar may be made a lawful dollar, and whether or not post-redemption issues and re-issues of such promises can be lawfully made, after twenty-one years of peace have superseded any real or imagined exigency of war, certain it is that every argument of policy now forbids the continuance of that legalized injustice. Had it ever been conferred, the Federal Government should be stripped of so dangerous a power. No executive and no legislature is fit to be trusted with the control it involves over the earnings and the savings of the people. No earthly sovereign or servant is capable of a just exercise of such authority to impair and pervert the obligations of contracts.

HOKE SMITH, late Secretary of the Interior; Speech at the Reform Club Sound Currency Dinner, New York, May 16, 1896:
If a President and Congress were elected in November committed to the free and unlimited coinage of 371¼ grains of silver into dollars, nearly six months would pass before they could be inaugurated, and six months more before the proposed legislation could become law. During that time creditors would seek to protect themselves against being paid in dollars worth only about 18 grains of gold, and they would endeavor to make collections before the unlimited coinage of depreciated dollars began. The debtors would not be allowed to remain debtors until they could get the advantage of paying off what they owed at fifty cents on the dollar; they would be forced to immediate settlements. Sheriffs and constables would call upon them without delay. Depositors in banks would withdraw their money. The large merchants, forced to settle their foreign indebtedness, would insist upon the immediate payment of debts due from smaller merchants. The smaller merchants, in turn, would be compelled to force collections from their customers. The great volume of business conducted upon credits would cease.

Manufacturing enterprises could not afford to continue business or make contracts until the value of the new dollar could be settled by the determination of just what 371¼ grains of silver would prove to be worth. Manufactories would close. Business houses would fail. Banks would be raided. The unemployed would be numbered by millions. The farmers would find few purchasers for their products. Want and famine would pervade the land.

Business interests, reaching from the richest banker to the poorest paid laborer, require the removal of all doubt about the meaning of a dollar. No man should be trusted, even with an unimportant nomination, who does not recognize that the value of a dollar is now measured by 23.22 grains of gold, and who is not willing openly to declare his purpose to help keep it there.

## STATISTICAL TABLES.

**Production of Gold and Silver in the World since the Discovery of America.**

[From 1493 to 1885 is from a Table of Averages for certain periods, compiled by Dr. Adolph Soetbeer. For the years 1886 to 1895 the production is the annual estimate of the Bureau of the Mint.]

| Period. | GOLD. | | | | SILVER. | | | |
|---|---|---|---|---|---|---|---|---|
| | Annual average for period. | | Total for period. | | Annual average for period. | | Total for period. | |
| | Ounces, fine. | Value. | Ounces, fine. | Value. | Ounces, fine. | Coining value. | Ounces, fine. | Coining value. |
| 1493–1520 | 186,470 | $3,855,000 | 5,221,160 | $107,931,000 | 1,511,050 | $1,954,000 | 42,309,400 | $54,703,000 |
| 1521–1544 | 230,194 | 4,759,000 | 5,524,650 | 114,205,000 | 2,899,930 | 3,749,000 | 69,596,320 | 89,948,000 |
| 1545–1560 | 273,596 | 5,656,000 | 4,377,544 | 90,492,000 | 10,017,940 | 12,952,000 | 160,287,010 | 207,240,000 |
| 1561–1580 | 219,906 | 4,546,000 | 4,398,120 | 90,917,000 | 9,628,925 | 12,450,000 | 192,578,500 | 248,990,000 |
| 1581–1600 | 237,267 | 4,905,000 | 4,745,340 | 98,095,000 | 13,467,635 | 17,413,000 | 269,352,700 | 348,254,000 |
| 1601–1620 | 273,918 | 5,662,000 | 5,478,300 | 113,248,000 | 13,596,285 | 17,579,000 | 271,924,700 | 351,579,000 |
| 1621–1640 | 266,845 | 5,516,000 | 5,336,900 | 110,324,000 | 12,654,340 | 16,361,000 | 253,084,900 | 327,221,000 |
| 1641–1660 | 281,955 | 5,828,000 | 5,639,110 | 116,671,000 | 11,776,545 | 15,226,000 | 235,530,900 | 304,525,000 |
| 1661–1680 | 297,709 | 6,154,000 | 5,954,180 | 123,084,000 | 10,834,550 | 14,008,000 | 216,691,000 | 280,166,000 |
| 1681–1700 | 346,095 | 7,154,000 | 6,921,895 | 143,088,000 | 10,992,085 | 14,212,000 | 219,841,700 | 284,240,000 |
| 1701–1720 | 412,163 | 8,520,000 | 8,243,260 | 170,403,000 | 11,432,640 | 14,781,000 | 228,650,800 | 295,629,000 |
| 1721–1740 | 613,422 | 12,681,000 | 12,268,440 | 253,611,000 | 13,863,050 | 17,924,000 | 277,961,000 | 359,480,000 |
| 1741–1760 | 791,211 | 16,356,000 | 15,824,230 | 327,116,000 | 17,140,612 | 22,162,000 | 342,812,235 | 443,232,000 |
| 1761–1780 | 665,666 | 13,761,000 | 13,313,315 | 275,211,000 | 20,985,591 | 27,133,000 | 419,711,820 | 542,658,000 |
| 1781–1800 | 571,948 | 11,823,000 | 11,438,970 | 236,464,000 | 28,261,779 | 36,540,000 | 565,235,580 | 730,810,000 |
| 1801–1810 | 571,568 | 11,815,000 | 5,715,627 | 118,152,000 | 28,746,922 | 37,166,000 | 287,469,225 | 371,677,000 |
| 1811–1820 | 367,957 | 7,606,000 | 3,679,566 | 76,063,000 | 17,385,755 | 22,479,000 | 178,857,555 | 224,786,000 |
| 1821–1830 | 457,044 | 9,448,000 | 4,570,444 | 94,479,000 | 14,807,004 | 19,144,000 | 148,070,040 | 191,444,000 |
| 1831–1840 | 652,291 | 13,484,000 | 6,522,913 | 134,841,000 | 19,175,867 | 24,793,000 | 191,758,675 | 247,930,000 |
| 1841–1850 | 1,760,502 | 36,393,000 | 17,605,018 | 363,928,000 | 25,090,342 | 32,440,000 | 250,903,422 | 324,400,000 |
| 1851–1855 | 6,410,324 | 132,513,000 | 32,051,621 | 662,566,000 | 28,488,597 | 36,824,000 | 142,442,995 | 184,160,000 |
| 1856–1860 | 6,486,262 | 134,083,000 | 32,431,312 | 670,415,000 | 29,095,428 | 37,618,000 | 145,477,142 | 188,092,000 |
| 1861–1865 | 5,949,582 | 122,989,000 | 29,747,913 | 614,944,000 | 35,401,972 | 45,772,000 | 177,009,862 | 228,861,000 |
| 1866–1870 | 6,270,086 | 129,614,000 | 31,350,430 | 648,071,000 | 43,051,583 | 55,663,000 | 215,257,914 | 278,313,000 |
| 1871–1875 | 5,591,014 | 115,577,000 | 27,955,008 | 577,883,000 | 63,317,014 | 81,864,000 | 316,585,069 | 409,322,000 |
| 1876–1880 | 5,543,110 | 114,586,000 | 27,715,550 | 572,931,000 | 78,775,602 | 101,851,000 | 393,878,009 | 509,256,000 |
| 1881–1885 | 4,704,755 | 99,116,000 | 23,973,773 | 495,582,000 | 92,003,914 | 118,935,000 | 460,019,722 | 594,673,000 |
| 1886 | 5,135,079 | 106,163,000 | 5,135,079 | 106,163,900 | 93,297,290 | 120,626,800 | 93,297,290 | 120,626,800 |
| 1887 | 5,116,861 | 107,774,700 | 5,116,861 | 105,774,900 | 96,123,586 | 124,281,000 | 96,123,586 | 124,281,000 |
| 1888 | 5,330,775 | 110,196,900 | 5,330,775 | 110,196,900 | 108,827,606 | 140,706,400 | 108,827,606 | 140,706,400 |
| 1889 | 5,973,790 | 123,489,200 | 5,973,700 | 123,489,200 | 120,213,611 | 155,427,700 | 120,213,611 | 155,427,700 |
| 1890 | 5,749,306 | 118,848,700 | 5,749,306 | 118,848,703 | 126,095,062 | 163,032,000 | 126,095,062 | 163,032,000 |
| 1891 | 6,320,194 | 130,650,000 | 6,320,194 | 130,650,000 | 137,170,919 | 177,352,300 | 137,170,919 | 177,352,300 |
| 1892 | 7,102,180 | 146,815,100 | 7,102,180 | 146,815,100 | 153,151,762 | 198,014,400 | 153,151,762 | 198,014,400 |
| 1893 | 7,608,787 | 157,287,600 | 7,608,787 | 157,287,600 | 166,092,047 | 214,745,300 | 166,092,047 | 214,745,300 |
| 1894 | 8,737,788 | 180,626,100 | 8,737,787 | 180,626,100 | 167,752,501 | 216,892,300 | 167,752,501 | 216,892,300 |
| 1895 | 9,820,125 | 203,000,000 | 9,820,125 | 203,000,000 | 174,790,875 | 226,000,000 | 174,790,875 | 226,000,000 |
| Total | | | 421,900,202 | 8,783,467,400 | | | 8,011,122,035 | 10,357,814,100 |

## STATISTICAL TABLES.

### Monetary Systems and Approximate Stocks of Money in the Aggre

| | Countries. | Monetary System. | Ratio between gold and full legal tender silver. | Ratio between gold and limited tender silver | Population. | Stock of gold |
|---|---|---|---|---|---|---|
| 1 | United States a.......... | Gold*... | 1 to 15.98 | 1 to 14.95 | 71,390,000 | $600,100,000 |
| 2 | United Kingdom....... | Gold.... | ........ | 1 to 14.28 | 38,900,000 | b580,000,000 |
| 3 | France................... | Gold*... | 1 to 15½ | 1 to 14.38 | 38,300,000 | b850,000,000 |
| 4 | Germany................. | Gold.... | ........ | 1 to 13.957 | 51,200,000 | b625,000,000 |
| 5 | Belgium.................. | Gold*... | 1 to 15½ | 1 to 14.38 | 6,300,000 | b55,000,000 |
| 6 | Italy ..................... | Gold*§.. | 1 to 15½ | 1 to 14.38 | 30,700,000 | c98,200,000 |
| 7 | Switzerland............. | Gold*... | 1 to 15½ | 1 to 14.38 | 3,000,000 | c14,900,000 |
| 8 | Greece ... ............... | Gold*§.. | 1 to 15½ | 1 to 14.38 | 2,200,000 | b500,000 |
| 9 | Spain ................... | Gold*§.. | 1 to 15½ | 1 to 14.38 | 17,500,000 | b40,000,000 |
| 10 | Portugal ................ | Gold§... | ........ | 1 to 14.08 | 5,100,000 | b38,000,000 |
| 11 | Roumania............... | Gold.... | ........ | ........ | 5,800,000 | c38,600,000 |
| 12 | Servia.................... | Gold§... | ........ | ........ | 2,300,000 | c3,000,000 |
| 13 | Austria-Hungary........ | Gold§... | ........ | 1 to 13.69 | 43,500,000 | b140,000,000 |
| 14 | Netherlands............. | Gold*... | 1 to 15⅝* | 1 to 15 | 4,700,000 | c29,200,000 |
| 15 | Norway................... | Gold.... | ........ | 1 to 14.88 | 2,000,000 | b7,500,000 |
| 16 | Sweden ................ | Gold.... | ........ | 1 to 14.88 | 4,800,000 | c8,000,000 |
| 17 | Denmark ............... | Gold.... | ........ | 1 to 14.88 | 2,300,000 | c14,500,000 |
| 18 | Russia.................... | Silver§.. | 1 to 15½ | 1 to 12.90 | 126,000,000 | b480,000,000 |
| 19 | Turkey .................. | Gold*... | 1 to 15⅞ | 1 to 15⅞ | 22,000,000 | b50,000,000 |
| 20 | Australia'................ | Gold... | ........ | 1 to 14.28 | 4,700,000 | b115,000,000 |
| 21 | Egypt..................... | Gold.... | ........ | 1 to 15.68 | 6,800,000 | b120,000,000 |
| 22 | Mexico ................... | Silver... | 1 to 16½ | ........ | 12,100,000 | b5,000,000 |
| 23 | Central American States. | Silver... | 1 to 15½ | ........ | 5,600,000 | b500,000 |
| 24 | South American States.. | Silvere.. | 1 to 15½ | ........ | 36,000,000 | b40,000,000 |
| 25 | Japan..................... | Silver... | 1 to 16.18 | ........ | 41,100,000 | c80,000,000 |
| 26 | India..................... | Silver... | 1 to 15 | ........ | 296,000,000 | .......... |
| 27 | China..................... | Silver... | ........ | ........ | 360,000,000 | .......... |
| 28 | Straits Settlements...... | Silver... | ........ | ........ | 3,800,000 | .......... |
| 29 | Canada .................. | Gold.... | ........ | 1 to 14.28 | 4,800,000 | 20,000,000 |
| 30 | Cuba...................... | Gold*... | 1 to 15½ | ........ | 1,800,000 | b18,000,000 |
| 31 | Haiti...................... | Gold*... | 1 to 15½ | ........ | 1,000,000 | b3,000,000 |
| 32 | Bulgaria.................. | Gold*... | 1 to 15½ | 1 to 14.38 | 4,300,000 | b800,000 |
|  | Total................ | ........ | ........ | ........ | ........ | $4,074,800,000 |

\* In these countries silver is a legal tender, but coined only to a limited extent and for government account, by which means the gold standard is maintained. In Germany and Austria-Hungary some old legal-tender silver is still current.
§ Actual standard, depreciated paper.
a July 1, 1806; all other countries, January 1, 1895.

STATISTICAL TABLES.

*gate and Per Capita in the Principal Countries of the World.*

| Stock of Silver. | | | Uncovered paper. | Per Capita. | | | | |
|---|---|---|---|---|---|---|---|---|
| Full Tender. | Limited Tender. | Total. | | Gold. | Silver. | Paper. | Total. | |
| $549,800,000 | $75,800,000 | $625,600,000 | $383,300,000 | $8.41 | $8.77 | $5.37 | $22.55 | 1 |
| ............ | b115,000,000 | 115,000,000 | c113,400,000 | 14.91 | 2.96 | 2.91 | 20.78 | 2 |
| b430,000,000 | c57,900,000 | 487,900,000 | f32,800,000 | 22.19 | 12.74 | .85 | 35.78 | 3 |
| b105,000,000 | b110,000,000 | 215,000,000 | c60,400,000 | 12.21 | 4.20 | 1.18 | 17.59 | 4 |
| b48,000,000 | b6,900,000 | 54,900,000 | c65,400,000 | 8.73 | 8.71 | 10.38 | 27.82 | 5 |
| bc21,400,000 | bc20,000,000 | 41,400,000 | c172,800,000 | 3.20 | 1.35 | 5.62 | 10.17 | 6 |
| b10,000,000 | 5,000,000 | 15,000,000 | f16,400,000 | 4.97 | 5.00 | 5.47 | 15.44 | 7 |
| b500,000 | b1,000,000 | 1,500,000 | c24,600,000 | .23 | .68 | 11.18 | 12.09 | 8 |
| b126,000,000 | b40,000,000 | 166,000,000 | c83,700,000 | 2.28 | 9.49 | 4.78 | 16.55 | 9 |
| ............ | b24,800,000 | 24,800,000 | c45,800,000 | 7.45 | 4.86 | 8.98 | 21.29 | 10 |
| ............ | c10,600,000 | 10,600,000 | c11,700,000 | 6.65 | 1.83 | 2.02 | 10.50 | 11 |
| ............ | c1,900,000 | 1,900,000 | f2,800,000 | 1.30 | .83 | 1.22 | 3.35 | 12 |
| b80,000,000 | b40,000,000 | 120,000,000 | c204,700,000 | 3.22 | 2.76 | 4.70 | 10.68 | 13 |
| c53,000,000 | c3,900,000 | 56,900,000 | c34,600,000 | 6.21 | 12.10 | 7.36 | 25.67 | 14 |
| ............ | b2,000,000 | 2,000,000 | c3,800,000 | 3.75 | 1.00 | 1.90 | 6.65 | 15 |
| ............ | c4,800,000 | 4,800,000 | f17,600,000 | 1.66 | 1.00 | 3.66 | 6.34 | 16 |
| ............ | c5,400,000 | 5,400,000 | c5,400,000 | 6.30 | 2.35 | 2.35 | 11.00 | 17 |
| ............ | b48,000,000 | 48,000,000 | c539,000,000 | 3.80 | .38 | 4.28 | 8.46 | 18 |
| b30,000,000 | d10,000,000 | 40,000,000 | ............ | 2.27 | 1.82 | ..... | 4.09 | 19 |
| ............ | b7,000,000 | 7,000,000 | ............ | 24.47 | 1.49 | ..... | 25.96 | 20 |
| ............ | b15,000,000 | 15,000,000 | ............ | 17.65 | 2.20 | ..... | 19.85 | 21 |
| b55,000,000 | ............ | 55,000,000 | b2,000,000 | .41 | 4.54 | .16 | 5.11 | 22 |
| c12,000,000 | ............ | 12,000,000 | c8,000,000 | .09 | 2.14 | 1.43 | 3.66 | 23 |
| b30,000,000 | ............ | 30,000,000 | b550,000,000 | 1.11 | .83 | 15.28 | 17.22 | 24 |
| c68,000,000 | c16,300,000 | 84,300,000 | 83,000,000 | 1.95 | 2.05 | 2.02 | 6.02 | 25 |
| b950,000,000 | ............ | 950,000,000 | b37,000,000 | ..... | 3.21 | .12 | 3.33 | 26 |
| b750,000,000 | ............ | 750,000,000 | ............ | ..... | 2.08 | ..... | 2.08 | 27 |
| b115,000,000 | ............ | 115,000,000 | ............ | ..... | 3.26 | ..... | 3.26 | 28 |
| ............ | 6,500,000 | 6,500,000 | 40,000,000 | 4.17 | 1.35 | 8.32 | 13.84 | 29 |
| b1,500,000 | ............ | 1,500,000 | ............ | 10.00 | .83 | ..... | 10.83 | 30 |
| b2,100,000 | b800,000 | 2,900,000 | c4,200,000 | 3.00 | 2.00 | 4.20 | 10.10 | 31 |
| b3,400,000 | 3,400,000 | 6,800,000 | ............ | .18 | 1.58 | ..... | 1.76 | 32 |
| $3,440,700,000 | $632,000,000 | $4,072,700,000 | $2,542,400,000 | ..... | ..... | ..... | ..... | |

b Estimate, Bureau of the Mint.
c Information furnished through United States representatives.
d Haupt.
e Except Venezuela and Chili.
f Bulletin de Statistique.

4.03

## STATISTICAL TABLES.

### Products of gold and silver from mines in the United States, 1873–1895.

The silver product is given at its commercial value, reckoned at the average market price of silver each year, as well as its coining value in United States dollars.

| Calendar Year. | Gold. | | Silver. | | |
|---|---|---|---|---|---|
| | Fine ounces. | Value. | Fine ounces. | Commercial value. | Coining value. |
| 1873 | 1,741,500 | $36,000,000 | 27,650,000 | $35,890,000 | $35,750,000 |
| 1874 | 1,620,563 | 33,500,000 | 28,849,000 | 36,869,000 | 37,300,000 |
| 1875 | 1,615,725 | 33,400,000 | 24,518,000 | 30,549,000 | 31,700,000 |
| 1876 | 1,930,162 | 39,900,000 | 30,000,000 | 31,690,000 | 38,800,000 |
| 1877 | 2,268,768 | 46,900,000 | 30,783,000 | 36,970,000 | 39,800,000 |
| 1878 | 2,476,800 | 51,200,000 | 34,960,000 | 40,270,000 | 45,200,000 |
| 1879 | 1,881,787 | 38,900,000 | 31,550,000 | 35,430,000 | 40,800,000 |
| 1880 | 1,741,500 | 36,000,000 | 30,320,000 | 34,720,000 | 39,200,000 |
| 1881 | 1,678,612 | 34,700,000 | 33,260,000 | 37,850,000 | 43,000,000 |
| 1882 | 1,572,187 | 32,500,000 | 36,200,000 | 41,120,000 | 46,800,000 |
| 1883 | 1,451,250 | 30,000,000 | 35,730,000 | 39,660,000 | 46,200,000 |
| 1884 | 1,480,950 | 30,800,000 | 37,800,000 | 42,070,000 | 48,800,000 |
| 1885 | 1,538,325 | 31,800,000 | 39,910,000 | 42,500,000 | 51,600,000 |
| 1886 | 1,693,125 | 35,000,000 | 39,440,000 | 39,230,000 | 51,000,000 |
| 1887 | 1,596,375 | 33,000,000 | 41,200,000 | 40,410,000 | 53,350,000 |
| 1888 | 1,604,841 | 33,175,000 | 45,780,000 | 43,020,000 | 59,195,000 |
| 1889 | 1,587,000 | 32,800,000 | 50,000,000 | 46,750,000 | 64,646,000 |
| 1890 | 1,588,880 | 32,845,000 | 54,500,000 | 57,225,000 | 70,465,000 |
| 1891 | 1,604,840 | 33,175,000 | 58,330,000 | 57,680,000 | 75,417,000 |
| 1892 | 1,596,375 | 33,000,000 | 63,500,000 | 55,563,000 | 82,101,000 |
| 1893 | 1,739,323 | 35,955,000 | 60,000,000 | 46,800,000 | 77,576,000 |
| 1894 | 1,910,813 | 39,500,000 | 49,500,000 | 31,422,000 | 64,000,000 |
| 1895 | 2,254,760 | 46,610,000 | 55,727,000 | 36,445,000 | 72,051,000 |
| Total | 40,183,481 | $830,660,000 | 939,576,000 | $943,083,000 | $1,214,751,000 |

### Average Yearly Wages in the U. S. in Manufacturing Industries.
As shown by Census Reports.

| Year. | Population | Employees | Total wages. | Equivalent total wages in gold. | Average Annual wages in gold. | Wages increased since previous census. |
|---|---|---|---|---|---|---|
| 1860 | 31,443,321 | 1,311,246 | $378,878,966 | $378,878,966 | $288 | — |
| 1870 | 38,558,371 | 2,053,996 | 775,584,343 | 674,421,168 | 328 | 14 per cent. |
| 1880 | 50,155,783 | 2,732,595 | 947,953,795 | 947,953,795 | 347 | 5½ " |
| 1890 | 62,831,900 | 4,712,622 | 2,283,216,529 | 2,283,216,529 | 484 | 39 " |

4.04

## STATISTICAL TABLES.

*Statement of the Coin and Paper Circulation of the United States on June 30, from 1860 to 1896, inclusive.*

[Prepared by Loans and Currency Division, Treasury Department.]

| Year. | Coin in United States, including Bullion in Treasury. | Paper Money in United States. | Total Money. | Coin Bullion and Paper Money in Treasury. | Total Money in Circulation. | Population. | Circulation per Capita. |
|---|---|---|---|---|---|---|---|
| 1860 | $235,000,000 | $207,102,477 | $442,102,477 | $6,695,225 | $435,407,252 | 31,443,321 | $13.85 |
| 1861 | 250,000,000 | 202,005,767 | 452,005,767 | 3,600,000 | 448,405,767 | 32,064,000 | 13.99 |
| 1862 | 25,000,000 | 333,452,079 | 358,052,079 | 23,754,335 | 334,697,744 | 32,704,000 | 10.22 |
| 1863 | 25,000,000 | 649,867,283 | 674,867,283 | 79,473,245 | 595,394,038 | 33,365,000 | 17.84 |
| 1864 | 25,000,000 | 680,588,067 | 705,588,067 | 35,946,589 | 669,641,478 | 34,046,000 | 19.67 |
| 1865 | 25,000,000 | 745,129,755 | 770,129,755 | 55,426,760 | 714,702,995 | 34,748,000 | 20.57 |
| 1866 | 25,000,000 | 729,827,254 | 754,827,254 | 80,839,010 | 673,488,244 | 35,469,000 | 18.99 |
| 1867 | 25,000,000 | 703,200,612 | 728,200,612 | 66,208,543 | 661,992,069 | 36,211,000 | 18.28 |
| 1868 | 25,000,000 | 691,553,578 | 716,553,578 | 36,449,917 | 680,103,661 | 36,973,000 | 18.39 |
| 1869 | 25,000,000 | 690,351,180 | 715,351,180 | 50,898,289 | 664,452,891 | 37,756,000 | 17 60 |
| 1870 | 25,000,000 | 697,868,461 | 722,868,461 | 47,655,667 | 675,212,794 | 38,558,371 | 17.60 |
| 1871 | 25,000,000 | 716,812,174 | 741,812,174 | 25,923,169 | 715,889,005 | 39,555,000 | 18.10 |
| 1872 | 25,000,000 | 737,721,565 | 762,721,565 | 24,412,016 | 738,309,549 | 40,596,000 | 18.19 |
| 1873 | 25,000,000 | 749,445,010 | 774,445,610 | 22,563,801 | 751,881,809 | 41,677,000 | 18.04 |
| 1874 | 25,000,000 | 781,024,781 | 806,024,781 | 29,911,750 | 776,083,031 | 42,796,000 | 18.13 |
| 1875 | 25,000,000 | 773,273,509 | 798,273,509 | 44,171,562 | 754,101,947 | 43,951,000 | 17.16 |
| 1876 | 52,418,734 | 738,264,550 | 790,683,284 | 63,073,896 | 727,609,388 | 45,137,000 | 16.12 |
| 1877 | 65,837,506 | 697,216,341 | 763,053,847 | 40,788,904 | 722,314,883 | 46,353,000 | 15.58 |
| 1878 | 102,047,907 | 649,205,669 | 791,253,576 | 62,120,942 | 729,132,634 | 47,598,000 | 15.32 |
| 1879 | 357,268,178 | 694,253,363 | 1,051,521,541 | 232,889,748 | 818,631,793 | 48,866,000 | 16.75 |
| 1880 | 494,363,884 | 711,565,313 | 1,205,929,197 | 232,546,969 | 973,332,228 | 50,155,783 | 19.41 |
| 1881 | 647,868,682 | 758,673,141 | 1,406,541,823 | 292,303,704 | 1,114,238,119 | 51,316,000 | 21.71 |
| 1882 | 703,974,839 | 776,556,880 | 1,480,531,719 | 306,241,300 | 1,174,290,419 | 52,495,000 | 22.37 |
| 1883 | 769,740,048 | 873,749,768 | 1,643,489,816 | 413,184,120 | 1,230,305,696 | 53,693,000 | 22.91 |
| 1884 | 801,068,939 | 904,385,250 | 1,705,454,189 | 461,528,220 | 1,243,925,969 | 54,911,000 | 22.65 |
| 1885 | 872,175,823 | 945,482,513 | 1,817,658,336 | 525,089,721 | 1,292,568,615 | 56,148,000 | 23.02 |
| 1886 | 903,027,304 | 905,532,390 | 1,808,559,694 | 555,859,160 | 1,252,700,525 | 57,404,000 | 21.82 |
| 1887 | 1,007,513,901 | 892,928,771 | 1,900,442,672 | 582,903,529 | 1,317,539,143 | 58,680,000 | 22.45 |
| 1888 | 1,092,391,690 | 970,564,259 | 2,062,955,949 | 690,785,079 | 1,372,170,870 | 59,974,000 | 22.88 |
| 1889 | 1,100,612,434 | 974,738,277 | 2,075,350,711 | 694,989,062 | 1,380,361,649 | 61,289,000 | 22.52 |
| 1890 | 1,152,471,983 | 991,754,521 | 2,144,226,159 | 714,974,889 | 1,429,251,270 | 62,622,250 | 22.82 |
| 1891 | 1,163,185,054 | 1,032,089,021 | 2,195,224,075 | 697,783,368 | 1,497,440,707 | 63,975,000 | 23.41 |
| 1892 | 1,232,854,331 | 1,139,745,170 | 2,372,599,501 | 771,252,314 | 1,601,347,187 | 65,580,000 | 24.44 |
| 1893 | 1,213,413,584 | 1,109,988,808 | 2,323,402,392 | 726,701,147 | 1,586,701,245 | 66,946,000 | 23.85 |
| 1894 | 1,251,543,158 | 1,168,891,623 | 2,420,434,781 | 759,626,073 | 1,660,808,708 | 68,397,000 | 24.28 |
| 1895 | 1,260,987,506 | 1,137,619,914 | 2,398,607,420 | 796,698,947 | 1,601,908,473 | 69,878,000 | 22.93 |
| 1896 | 1,225,618,792 | 1,120,012,536 | 2,345,631,328 | 839,000,302 | 1,506,631,026 | 71,390,000 | 21.10 |

NOTE 1.—Specie payments were suspended from January 1, 1862, to January 1, 1879. During the greater part of that period gold and silver coins were not in circulation except on the Pacific coast, where, it is estimated, the specie circulation was generally about $25,000,000. This estimated amount is the only coin included in the above statement from 1862 to 1875, inclusive.

NOTE 2.—In 1876 subsidiary silver again came into use, and is included in this statement, beginning with that year.

NOTE 3.—The coinage of standard silver dollars began in 1878 under the act of February 28, 1878.

NOTE 4.—Specie payments were resumed January 1, 1879, and all gold and silver coins, as well as gold and silver bullion in the Treasury, are included in this statement from and after that date.

*Highest, lowest and average price of silver bullion and bullion value of a United States silver dollar, measured by the market price of silver, and the quantity of silver purchasable with a dollar at average London price of silver,* 1873-95.

| Calendar Year. | Price of Silver Bullion. | | | | Bullion value of a silver dollar. | | | Grains of pure silver at average price purchasable with a United States silver dollar.* |
|---|---|---|---|---|---|---|---|---|
| | Lowest. | Highest | Average | Value of a fine ounce at average quotation | Highest | Lowest. | Average | |
| 1873 | 57 7/8 | 59 15/16 | 59 1/4 | 1.298 | $1.016 | $0.981 | $1.004 | 369.77 |
| 1874 | 57 1/4 | 59 1/2 | 58 5/16 | 1.273 | 1.003 | .970 | .988 | 375.76 |
| 1875 | 55 1/2 | 57 5/8 | 56 7/8 | 1.246 | .977 | .941 | .964 | 385.11 |
| 1876 | 46 3/4 | 58 1/2 | 52 3/4 | 1.156 | .991 | .792 | .894 | 415.27 |
| 1877 | 53 1/4 | 58 1/4 | 54 13/16 | 1.201 | .987 | .902 | .929 | 398.62 |
| 1878 | 49 1/2 | 55 1/4 | 52 9/16 | 1.152 | .936 | .839 | .891 | 419.66 |
| 1879 | 48 7/8 | 53 3/4 | 51 1/4 | 1.123 | .911 | .868 | .868 | 427.70 |
| 1880 | 51 5/8 | 52 7/8 | 52 1/4 | 1.145 | .896 | .875 | .886 | 419.49 |
| 1881 | 50 7/8 | 52 7/8 | 51 15/16 | 1.138 | .896 | .862 | .881 | 421.87 |
| 1882 | 50 | 52 3/8 | 51 13/16 | 1.136 | .887 | .847 | .878 | 422.83 |
| 1883 | 50 | 51 3/16 | 50 5/8 | 1.110 | .868 | .847 | .858 | 472.69 |
| 1884 | 49 1/2 | 51 3/8 | 50 3/4 | 1.113 | .871 | .839 | .861 | 431.18 |
| 1885 | 46 7/8 | 50 | 48 9/16 | 1.0645 | .847 | .794 | .823 | 451.09 |
| 1886 | 42 | 47 | 45 3/8 | .9946 | .797 | .712 | .769 | 482.77 |
| 1887 | 43 1/4 | 47 1/8 | 44 5/8 | .97823 | .799 | .733 | .758 | 489.78 |
| 1888 | 41 5/8 | 44 9/16 | 42 7/8 | .93897 | .755 | .706 | .727 | 510.66 |
| 1889 | 42 | 44 3/8 | 41 11/16 | .93519 | .752 | .746 | .724 | 512.93 |
| 1890 | 43 5/8 | 54 5/8 | 47 3/4 | 1.04633 | .926 | .740 | .810 | 458.83 |
| 1891 | 43 1/2 | 48 3/4 | 45 1/16 | .98782 | .827 | .738 | .764 | 485.76 |
| 1892 | 37 7/8 | 43 3/4 | 39 3/4 | .87106 | .742 | .642 | .674 | 550.79 |
| 1893 | 30 1/2 | 38 3/4 | 35 9/16 | .78031 | .655 | .513 | .604 | 615.10 |
| 1894 | 27 | 31 3/4 | 28 7/8 | .63479 | .538 | .457 | .491 | 756.04 |
| 1895 | 27 3/16 | 31 3/8 | 29 13/16 | .68406 | .532 | .461 | .505 | 733.87 |
| 1896 (6 months). | 30 1/2 | 31 13/16 | 31 3/16 | .68158 | .539 | .517 | .528 | 704.03 |

* 371.25 grains of pure silver are contained in a silver dollar.

## STATISTICAL TABLES.

### Commercial ratio of silver and gold each year 1687–1895.

[NOTE—From 1687 to 1832 the ratios are taken from Dr. A. Soetbeer; from 1833 to 1878 from Pixley and Abell's tables, and from 1879 to 1894 from daily cablegrams from London to the Bureau of the Mint.]

| Year. | Ratio. | Year. | Ratio. | Year. | Ratio. | Year. | Ratio. | Year. | Ratio. | Year. | Ratio. |
|---|---|---|---|---|---|---|---|---|---|---|---|
| 1687... | 14.94 | 1723.. | 15.20 | 1759.. | 14.15 | 1795.. | 15.55 | 1831.. | 15.72 | 1867... | 15.57 |
| 1688... | 14.94 | 1724.. | 15.11 | 1760.. | 14.14 | 1796.. | 15.65 | 1832.. | 15.73 | 1868... | 15.59 |
| 1689... | 15.02 | 1725.. | 15.11 | 1761.. | 14.54 | 1797.. | 15.41 | 1833.. | 15.93 | 1869... | 15.60 |
| 1690... | 15.02 | 1726.. | 15.15 | 1762.. | 15.27 | 1798.. | 15.59 | 1834.. | 15.73 | 1870.. | 15.57 |
| 1691... | 14.98 | 1727.. | 15.24 | 1763.. | 14.99 | 1799.. | 15.74 | 1835.. | 15.80 | 1871... | 15.57 |
| 1692... | 14.92 | 1728.. | 15.11 | 1764. | 14.70 | 1800.. | 15.68 | 1836.. | 15.72 | 1872... | 15.63 |
| 1693... | 14.83 | 1729. | 14.92 | 1765.. | 14.83 | 1801.. | 15.46 | 1837·· | 15.83 | 1873... | 15.92 |
| 1694... | 14.87 | 1730.. | 14.81 | 1766.. | 14.80 | 1802.. | 15.26 | 1838.. | 15.85 | 1874... | 16.17 |
| 1695... | 15.02 | 1731.. | 14.94 | 1767.. | 14.85 | 1803.. | 15.41 | 1839.. | 15.62 | 1875... | 16.59 |
| 1696... | 15.00 | 1732.. | 15.09 | 1768.. | 14.80 | 1804.. | 15.41 | 1840.. | 15.62 | 1876... | 17.88 |
| 1697... | 15.20 | 1733.. | 15.18 | 1769.. | 14.72 | 1805.. | 15.79 | 1841.. | 15.70 | 1877... | 17.22 |
| 1698... | 15.07 | 1734.. | 15.39 | 1770.. | 14.62 | 1806.. | 15.52 | 1842.. | 15.87 | 1878... | 17.94 |
| 1699... | 14.94 | 1735.. | 15.41 | 1771.. | 14.66 | 1807.. | 15.43 | 1843.. | 15.93 | 1879... | 18.40 |
| 1700... | 14.81 | 1736.. | 15.18 | 1772.. | 14.52 | 1808.. | 16.08 | 1844.. | 15.85 | 1880... | 18.05 |
| 1701... | 15.07 | 1737.. | 15.02 | 1773.. | 14.62 | 1809.. | 15.96 | 1845.. | 15.92 | 1881... | 18.16 |
| 1702... | 15.52 | 1738.. | 14.91 | 1774.. | 14.62 | 1810.. | 15.77 | 1846.. | 15.90 | 1882... | 18.19 |
| 1703... | 15.17 | 1739.. | 14.91 | 1775.. | 14.72 | 1811.. | 15.53 | 1847.. | 15.80 | 1883... | 18.64 |
| 1704... | 15.22 | 1740.. | 14.94 | 1776.. | 14.55 | 1812.. | 16.11 | 1848.. | 15.85 | 1884... | 18.57 |
| 1705... | 15.11 | 1741.. | 14.92 | 1777.. | 14.54 | 1813.. | 16.25 | 1849.. | 15.78 | 1885... | 19.41 |
| 1706... | 15.27 | 1742.. | 14.85 | 1778.. | 14.68 | 1814.. | 15.04 | 1850.. | 15.70 | 1886... | 20.78 |
| 1707... | 15.44 | 1743.. | 14.85 | 1779.. | 14.80 | 1815.. | 15.26 | 1851.. | 15.46 | 1887... | 21.13 |
| 1708... | 15.41 | 1744.. | 14.87 | 1780.. | 14.72 | 1816.. | 15.28 | 1852.. | 15.59 | 1888... | 21.99 |
| 1709... | 15.31 | 1745.. | 14.98 | 1781.. | 14.78 | 1817.. | 15.11 | 1853.. | 15.33 | 1889.. | 22.10 |
| 1710... | 15.22 | 1746.. | 15.13 | 1782.. | 14.42 | 1818.. | 15.35 | 1854.. | 15.33 | 1890... | 19.76 |
| 1711... | 15.29 | 1747.. | 15.26 | 1783.. | 14.48 | 1819.. | 15.83 | 1855.. | 15.38 | 1891... | 20.92 |
| 1712... | 15.31 | 1748.. | 15.11 | 1784.. | 14.70 | 1820 . | 15.62 | 1856.. | 15.38 | 1892... | 23.72 |
| 1713... | 15.24 | 1749.. | 14.80 | 1785.. | 14.92 | 1821.. | 15.95 | 1857.. | 15.27 | 1893... | 26.49 |
| 1714... | 15.13 | 1750.. | 14.55 | 1786.. | 14.96 | 1822.. | 15.80 | 1858.. | 15.38 | 1894... | 32.56 |
| 1715... | 15.11 | 1751.. | 14.39 | 1787.. | 14.92 | 1823.. | 15.84 | 1859.. | 15.19 | 1895... | 31.60 |
| 1716... | 15.09 | 1752.. | 14.54 | 1788.. | 14.65 | 1824. | 15.82 | 1860.. | 15.29 | 1896 (6 months) | 30.32 |
| 1717... | 15.13 | 1753.. | 14.54 | 1789.. | 14.75 | 1825.. | 15.70 | 1861.. | 15.50 | | |
| 1718... | 15.11 | 1754.. | 14.48 | 1790.. | 15.04 | 1826.. | 15.76 | 1862.. | 15.35 | | |
| 1719... | 15.09 | 1755.. | 14.68 | 1791.. | 15.05 | 1827.. | 15.74 | 1863.. | 15.37 | | |
| 1720... | 15.04 | 1756.. | 14.94 | 1792.. | 15.17 | 1828 . | 15.78 | 1864 . | 15.37 | | |
| 1721... | 15.05 | 1757.. | 14.87 | 1793.. | 15.00 | 1829.. | 15.78 | 1865.. | 15.44 | | |
| 1722... | 15.17 | 1758.. | 14.85 | 1794.. | 15.37 | 1830.. | 15.82 | 1866.. | 15.43 | | |

## STATISTICAL TABLES.

### *Comparative Statement of the Exchanges of certain Clearing-houses of the United States for Four Years.*

| Clearing-house at— | Exchanges for years ending September 30— | | | |
|---|---|---|---|---|
| | 1895. | 1894. | 1893. | 1892. |
| New York............ | $28,264,379,126 | $24,230,145,368 | $34,421,379,870 | $36,279,905,236 |
| Boston............... | 4,029,303,920 | 4,095,997,060 | 4,864,779,750 | 4,901,096,976 |
| Chicago. .;........ | 4,541,435,824 | 4,263,560,459 | 4,970,913,387 | 4,959,861,142 |
| Philadelphia... .... | 3,395,864,543 | 2,902,542,206 | 3,656,677,140 | 3,671,140,407 |
| St. Louis............ | 1,218,425,062 | 1,106,770,443 | 1,188,378,457 | 1,211,370,719 |
| San Francisco....... | 671,852,105 | 647,848,503 | 732,949,766 | 833,617,126 |
| Baltimore........... | 685,004,866 | 664,214,307 | 737,568,241 | 772,435,133 |
| Pittsburgh.......... | 711,773,043 | 630,268,350 | 711,547,291 | 743,635,356 |
| Cincinnati ......... | 653,228,500 | 630,364,800 | 679,051,000 | 728,711,350 |
| Kansas City. ....... | 507,805,333 | 464,394,146 | 507,454,919 | 494,906,132 |
| New Orleans........ | 451,679,488 | 445,671,110 | 523,996,645 | 488,931,005 |
| Minneapolis ........ | 337,201,924 | 298,085,000 | 377,785,380 | 427,287,201 |
| Detroit............. | 338,313,355 | 282,755,354 | 353,558,369 | 347,737,582 |
| Louisville........... | 309,894,324 | 308,993,881 | 356,301,823 | 368,693,612 |
| Other cities.'....... | 4,395,300,093 | 4,007,886,111 | 4,778,280,417 | 4,054,229,071 |
| Total. ........ | $51,111,591,928 | $45,028,490,746 | $58,880,682,455 | $60,833,572,438 |

### *Transactions of the New York Clearing House for Thirty-six Years.*

| Year. | No. of Banks. | Capital. | Clearings. | Balances Paid in Money. | Average Daily Clearings. | Average Daily Balances Paid in Money. | Balances to Clearings. |
|---|---|---|---|---|---|---|---|
| 1860..... | 50 | $69,907,435 | $7,231,143,057 | $380,693,438 | $23,401,757 | $1,232,018 | 5.3% |
| 1861..... | 50 | 68,900,605 | 5,915,742,758 | 353,383,944 | 19,269,520 | 1,151,088 | 6.0 |
| 1862..... | 50 | 68,375,820 | 6,871,443,591 | 415,530,331 | 22,237,682 | 1,344,758 | 6.0 |
| 1863..... | 50 | 68,972,508 | 14,867,597,849 | 677,626,483 | 48,428,657 | 2,207,252 | 4.6 |
| 1864..... | 49 | 68,586,763 | 24,097,196,656 | 885,719,205 | 77,984,455 | 2,866,405 | 3.7 |
| 1865..... | 55 | 80,363,013 | 26,032,384,342 | 1,035,765,108 | 84,796,040 | 3,373,828 | 4.0 |
| 1866..... | 58 | 82,370,200 | 28,717,146,914 | 1,066,135,106 | 93,541,195 | 3,472,753 | 3.7 |
| 1867..... | 58 | 81,770,200 | 26,675,159,472 | 1,144,963,451 | 93,101,167 | 3,717,414 | 4.0 |
| 1868..... | 59 | 82,270,200 | 28,484,288,637 | 1,125,455,237 | 92,182,104 | 3,642,250 | 4.0 |
| 1869..... | 59 | 82,720,200 | 37,407,028,987 | 1,120,318,308 | 121,451,393 | 3,637,397 | 3 0 |
| 1870..... | 61 | 83,620,200 | 27,804,539,406 | 1,036,484,822 | 90,274,479 | 3,365,210 | 3.7 |
| 1871..... | 62 | 84,420,200 | 29,300,986,682 | 1,209,721,029 | 95,133,074 | 3,927,606 | 4 1 |
| 1872..... | 61 | 84,420,200 | 33,844,369,568 | 1,428,582,707 | 109,884,317 | 4,636,632 | 4.2 |
| 1873..... | 59 | 83,370,200 | 35,461,052,826 | 1,474,508,025 | 115,885,794 | 4,818,654 | 4.1 |
| 1874..... | 59 | 81,635,200 | 22,855,927,636 | 1,286,753,176 | 74,692,574 | 4,205,076 | 5.7 |
| 1875..... | 58 | 80,435,200 | 25,061,237,902 | 1,408,608,777 | 81,899,470 | 4,603,297 | 5.6 |
| 1876..... | 59 | 81,731,200 | 21,597,274,247 | 1,295,042,029 | 70,349,428 | 4,218,378 | 5.9 |
| 1877..... | 58 | 71,085,200 | 23,289,243,701 | 1,373,996,302 | 76,358,176 | 4,504,900 | 5.9 |
| 1878..... | 57 | 63,611,500 | 22,508,438,442 | 1,307,843,857 | 73,555,988 | 4,274,000 | 5.8 |
| 1879..... | 59 | 60,800,200 | 25,178,770,691 | 1,400,111,068 | 82,015,540 | 4,560,622 | 5.6 |
| 1880..... | 57 | 60,475,200 | 37,182,128,621 | 1,516,538,631 | 121,510,224 | 4,956,000 | 4.1 |
| 1881..... | 60 | 61,162,700 | 48,565,818,212 | 1,776,018,162 | 159,232,191 | 5,823,010 | 3.5 |
| 1882..... | 61 | 60,962,700 | 46,552,846,161 | 1,595,000,245 | 151,037,985 | 5,195,440 | 3.4 |
| 1883..... | 63 | 61,162,700 | 40,293,165,258 | 1,568,983,196 | 132,548,307 | 5,161,129 | 3.9 |
| 1884..... | 61 | 60,412,700 | 34,092,037,338 | 1,524,930,904 | 111,048,983 | 4,967,202 | 4.5 |
| 1885..... | 64 | 58,612,700 | 25,250,791,440 | 1,295,355,252 | 82,780,480 | 4,247,069 | 5.1 |
| 1886..... | 63 | 59,312,700 | 33,374,682,216 | 1,519,565,885 | 109,067,580 | 4,965,900 | 4.5 |
| 1887..... | 64 | 60,862,700 | 34,872,848,786 | 1,569,626,325 | 114,337,209 | 5,146,316 | 4.5 |
| 1888. .. | 63 | 60,762,700 | 30,863,696,609 | 1,570,198,528 | 101,192,415 | 5,148,192 | 5.1 |
| 1889..... | 63 | 60,762,700 | 34,796,465,520 | 1,757,637,478 | 114,839,820 | 5,800,784 | 5.0 |
| 1890..... | 64 | 60,812,700 | 37,660,686,572 | 1,753,040,145 | 123,074,139 | 5,726,889 | 4.7 |
| 1891..... | 63 | 60,772,700 | 34,053,698,770 | 1,584,635,500 | 111,651,471 | 5,195,520 | 4.6 |
| 1892..... | 64 | 60,422,700 | 36,279,905,236 | 1,861,500,575 | 118,561,782 | 6,093,835 | 5 1 |
| 1893..... | 64 | 60,022,700 | 34,421,380,870 | 1,696,207,176 | 113,078,082 | 5,616,580 | 4.9 |
| 1894..... | 65 | 61,622,700 | 24,230,145,368 | 1,585,241,634 | 79,704,426 | 5,214,611 | 6.5 |
| 1895..... | 66 | 62,622,700 | 28,264,379,126 | 1,396,574,349 | 92,670,095 | 6,218,276 | 0.7 |

4.08

STATISTICAL TABLES.

*Coinage of the U. S. Mints from Organization, 1792, to June 30, 1896.*

| Denomination. | Pieces. | Value. |
|---|---|---|
| **Gold.** | | |
| Double Eagles | 63,884,661 | $1,277,693,220 00 |
| Eagles | 26,653,827 | 266,538,270 00 |
| Half Eagles | 44,126,207 | 220,631,035 00 |
| Three-dollar pieces, 1858–1890 | 539,792 | 1,619,376 00 |
| Quarter Eagles | 11,484,406 | 28,711,015 00 |
| Dollars, 1849–1890 | 19,499,337 | 19,499,337 00 |
| Total gold | 166,188,230 | $1,814,692,253 00 |
| **Silver.** | | |
| Dollars | 438,821,279 | $438,821,279 00 |
| Trade dollars | 35,965,924 | 35,965,924 00 |
| Half dollars | 265,324,616 | 132,662,308 00 |
| Columbian half dollars | 5,002,105 | 2,501,052 50 |
| Quarter dollars | 204,664,667 | 51,166,166 75 |
| Columbian quarter dollars | 40,023 | 10,005 75 |
| Twenty-cent pieces, 1875–1878 | 1,355,000 | 271,000 00 |
| Dimes | 289,043,005 | 28,904,300 50 |
| Half dimes, 1792–1873 | 97,604,388 | 4,880,219 40 |
| Three-cent pieces, 1851–1873 | 42,736,240 | 1,282,087 20 |
| Total silver | 1,380,557,247 | $696,464,343 10 |
| Total gold and silver | 1,546,745,477 | $2,511,156,596 10 |
| Minor coinage | 1,535,261,002 | 27,830,048 67 |
| Grand total | 3,082,006,479 | $2,538,986,644 77 |

*Railroad Freight Earnings and Rates per Ton, 1873–95.*
Compiled from Henry W. Poor's Figures.

| Year. | Earnings from Freight. | Tons Freight Moved. | Average Rate Per Ton Per Mile. |
|---|---|---|---|
| 1873 | $389,025,508 | 188,000,000 | 2.210 |
| 1874 | 379,466,935 | 190,000,000 | 2.040 |
| 1875 | 368,960,234 | 190,000,000 | 1.810 |
| 1876 | 361,137,376 | 210,000,000 | 1.585 |
| 1877 | 347,704,548 | 210,000,000 | 1.524 |
| 1878 | 365,496,061 | 231,700,000 | 1.401 |
| 1879 | 386,676,108 | 280,000,000 | 1.201 |
| 1880 | 467,748,928 | 326,000,000 | 1.348 |
| 1881 | 551,963,477 | 336,000,000 | 1.264 |
| 1882 | 485,778,341 | 360,490,375 | 1.236 |
| 1883 | 559,509,831 | 400,453,489 | 1.224 |
| 1884 | 502,869,910 | 399,074,749 | 1.125 |
| 1885 | 509,690,992 | 437,040,099 | 1.036 |
| 1886 | 570,359,054 | 482,245,254 | 1.042 |
| 1887 | 636,666,228 | 552,074,752 | 1.034 |
| 1888 | 639,200,723 | 590,857,353 | 0.977 |
| 1889 | 665,962,631 | 619,165,630 | 0.970 |
| 1890 | 731,821,733 | 691,344,437 | 0.927 |
| 1891 | 754,185,910 | 704,398,609 | 0.929 |
| 1892 | 794,526,500 | 730,605,011 | 0.941 |
| 1893 | 808,494,668 | 757,464,480 | 0.898 |
| 1894 | 700,477,409 | 674,714,747 | 0.864 |
| 1895 | 743,784,751 | 763,799,883 | 0.839 |

## STATISTICAL TABLES.

### Crop and Yearly Prices of Cotton, 1872-95.

| Year. | Annual Crop of Cotton in Bales. | Year's Price, N. Y., in Cents. |
|---|---|---|
| 1872 | 2,974,351 | 22.19 |
| 1873 | 3,930,508 | 20.14 |
| 1874 | 4,170,388 | 17.95 |
| 1875 | 3,827,845 | 15.46 |
| 1876 | 4,632,313 | 12.98 |
| 1877 | 4,474,069 | 11.82 |
| 1878 | 4,773,865 | 11.22 |
| 1879 | 5,074,155 | 10.84 |
| 1880 | 5,761,252 | 11.51 |
| 1881 | 6,605,750 | 12.03 |
| 1882 | 5,456,048 | 11.56 |
| 1883 | 6,949,756 | 11.88 |
| 1884 | 5,513,200 | 10.88 |
| 1885 | 5,706,165 | 10.45 |
| 1886 | 6,575,691 | 9.28 |
| 1887 | 6,505,087 | 10.21 |
| 1888 | 7,046,833 | 10.03 |
| 1889 | 6,938,290 | 10.65 |
| 1890 | 7,311,322 | 11.07 |
| 1891 | 8,652,597 | 8.60 |
| 1892 | 9,035,379 | 7.71 |
| 1893 | 6,700,365 | 8.56 |
| 1894 | 7,549,817 | 6.94 |
| 1895 | 9,901,251 | 7.44 |

### Gold Values for Wheat per Bushel, Minnesota, New York and London, 1862-94.

| Year. | Minn. | New York. | London. | Differences. | |
|---|---|---|---|---|---|
| | | | | Minn. and New York. | Minn. and London. |
| 1862-66 | 56.5 | 115.0 | .... | 58.5 | .... |
| 1867-70 | 65.3 | 138.6 | 175.6 | 73.3 | 110.8 |
| 1871-74 | 73.1 | 134.1 | 176.3 | 61.1 | 103.2 |
| 1875-78 | 72.7 | 110.5 | 149.2 | 37.8 | 76.5 |
| 1879-82 | 92.2 | 132.4 | 149.6 | 40.2 | 57.4 |
| 1883-86 | 64.2 | 92.4 | 113.5 | 39.2 | 48.3 |
| 1887-90 | 73.4 | 95.3 | 106.1 | 21.9 | 38.7 |
| 1891-94 | 62.1 | 83.5 | .... | 21.4 | .... |

## STATISTICAL TABLES.

### Average Farm Prices Per Ton in Gold in Illinois, 1862-94.
Compiled by L. G. Powers of Minnesota.

| CROPS. | 1862 to 1866 | 1867 to 1870 | 1871 to 1874 | 1875 to 1878 | 1879 to 1882 | 1883 to 1886 | 1887 to 1890 | 1891 to 1894 | 1862 to 1894 | Percentages. |
|---|---|---|---|---|---|---|---|---|---|---|
| Corn | $10.57 | $13.08 | $10.97 | $9.84 | $14.55 | $11.43 | $11.60 | $12.91 | $11.82 | 50.36 |
| Oats | 16.42 | 18.35 | 16.33 | 13.62 | 20.68 | 15.63 | 15.90 | 17.92 | 16.77 | 9.81 |
| Wheat | 29.17 | 30.44 | 32.49 | 28.34 | 33.10 | 24.59 | 26.18 | 20.96 | 29.55 | 8.49 |
| Barley | 24.22 | 29.60 | 28.16 | 24.74 | 29.41 | 22.39 | 24.77 | 18.25 | 25.72 | 0.27 |
| Buckwheat | 20.95 | 26.05 | 29.01 | 25.76 | 31.65 | 25.99 | 24.87 | 29.58 | 25.54 | 0.04 |
| Rye | 16.81 | 20.62 | 18.82 | 17.25 | 23.68 | 17.98 | 18.65 | 15.04 | 19.04 | 0.63 |
| Potatoes | 14.80 | 17.39 | 23.04 | 13.51 | 19.87 | 12.86 | 17.11 | 23.02 | 17.39 | 2.87 |
| Hay | 7.16 | 7.55 | 8.70 | 6.19 | 9.54 | 6.81 | 8.70 | 7.62 | 7.82 | 27.99 |
| Tobacco | 167.24 | 134.04 | 156.63 | 96.08 | 134.25 | 147.60 | 168.14 | 143.68 | 145.65 | 0.03 |
| Corn, Oats and Wheat (1) | 14.26 | 16.38 | 14.26 | 12.05 | 18.21 | 13.28 | 14.06 | 14.83 | 14.59 | |
| Corn, Oats and Wheat (2) | 13.69 | 15.97 | 14.40 | 12.66 | 17.72 | 18.66 | 14.01 | 14.61 | 14.59 | |
| All Crops (1) | 12.45 | 13.83 | 13.17 | 10.60 | 16.25 | 11.31 | 12.65 | 13.31 | 12.88 | |
| All Crops (2) | 11.98 | 13.75 | 13.13 | 10.98 | 15.59 | 11.83 | 12.72 | 13.19 | 12.88 | |

No. 1. General averages of all.    No. 2. Averaged on relative importance.

### Farm Prices in Indiana, 1862-95.
Compiled by Lucius B. Swift of Indianapolis.

| | 1873-1877. | 1878-1882. | 1883-1887. | 1888-1892. |
|---|---|---|---|---|
| Corn, per bushel | 35.6 | 41.8 | 37 | 39.8 |
| Oats, per bushel | 29.6 | 31.6 | 28.8 | 35.2 |
| Wheat, per bushel | 95 | 102.6 | 79 | 87.2 |
| Rye, per bushel | 52.8 | 70.4 | 57.6 | 68 |
| Potatoes, per bushel | 53 | 60.6 | 50.8 | 59.4 |
| Hay, per ton | $9.31 | $9.47 | $8.21 | $9.54 |

### Prices of Farm Implements in Bushels of Grain, 1873 and 1889.

| IMPLEMENTS. | BUSH. WHEAT. | | BUSH. CORN. | | BUSH. OATS. | |
|---|---|---|---|---|---|---|
| | 1873. | 1889. | 1873. | 1889. | 1873. | 1889. |
| One-horse steel plow (wood beam) | 6.4 | 3.8 | 19.1 | 8.5 | 27.0 | 11.5 |
| One-horse iron plow (wood beam) | 4.9 | 2.7 | 14.7 | 6.2 | 20.8 | 8.3 |
| Two-horse side-hill, or reversible plow | 17.6 | 13.7 | 52.9 | 31.2 | 75.0 | 41.7 |
| One potato digger | 19.6 | 10.2 | 58.8 | 23.4 | 83.3 | 31.2 |
| Old-fashioned tooth harrow | 14.7 | 8.9 | 44.1 | 20.3 | 62.5 | 27.0 |
| One-horse cultivator | 6.8 | 4.7 | 20.5 | 10.9 | 29.1 | 14.5 |
| One-horse mower | 83.3 | 61.6 | 250.0 | 140.6 | 354.1 | 187.5 |
| Com. iron garden rake (10-tooth steel), doz. | 11.7 | 5.1 | 35.2 | 11.7 | 50.0 | 15.6 |
| One-horse horse-power | 44.1 | 34.2 | 132.8 | 78.1 | 187.5 | 104.1 |
| Binder | 277.7 | 184.9 | 769.2 | 421.8 | 857.1 | 562.5 |
| Corn-sheller (1 hole) | 11.2 | 8.2 | 38.8 | 18.7 | 47.9 | 25.0 |
| Common hoes (cast-steel socket), per doz. | 6.3 | 4.7 | 19.1 | 10.9 | 27.0 | 14.5 |
| Common rakes (wood), per doz. | 2.9 | 2.4 | 8.8 | 6.2 | 12.5 | 8.3 |
| Scythes (Ames' grass), per doz | 15.7 | 10.2 | 47.0 | 23.4 | 66.6 | 31.2 |
| Scythe snaths (patent), per doz. | 10.8 | 6.1 | 32.3 | 14.0 | 45.8 | 18.7 |
| Shovel (Ames), per doz | 17.6 | 13.0 | 52.9 | 29.6 | 75.0 | 39.5 |
| Spades (Ames), per doz | 13.1 | 13.7 | 54.4 | 31.2 | 27.0 | 46.6 |
| Total | 569.4 | 388.1 | 1,615.1 | 886.7 | 2,048.2 | 1,187.7 |

## STATISTICAL TABLES.

*Freight Rates on Wheat, by Lake, Canal, and Rail, from Chicago to New York, 1860–95.*

[Prepared by J. C. Brown, statistician, New York Produce Exchange.]

| Calendar year. | Average rates per bushel. | | | Calendar year. | Average rates per bushel. | | |
|---|---|---|---|---|---|---|---|
| | By lake and canal. a | By lake and rail. | By all rail. | | By lake and canal. a | By lake and rail. | By all rail. |
| | Cents. | Cents. | Cents. | | Cents. | Cents. | Cents. |
| 1860 | 24.83 | .... | .... | 1878 | 9.15 | 11.4 | 17.7 |
| 1861 | 26.55 | .... | .... | 1879 | 11.6 | 13 3 | 17.3 |
| 1862 | 26.33 | .... | .... | 1880 | 12 27 | 15.7 | 10.9 |
| 1863 | 22.91 | .... | .... | 1881 | 8.19 | 10.4 | 14.4 |
| 1864 | 28.36 | .... | .... | 1882 | 7.89 | 10.9 | 14.6 |
| 1865 | 26.62 | .... | .... | 1883 | 8.37 | 11.5 | 16.5 |
| 1866 | 29.61 | .... | .... | 1884 | 6.31 | 9.55 | 13.125 |
| 1867 | 22.36 | .... | .... | 1885 | 5.87 | 9.02 | 14 |
| 1868 | 22.79 | 29 | 42.6 | 1886 | 8.71 | 12 | 16.5 |
| 1869 | 25.12 | 25 | 35.1 | 1887 | 8.51 | 12 | b 15.74 |
| 1870 | 17.1 | 22 | 33.3 | 1888 | 5.93 | 11 | b 14.5 |
| 1871 | 20.24 | 25 | 31 | 1889 | 6.89 | b 8.7 | 15 |
| 1872 | 24.47 | 28 | 33.5 | 1890 | 5.85 | 8.5 | 14.31 |
| 1873 | 19.19 | 26.9 | 33.2 | 1891 | 5.96 | 8.53 | 15 |
| 1874 | 14.1 | 16.9 | 28.7 | 1892 | 5.61 | 7.55 | 14.23 |
| 1875 | 11.43 | 14.6 | 24.1 | 1893 | 6.33 | 8.44 | 14.7 |
| 1876 | 9.58 | 11.8 | 16.5 | 1894 | 4.44 | 7 | 12.88 |
| 1877 | 11.24 | 15.8 | 20.3 | 1895 | 4.11 | 6.95 | 12.17 |

a Including canal tolls until 1882, but not Buffalo transfer charges.
b Averages of officially published tariffs.

*Freight Rates on Grain and Flour from St. Louis to Various Points during each Year from 1876–95.*

[Prepared by George H. Morgan, secretary Merchant's Exchange, St. Louis, Mo.]

| Calendar year. | To New Orleans by river. | | To New York by rail. | | To Liverpool. | |
|---|---|---|---|---|---|---|
| | On grain in sacks per 100 pounds. | On wheat in bulk by barges per bushel. | On wheat per 100 pounds. | On flour per barrel. | Via New Orleans on wheat per bushel. | Via New York on wheat per bushel. |
| | Cents. | Cents. | Cents. | Cents. | Cents. | Cents. |
| 1876 | .... | .... | 39.5 | 79 | .... | .... |
| 1877 | 21 | 8.5 | 41 | 82 | .... | .... |
| 1878 | 17.5 | 7.25 | 34 | 76 | .... | .... |
| 1879 | 18 | 7.75 | 33.5 | 67 | .... | .... |
| 1880 | 19 | 8.25 | 42 | 84 | .... | .... |
| 1881 | 20 | 6 | 32 | 64 | .... | .... |
| 1882 | 20 | 6.42 | 29.5 | 59 | 23.66 | 23.66 |
| 1883 | 17.75 | 5.5 | 33 | 66 | 19.58 | 27 |
| 1884 | 14 | 6.63 | 26 | 52 | 14.58 | 21.25 |
| 1885 | 15 | 6.4 | 22.14 | 44.29 | 15.11 | 20 5 |
| 1886 | 16 | 6.5 | 29 | 58 | 16.17 | 24 |
| 1887 | 19 | 6.5 | 32.13 | 64.25 | 14.8 | 21.8 |
| 1888 | 15 | 6.5 | 29.5 | 59 | 15.17 | 22.95 |
| 1889 | 17.93 | 5.95 | 28.5 | 58 | 17.33 | 24.97 |
| 1890 | 15.66 | 6.58 | 27.63 | 52.63 | 14.33 | 21.48 |
| 1891 | 16.28 | 6.88 | 29 | 58 | 15.75 | 23.55 |
| 1892 | 16.87 | 6.50 | 26.62 | 58 | 14 | 21 |
| 1893 | 17.54 | 6.55 | 28.5 | 57 | 14.71 | 21.72 |
| 1894 | 17.14 | 5.89 | 24.73 | 50 | 11.69 | 18.71 |
| 1895 | 13.00 | 5.95 | a23.57 | 47 | 12.13 | 18.33 |

a The figures represent published rates. Lower rates were probably secured.

STATISTICAL TABLES.

## Time Table of Procedure—The Act of 1873.
### Summarized by Prof. Laughlin.

|  | SENATE. | HOUSE. |
|---|---|---|
| Submitted by Secretary of the Treasury............................. | April 25, 1870 | ............... |
| Referred to Senate Finance Committee........................ | April 28, 1870 | ............... |
| Five hundred copies ordered printed......... .......... ..... | May 2, 1870 | ............... |
| Submitted to House, with supplementary report and correspondence ............... | ............... | June 25, 1870 |
| Reported, amended and ordered printed..................... | Dec. 19, 1870 | ............... |
| Debated .......... ........................................... | Jan. 9, 1871 | ............... |
| Passed the Senate by a vote of 36 to 14 ........................ | Jan. 10, 1871 | ............... |
| Senate Bill ordered printed.......... ................ | ............... | Jan. 18, 1871 |
| Bill reported with substitute, and recommitted ............... | ............... | Feb. 25, 1871 |
| Original bill reintroduced and printed................... | ............... | Mar. 9, 1871 |
| Reported and debated ............................................. | ............... | Jan. 9, 1872 |
| Recommitted ............................................... | ............... | Jan. 10, 1872 |
| Reported from Coinage Committee, printed and recommitted.. | ............... | Feb. 9, 1872 |
| Reported back, amended and printed......................... | ............... | Feb. 13, 1872 |
| Debated .......................................................... | ............... | April 9, 1872 |
| Amended and passed by vote 110 to 13......................... | ............... | May 27, 1872 |
| Printed in Senate................................................ | May 29, 1872 | ............... |
| Reported with amendments and printed....... ............ | Dec. 16, 1872 | ............... |
| Reported with additional amendments and printed ......... | Jan. 7, 1873 | ............... |
| Passed Senate. .................................. ............... | Jan. 17, 1873 | ............... |
| Printed with amendments........................................ | ............... | Jan. 21, 1873 |
| Conference committee appointed............................. | Jan. 27, 1873 | Jan. 25, 1873 |
| Report of conference committee presented and concurred in.. | Feb. 6, 1873 | Feb. 7, 1873 |
| Became a law February 12, 1873................................. | ............... | ............... |

## Prices, Wages, Purchasing Power, 1845–90.
### Condensed from the Senate Report of 1892.

|  | 1845 | 1850 | 1855 | 1860 | 1865 | 1870 | 1875 | 1880 | 1885 | 1890 |
|---|---|---|---|---|---|---|---|---|---|---|
| Meat............................. | 79.4 | 86.6 | 104.7 | 100 | 197 | 174.3 | 140.4 | 108.6 | 107.6 | 99.6 |
| Other food...................... | 82.8 | 80.7 | 114.5 | 100 | 240.3 | 146.3 | 125 | 116.9 | 97.2 | 103.5 |
| Cloths and clothing........... | 97.1 | 91.3 | 94.7 | 100 | 299.2 | 139.4 | 120.1 | 104.5 | 84.8 | 82.4 |
| Fuel and lighting............. | .... | 102.6 | 121.1 | 100 | 237.8 | 196.5 | 155.5 | 100.2 | 89.6 | 92.5 |
| Metals and implements....... | 110.8 | 114.8 | 117.8 | 100 | 191.4 | 127.8 | 117.5 | 96.3 | 77.4 | 73.2 |
| Lumber and building materials ........................ | 106.7 | 102.2 | 103.4 | 100 | 182.1 | 148.3 | 143.7 | 130.9 | 126.6 | 123.7 |
| Drugs and Chemicals......... | 121 | 123.6 | 129.2 | 100 | 271.6 | 149.6 | 144.2 | 113.1 | 86.9 | 87.9 |
| House furnishing ............. | 102.3 | 125.6 | 121.1 | 100 | 181.1 | 121.6 | 95 | 85.2 | 70.1 | 69.5 |
| Miscellaneous................... | 114.8 | 107.7 | 115.2 | 100 | 202.8 | 148.7 | 122.9 | 109.8 | 97.5 | 89.7 |
| Average of all prices......... | 102.8 | 102.3 | 113.1 | 100 | 216.8 | 142.3 | 127.6 | 106.9 | 93 | 92.3 |
| Average of all wages......... | 86.8 | 92.7 | 98 | 100 | 143.1 | 162.2 | 158.4 | 141.5 | 150.7 | 158.9 |
| Average wages by importance | 85.7 | 90.9 | 97.5 | 100 | 148.6 | 167.1 | 158 | 143 | 155.9 | 63.2 |
| Salaries of city teachers...... | 74.6 | 83.8 | 91.4 | 100 | 134.7 | 186.3 | 188.1 | 182.8 | 186.3 | 88.3 |
| Paper money................... | 100 | 100 | 100 | 100 | 49.5 | 81.1 | 88.8 | 100 | 100 | 100 |
| Gold prices of silver bullion in London................... | 95.3 | 97.3 | 100 | 100 | 99 | 98.2 | 92.2 | 84.7 | 78.7 | 77.4 |
| Purchasing power of wages. | 84.4 | 90.6 | 86.6 | 100 | 66 | 114.1 | 124.1 | 132.3 | 162 | 172.1 |

## STATISTICAL TABLES.

*Wages in U. S. and Other Countries.   From Report of Senate Committee of 1892.*

| TRADES AND OCCUPATIONS. | U. S. | JAPAN. | MEXICO. | PERSIA. | PERU. | VENEZ. |
|---|---|---|---|---|---|---|
| | 1891. | 1892. | 1891. | 1884. | 1884. | 1884. |
| Bricklayers | $21.18 | $2.04 | $10.00 | $2.40 | $9.00 | $9.00 |
| Hodcarriers | 13.38 | 1.14 | 3.60 | 1.90 | 5.40 | 4.63 |
| Masons | 21.00 | 2.18 | 10.80 | 1.80 | 14.76 | 9.74 |
| Tenders | 9.60 | 1.14 | 3.50 | 1.20 | 4.90 | 8.81 |
| Plasterers | 23.10 | 1.56 | 4.25 | 2.40 | 9.00 | 9.40 |
| Slaters | 21.00 | | | | | 13.20 |
| Roofers | 17.30 | 1.80 | 8.40 | 1.80 | | 8.70 |
| Plumbers | 19.00 | | | | | |
| Assistants | | | | | | 9.60 |
| Carpenters | 15.25 | 1.56 | | 2.40 | 9.00 | 9.84 |
| Gasfitters | 11.90 | | | | | 18.00 |
| Bakers | | | 7.60 | 3.72 | 3.60 | 12.00 |
| Blacksmiths | 16.02 | 1.85 | 8.00 | 3.04 | 16.30 | 12.83 |
| Bookbinders | | | 5.50 | | 13.80 | 10.25 |
| Brickmakers | | | 6.00 | 3.78 | 9.20 | 9.16 |
| Brewers | | | 6.00 | | 20.00 | |
| Butchers | | | 5.40 | 1.68 | 12.30 | 11.75 |
| Brass-founders | | 3.00 | 10.00 | | | |
| Cabinetmakers | 13.32 | | 10.00 | | 14.76 | 14.45 |
| Confectioners | | | 5.00 | 2.88 | 4.20 | 10.38 |
| Cigarmakers | | | 4.50 | 1.68 | 7.50 | 12.50 |
| Coopers | 16.08 | | 7.25 | | 7.50 | |
| Cutlers | | | | | | |
| Distillers | | | 4.00 | 1.25 | | 13.50 |
| Draymen and teamsters | 10.80 | | 3.60 | | 3.50 | |
| DRIVERS.— | | | | | | |
|   Cab and carriage | | 1.50 | 3.60 | 1.75 | 3.50 | |
|   Street car | | | 3.00 | | 7.40 | 8.50 |
| Dyers | 9.00 | | 3.16 | 2.40 | | 10.00 |
| Furriers | | | 3.66 | | | 13.00 |
| Gardeners | 13.50 | | 3.90 | 1.48 | 5.00 | 6.50 |
| Hatters | | | 5.10 | 3.84 | 9.00 | |
| Horseshoers | | | 3.75 | 1.68 | | |
| Jewelers | | | 4.15 | 6.30 | 13.90 | |
| Laborers, porters, etc | 8.88 | 1.14 | 2.90 | 1.92 | 3.50 | 7.85 |
| Millwrights | 16.80 | | 3.30 | | | |
| Printers | 16.42 | 1.75 | 5.76 | 1.92 | 9.42 | 12.00 |
| Potters | | 1.80 | 5.76 | 3.00 | | |
| Sailmakers | | | 2.60 | | | 14.00 |
| Shoemakers | | | 2.95 | 3.84 | | 10.00 |
| Stevedores | | | 9.00 | | 4.92 | |
| Stonecutters | 21.00 | 2.18 | | | | |
| Tanners | | | 3.00 | 3.84 | 4.92 | 12.00 |
| Tailors | | 2.95 | 7.14 | 2.88 | 4.92 | 12.50 |
| Telegraph operators | | | 11.50 | | 12.10 | 11.38 |
| Tinsmiths | 14.35 | | 7.50 | 1.92 | 7.50 | 14.00 |

*Diagram Showing Prices of Silver, Wheat, Pork, Freight, Telegrams, etc., 1873-95.*

From Wheeler's "Real Bi-Metallism" (Copyright, 1895, by G. P. Putnam's Sons) by permission of Messrs. Putnam's Sons.

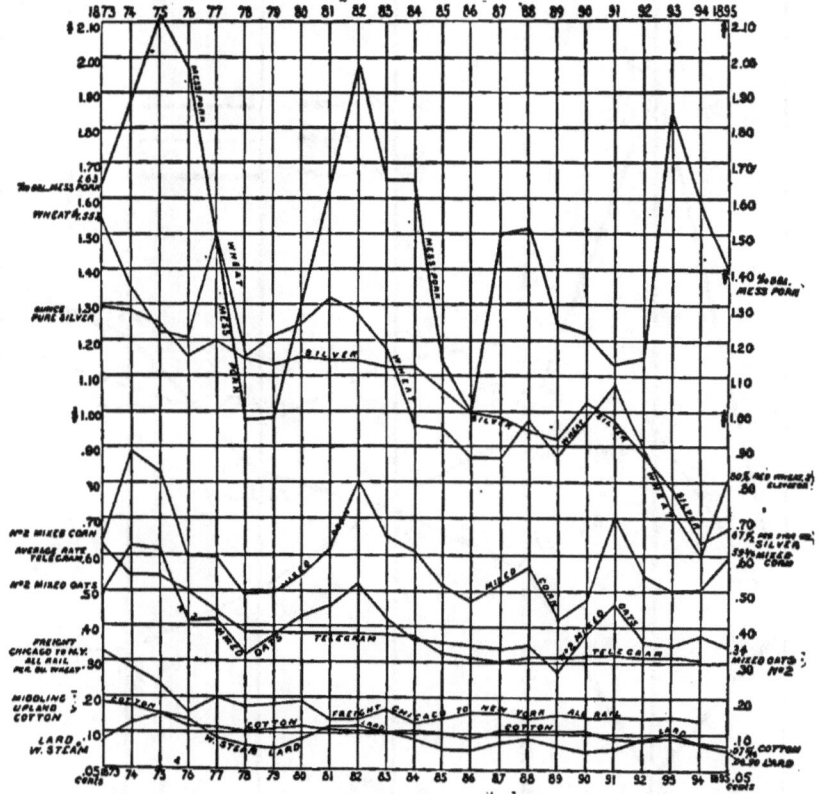

Diagram showing comparison between prices of silver per fine ounce from 1873 to 1895 (May 23d), and the following: 1-10 bbl. Mess Pork; 1 bushel No. 2 Red Winter Wheat (from 1873 to 1877, Milwaukee No. 2 Spring Wheat); 1 bushel No. 2 Mixed Corn; 1 bushel No. 2 Mixed Oats; and 1 pound Western Steam Lard.
Also average price of Telegrams in the United States, and freight per bushel Wheat, Chicago to New York—all rail.
All the prices are in currency, except that of silver from 1873 to 1878, and all in the New York Market.

## STATISTICAL TABLES.

*Diagram showing the Course of Prices, Wages, and the Purchasing Power of Wages, 1860 to 1890.*

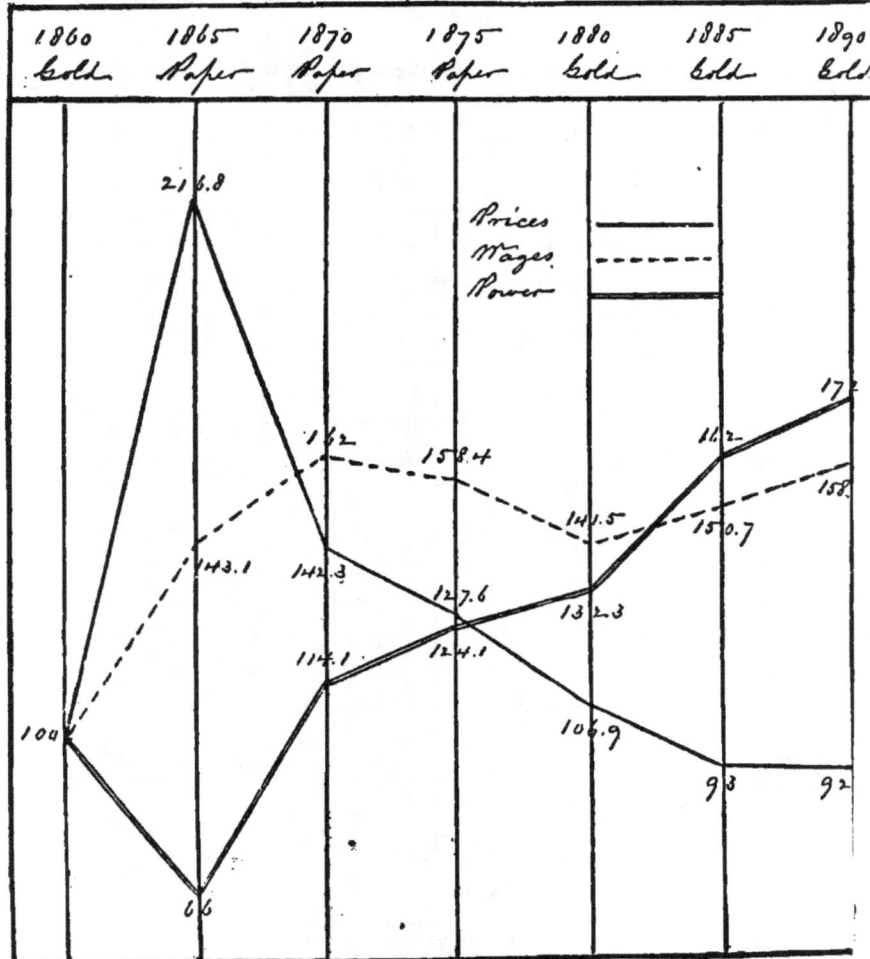

The course of prices shows the average variation from a standpoint of 100 in 1860 computed upon the market prices of over 200 articles.
The course of wages is computed on the general average of mechanical and manufacturing industries.
The data on which this diagram is based are given in the Report of the Finance Committee of the Senate on Prices and Wages for 52 years, compiled under the direction of Commissioner Carroll D. Wright.

www.ingramcontent.com/pod-product-compliance
Lightning Source LLC
Chambersburg PA
CBHW020902230426
43666CB00008B/1279